BRISTOL RECORD SOCIETY'S
PUBLICATIONS

General Editor: JOSEPH BETTEY, M.A., Ph.D., F.S.A.
Assistant Editor: MISS ELIZABETH RALPH, M.A., D. Litt., F.S.A.

VOL. XLVI

THE PRE-REFORMATION RECORDS OF

ALL SAINTS', BRISTOL: PART I

THE PRE-REFORMATION RECORDS OF ALL SAINTS', BRISTOL: PART I

EDITED BY
CLIVE BURGESS

Published by
BRISTOL RECORD SOCIETY
1995

ISBN 0 901538 16 7

The Bristol Record Society is grateful to the following charitable trusts for grants towards the cost of this publication:

The late Isobel Thornley's Bequest to the University of London
The Greater Bristol Trust
The J & M Britton Charitable Trust

The editor would also like to express his gratitude to the Leverhulme Trust.

Produced for the Society by
Alan Sutton Publishing Limited, Stroud, Glos.
Printed in Great Britain by
Alden Press,
Oxford and Northampton.

CONTENTS

	Page
Note on Bristol Record Society	vi
Preface	viii
Introduction	xi
Glossary	xlv
Text	1
Parish Account, 1427–8. Fox Ms. 70.	139
Index	143

BRISTOL RECORD SOCIETY

The Society exists to encourage the preservation, study and publication of documents relating to the history of Bristol, and since its foundation in 1929 has published forty-six major volumes of historic documents concerning the city. All the volumes, together with their authoritative introductions, are edited by scholars who are experts in the chosen field.

Recent volumes have included: *Tudor Wills Proved in Bristol 1546–1603*, edited by Sheila Lang and Margaret McGregor (Vol.XLIV), and *Reformation and Revival in Eighteenth-Century Bristol*, edited by Jonathan Barry and Kenneth Morgan (Vol. XLV).

Forthcoming volumes will include further publications of the All Saints' records, the final part of David Richardson's important work on Bristol and the Slave Trade, and a volume with maps and plans illustrating the development of the topography of central Bristol which is being edited by Roger Leech.

In return for the modest subscription, members of the Society receive the volumes as they are published. The subscription for private members is £7.50 per annum, for U.K. Institutions £10.00, and for Overseas membership £12.00. Subscriptions and enquiries should be sent to the Hon. Secretary, School of Historical Studies, University of Bristol, 13–15 Woodland Road, Bristol BS8 1TB.

THE PRE-REFORMATION RECORDS OF ALL SAINTS', BRISTOL.
PART I: THE ALL SAINTS' CHURCH BOOK.

PREFACE

The late medieval parish was a topic which excited but little interest some twenty years ago when I embarked on research. Recent debate on the Reformation, however, has greatly stimulated the need to know more about the state of the church before the changes in the sixteenth century; it should also be noted that students have found the area to be of considerable interest in its own right. As a result the beliefs, practices and devotional lives of the fourteenth- and fifteenth-century laity now attract increasing attention. In the circumstances I count myself lucky that I have lived with the parish and parishioners of All Saints', Bristol, for so long. I was by no means the first to discover the archive surviving for All Saints' late medieval parishioners, but I would be the first to admit that I am profoundly thankful for the wealth of detail and insight which it has afforded both during my doctoral research and since. Examples from the archive and the wider understanding made possible by such plentiful materials have done much to formulate my impressions and conclusions. My thesis benefited greatly; so too has my published work. Recent forays into the archives and histories of late medieval London's parishes have served only to confirm what I already suspected: that the All Saints' archive has a variety and breadth which render it quite exceptional. Hence my return. Ironically, without London this might never have happened. I sincerely hope that my findings for All Saints', Bristol, will cast light on activities in many another parish in London and elsewhere.

This is the first of a short series which will retrieve and publish the All Saints' archive. Bringing the work to fruition has been a long process during which I have incurred many debts. It is a pleasure to acknowledge these. I am particularly grateful to my parents for their unfailing support and encouragement, grateful also to the staff at the Bristol Record Office for their unerring efficiency and courtesy, to Dr Joseph Bettey for enabling me to publish this material and for being patient, to Miss Patricia Crimmin and the other trustees of the Thornley Bequest for arranging a generous subvention towards the costs of publication, and to Miss Barbara Harvey and Dr Caroline Barron both for setting standards I can only hope to emulate and for advice and encouragement in many areas. My debt to the Leverhulme Trust is fundamental: without its support the project could never have been completed. I also want to thank Tony and Cathy Benjamin for their hospitality when first I started this work. More recently I have incurred a very deep debt to Mark Owen and Timothy Goodchild in Cardiff, for without their friendship and generosity time spent in Bristol would have been both short and infinitely less enjoyable. The book is dedicated to another friend whom I associate closely with Cardiff but who, in my memory at least, was very much a presence when this work was in preparation.

For Richard Thomas: so that
'he shall not be forgotten but had in remembrance'.

INTRODUCTION[1]

For any who wish to understand something of religion as it affected the late medieval English laity, one of the easiest points of access is study of the beliefs and practices prevalent in a large town. Quite simply, records survive for these centres in relative abundance. Wills are plentiful and may, with luck, be supplemented by materials produced by and designed to serve the laity who managed parishes. Indeed, the analysis of wills and parish materials in combination proves to be particularly revealing when examining the practices and priorities of contemporaries. Bristol is fortunate here as its archives offer the historian a perfectly adequate cache of late medieval wills and unexpectedly abundant parish records: most of its fifteen or so parishes have something, be it an inventory or accounts or property deeds. This has made the study of pre-Reformation pious mores within Bristol notably rewarding. But for reasons which are far from apparent – indeed good luck rather than any good reason seems to be the best explanation – one parish, All Saints', in the centre of the old town, has late fifteenth- and early sixteenth-century records which are quite exceptional. Other parishes may have better inventories or fuller accounts but overall none can match it, and some of the material has no equivalent in any other Bristol parish archive. One could venture further. Very few other late medieval English parishes are likely to have an archive of comparable range, variety and detail. Now it must be admitted that conditions in a town like Bristol and an urban parish like All Saints' were far from typical in late medieval England; but, given the dearth of material for the great majority of parishes and our ignorance of the factors governing the life and behaviour of laity before the Reformation, the promise of the material from and for All Saints' makes it imperative to gather the archive together and publish it in as full a form as possible. If nothing

---

[1] Note that references to page numbers in the All Saints' Church Book correspond to the pagination in the manuscript; this is indicated in the printed text by the numbers in round brackets.

else, it will prove a useful benchmark facilitating comparisons and contrasts to illuminate practice elsewhere, both in town and countryside. The present volume, the first of three which are planned, contains the All Saints' Church Book, a tome which forms perhaps the core of the material in the archive. The second volume will print All Saints' unbound parish accounts, taking the run until c.1530; the third will publish any remaining documentation, including wills, chantry materials and a digest of the property deeds. As it is my intention to write a full study of the pre-Reformation parish of All Saints', Bristol, which will itself be closely based on the surviving archive, detailed commentaries on the transcripts as printed in the Bristol Record Series are superfluous. The introductions to each of the three volumes willprovide only what seems necessary for the better understanding of the material presented in the text.

All Saints', Bristol

As mentioned, All Saints' was and is situated at Bristol's centre, just to the south-west of the carfax where High Street, Corn Street, Broad Street and Wine Street meet. It was a compact parish, comprising the eastern half (very roughly) of the block of property bounded by Corn Street to the north and the sweep of St Nicholas Street to the south and west, and which extended over the High Street to incorporate some of the tenements on the eastern side of this artery.[2] It was also a relatively small parish, with a houseling (that is, communicant) population given as just less than 200 in the mid-sixteenth century Chantry Certificate; this may be set against the populations given for St Nicholas and St Mary Redcliffe at, respectively, 800 and 600, and a Bristol average of perhaps 400.[3] The site of the parish in so central a location argues for antiquity, but anything as precise as a foundation date is lacking. Nevertheless, at some time in the reign of Henry II [1154–89] the Augustinian Abbey of St Augustine's, Bristol, founded by Robert Fitzharding during the 1140s, acquired the patronage of All Saints'.[4] Successive abbots maintained their right of appointment to the living, as well as preserving the role of final arbiter in parish affairs. It should nevertheless be emphasized that, to judge from the surviving parish archive, the abbot of St Augustine's was not unduly intrusive in parish life. Rather, our attention is drawn towards a number of incumbents and

[2] The best impression of Bristol's topography and parish boundaries is to be had in M.D. Lobel and M.D. Carus-Wilson, 'Bristol', *The Atlas of Historic Towns*, II, ed. M.D. Lobel and W.H. Johns (London, 1975).

[3] John Maclean, 'Chantry Certificates, Gloucestershire', *Trans. Bristol and Gloucestershire Archaeological Society* [hereafter *T.B.G.A.S.*], viii (1883–4), 232–51.

[4] N. Orme, 'The Guild of Kalendars, Bristol', *T.B.G.A.S.*, xcvi (1978), 33–4 and notes 7 and 8.

parishioners, eminent both because of their generosity and because of the frequency with which they were involved in decisions and activities of moment. Neither 'side' was dominant: one of the most instructive aspects to emerge from the All Saints' archive is the impression that clergy and laity acted together, depending upon each other to secure the broader benefit of the parish.

The parish church of All Saints' is tucked into a confined site, separated from the High Street to the east by a row of tenements and with its main entrace on a side-street, Venny Lane now called All Saints' Lane.[5] In plan it is a compact, squarish church, consisting of a nave and a chancel with north and south aisles. To judge from payments made by various parishioners, the southern aisle seems to have been rebuilt in the 1430s; the northern aisle was rebuilt in the 1440s by Richard Haddon, who apparently depended in large part on the legacy left to him by his father, John. At the eastern end of the north aisle, against the chancel, is a tower, rebuilt in the early eighteenth century. At the western end of the both aisles, encroaching into the church at first-floor level, were two houses: in the south aisle, a house for the vicars of the parish rebuilt by Sir Thomas Marshall, vicar, who died in 1434; in the north aisle a house, rebuilt in the 1440s, in which the priests serving the fraternity of Kalendars lived. Space, clearly, was at a premium and the adjacent churchyard inadequate for new building. In the fifteenth century, in addition to the high altar in the chancel, there were four low altars in the church. In the north aisle, which for the greater part of the fifteenth century was called Our Lady aisle, but which towards the end of the century was known as the Jesus aisle, stood the altar of Our Lady, later called the Jesus altar. At the eastern end of the south aisle, known as the Rood or Cross aisle, was the Rood altar. There was a rood loft dividing nave from chancel, and standing before it on the nave side were the two remaining low altars, to the northern side (according to Cuthbert Atchley's deductions) was one dedicated to St Thomas, and to the south the other dedicated to Saints John the Baptist, John the Evangelist and Dunstan. The second of these was the Morrow-Mass altar, and it was for instance also at this altar that Halleway's chantry priest celebrated.

One final preliminary should be dealt with very briefly. Anyone perusing the records of All Saints' will encounter references to the fraternity of Kalendars.[6] During the reign of Henry II, Robert Fitzharding had moved this fraternity from its first home in the parish of Holy Trinity to All Saints'. The Kalendars remained there until the Dissolution in the 1540s. It was a fraternity for secular priests and laity,

---

[5] E.G.C. Atchley, 'Some Documents relating to the parish of All Saints', Bristol', *Archaeological Journal*, lviii (1901), 147–81, has a useful discussion on the site and the internal features of the church.

[6] N. Orme, *art. cit.*, is essential reading on the Kalendars and the following paragraph rests on his work.

the clergy assuming seniority in the partnership. In addition to clergy who were brothers and who may have been drawn from any of Bristol's parishes, there were some three or four priests perpetually maintained by endowments entrusted to the fraternity – it was these priests who occupied the house over the western end of the north aisle. Their chief was the prior who effectively seems to have been head of the guild. It is worth mentioning, first, that the fraternity met on or near the first day of the month (hence the name Kalendars) at a Mass celebrated for living and dead members. In addition each of the fraternity priests was obliged to celebrate daily for the benefit of members' souls, and all, clerical or lay, were to say thirteen *Pater nosters* and thirteen *Ave Marias* daily. Second, in 1464 Bishop Carpenter of Worcester sought to ensure that the Kalendars make a more tangible contribution towards strengthening orthodoxy in Bristol: to this end he obliged the prior to preach four times annually at specified sites within the town and entrusted the Kalendars with a library to be kept in their house and to assist in educating the townspeople. It may be speculation but it seems reasonable to deduce that, third, All Saints', if small, was in no way disadvantaged by size. Apart from anything else, the presence of so many clergy in the parish doubtless had an appreciable impact on the spiritual life of the community and on its liturgical sophistication.

The All Saints' Church Book

The Book [BRO: P/AS/ChW/1], bound in brown leather, has pages 29cms high and 21 cms broad, and while its frontispiece has the title 'The Minutes of All Saints' Parish in the Reign of Edward IV', this probably dates from the occasion of its present binding at some stage in the eighteenth or early nineteenth century. The Book contains upward of 1100 pages most of which have been numbered in a hand which post-dates its contents. Substantial sections of the Book are the work of one scribe, but there are also many additions often in very inferior scripts. It is, however, to be emphasized that the great majority of the Book's pages are blank. The uniformity of the watermark in the paper throughout the Book (of a bull's head with ears and horns, with a line between the horns marked with an X), when taken together with the underlying scribal uniformity, may suggest that the Book as it exists was conceived and executed as part of a single project. Its origins could, however, have been more complex. It is, for instance, possible that different sections in the Book were kept separately at first and only later bound together as a single, rather cumbersome volume. On further consideration, it seems increasingly likely that its parts were compiled as a result of different initiatives, but that at a later date someone, evidently with a particular intention in mind, conceived of the volume and copied suitable material into it.

The substance of the Book falls into three. The first section starts with a contents page, and while subsequent sub-sections are set out in accordance with this directive, only a few of these were written up. A number of parish ordinances are recorded on pages 3 to 6, and the pages following contain headings indicating that lists of names were to have been recorded, names of conducts (that is, lesser or stipendiary clergy) and the equipment that had been entrusted to them, names of debtors, and names of key-holders. But pages 7 to 67, apart from the headings, are blank. The list of parish benefactors, starting on page 68, has been compiled and entered, however. It comprises, first, a list of parish endowments and who had given them; second, from page 78 to page 86, a list of clergy who had been benefactors and what each had given; and third, from page 133 to 167, lists of the laity and what they had given. The second section of material starts on page 315. From page 315 to 358 there are two inventories of the goods in the church, one compiled in 1395 when William Lenche and Stephen Knyght were churchwardens, the other in 1469 when Richard Haddon and John Schoppe were churchwardens. Thereafter, on pages 375 to 382, there is a list, mainly in chronological order, of the churchwardens who had served the church in the earlier part of the fifteenth century up until the 1460s with a short description of what each pair had achieved. The third section, running from page 437 to 597, comprises churchwardens' accounts, starting in c.1410 and extending, with some gaps, until the early 1480s. Thereafter the volume is blank, apart from some miscellaneous memoranda towards its end. Here, among other scribble, on page 997 is material descriptive of some of the anniversaries running in the parish; on pages 1055 to 1057 brief transcripts of some Jesus Guild accounts from the early 1480s; and finally, on pages 1090 to 1093, a list of parish keyholders also, apparently, from the late fifteenth century.

Compiling the Book

If we discount the jottings at the end of the Book, we are dealing with three main sections of material. On close examination it appears that the bulk of the second and third sections was conceived and compiled in an initiative which pre-dated that responsible for the first section. It is, to start with, reasonably clear that the second inventory was compiled under the aegis of the churchwardens Richard Haddon and John Schoppe who were in office together in 1469. The same initiative gave us the list of churchwardens and what they had done for the church; it perhaps gave us the accounts down to the late 1460s in the third section of the Book, although, significantly, failing to include an account for the year when Haddon and Schoppe were wardens. The key information is to be found in the last of the entries concerning the wardens and what each set had done for All Saints'. We are told concerning Haddon and Schoppe '. . . as for 1 evidence to be had for ever [they] let ordained this book for every man's account to be written in as for 1 evidence of old time of rents that have been gathered and paid time out of mind, and also in the said year they let made an inventory of all the goods of the church where none before might be found.' It should be noted, however, that accounts in the Book subsequent to Haddon and Schoppe's wardenship, extending from 12 Edward IV [1472–3] to 21 Edward IV [1481–2], are much fuller than the previous and in a very different hand. They are clearly a later addition. Nevertheless, the churchwardens' list which, incidentally, starts with the wardenship of Derby and Backe just as the first account also records their financial stewardship, continues in roughly chronological order down to 1469 and effectively mirrors the main run of accounts. The list is an epitome of the accounts. If Haddon and Schoppe seem to have been instrumental in compiling an inventory and commissioning a roll of honour for previous wardens, in addition to instigating the accounts in the Book, then it must be emphasized that the last of these initiatives was in the main a duplication and tidying of existing material. In all probability the accounts in the Book were based on unbound accounts kept year by year probably from some point in the fourteenth century. One early account survives and is lodged now in the Fox collection in the Bristol Record Office.[7] It dates from 1428 and is in Latin, which may explain why later wardens seeking to make their predecessors' achievements accessible rendered all that they could find in English. Even if the accounts recorded in the Book are summaries of fuller versions, which, in point of fact, survive in some number from the mid-fifteenth century, Haddon and Schoppe's initiative certainly preserved a great deal of material which would otherwise have been lost.[8] But before moving on to consider the first section of the Book and its genesis, it is worth noting that two entries in the list of churchwardens and their deeds are out of chronological sequence and, in fact, concern two sets of wardens who pre-date those otherwise in the list. On page 376, Lenche and Knyght, whom we know were wardens in 1395, are said to have compiled an inventory, and similarly Aschton and Torner, wardens apparently in 1390–91, are said to have compiled a list of benefactors who gave livelode, that is endowments, to the church. It is to be emphasized that both Haddon and Schoppe in compiling an inventory and whoever compiled the benefaction list in the first section of the Book were, to some extent, imitating earlier initiatives. Indeed, headings in the Book on page 225 and following indicate that there was to be a section devoted to 'Evidence abounding of all the livelode of the church'; on page 225 the names John Aschton and John Torner have been written, indicating that the information that they had gathered was at hand and would have been used. But the pages are blank. The bulk of the information had

---

[7] Bristol Record Office, 08153(1), no. 70, printed as the final item in the text of this volume (below, pp. 139–41).

[8] These accounts are to be printed in the next volume of All Saints' records.

perhaps already been used in the benefaction list, or else towards the end of Haddon and Schoppe's inventory where there is a short section listing 'all manner of evidence that has been found in the church' a good deal of which was late fourteenth century in origin; another repetition was hardly a high priority.[9]

There is every indication that Richard Haddon, working in conjunction with John Schoppe, compiled a considerable quantity of material intended to stand as a 'memorial and remembrance'. Ironically, Haddon's own memory has been obscured. He fell from grace with the parish even though he had been a very generous benefactor and competent manager. As a vintner he had very probably been hard hit by the loss of Bordeaux in the 1450s; in the 1470s he seems to have reneged on arrangements he had made for his father's perpetual chantry and alienated the endowment to one John Hawkes of St Leonard's parish.[10] It is tempting to speculate whether this was in default for debt. In 1473–74 the parish fought a law-suit to recover the endowment, but to no avail.[11] Haddon was thereafter very largely excised from the collective memory of the parish. As noted, his accounts as churchwarden do not survive even though they must surely have been compiled. Nor is Haddon ever mentioned as a parish benefactor in his own right although, even discounting the chantry, he was among the most generous. The parish was obdurate; it may also have been rattled. The loss of Haddon's chantry came hard on the heels of another blow which, if ultimately rectified, doubtless unsettled the parish authorities. We are told in the first section of the Book, the benefaction list, that Sir Maurice Hardwick, vicar of All Saints' from 1455 until 1472, 'procured, moved and stirred' Agnes Fyler to give her dwelling house in the High Street to the parish. Agnes Fyler, a member of a prominent parish family and widow of a churchwarden, died in 1467. Her son Thomas, a London mercer, contested the will, forcing a court case.[12] According to the benefaction list, Thomas Fyler 'would have broken her last will and alienated the house to his own use, [and he] promised the said Sir Maurice great good to assist him', that is he would have appropriated the property

---

[9] Aschton and Torner's list is also referred to on page 358 of the All Saints' Church Book; it survives in All Saints' Deeds, NA 19. The year of its compilation, 14 Richard II, is significant: 1391 was the year when the government was proceeding towards a review of current mortmain practice; by Statute, 15 Richard II, c.5, evasion of proper mortmain procedures was forbidden. In these circumstances, survey of parish possessions and evidence would certainly have been apposite.

[10] This is tersely referred to on pages 81–2 of the Book; I hope to deal with this episode more fully in my monograph on All Saints'.

[11] Referred to on page 562 of the Book.

[12] The references to Hardwick's activities are in the Book on page 83; the court case is mentioned in the accounts for 1467 on page 547; Agnes Fyler's will is to be found in the Great Orphan Book (in Bristol Record Office), fo. 186–186v.

and to do so tried to bribe the vicar. Hardwick resisted. A compromise resulted with the property going in the first instance to Thomas Fyler and, after his death, to his sister, although both were to keep an anniversary in All Saints' for their parents' souls. After the death of the sister, the property was to revert to the parish. All Saints' was to keep the anniversary and also any surplus revenues accruing from the endowment. This the parish was doing by 1485–86, somewhat later than Agnes had intended or Sir Maurice had hoped. It is, however, instructive that on the same page of the Book as the information concerning the Fyler bequest and the ensuing struggle, Hardwick is said to have given All Saints' a 'coffer with lock and key to put in the evidence of the livelode of the church where before they lay abroad likely to be embezzled and mischiefed'. In another entry on the same page we are told that Hardwick 'laboured to compile and make this book for to be a memorial and remembrance for ever for the curates and the churchwardens that shall be, for the time that every man to put yearly his account for one evidence of the livelode of the church, and for to put in names of the good doers and the names of the wardens of the church and what good they did in their days that they must yearly be prayed for'. In circumstances which, rightly, suggested to the parish authorities that a more professional approach to property management was prudent, what with two eminent men of or from All Saints' acting in ways contrary to its interests, the parish reacted by keeping evidence safe and by moving to compile a memorial and remembrance.

The Fyler episode may have been the incident which, in 1469, decided Haddon and Schoppe to keep records of benefactors and benefactions; or, given that Hardwick, too, is said to have 'laboured to compile', the wardens may have worked either on the vicar's instructions or closely in consultation with him. When Haddon was blackballed it is possible that there were others who, quite consciously, sought to emulate or even exceed his achievements and who continued the initiative by compiling the benefaction list from which Haddon is effectively excluded. Given that this list consciously minimises Haddon's contribution, it is difficult not to conclude that the intention was to kick over certain traces. Given also that the Chestre family emerged to replace Haddon as leading lights within the parish in the 1470s and 80s, and that it transpires that the priest and scribe probably responsible for the benefaction list and for writing out much of the Book in its present form had family links with the Chestres, it is hard to escape the conclusion that pique or rivalry may have been as potent as the need for security in producing the first section of the Book.

On the same page as the references to Hardwick's initiatives there is an addition to the effect that one Sir John Thomas 'helped too and wrote this book up'. Sir John Thomas is a character of considerable interest. His will reveals that he was related to the Chestres and through them to other eminent parish families, so he may have had origins in the locality.[13] He was vicar from 1479 to 1503 but was also a scribe. We are told for instance that he had written the testament of a parishioner called John Jenkyns and then at the latter's request altered the document.[14] It is likely too that as 'Thomas clerk' he had written out the earliest of the Halleways' chantry accounts in 1464. He had a long, perhaps a life-long, association with the parish. He could have written up the material compiled by Haddon and Schoppe, 'this book for every man's account to be written in'. He may also have laboured on Hardwick's 'book for to be a memorial and remembrance for ever for the curates and the churchwardens that shall be'. But, what seems most likely, given the uniformity of much of the handwriting in different sections of the Book, which may reasonably be taken to be his, and given also the date of some of the material which this hand records, from the later 1480s and thus too late to be from Hardwick's era, is that Sir John Thomas built on earlier initiatives and compiled a volume properly fulfilling Hardwick's intentions, celebrating 'names of good doers and names of wardens . . . that they must yearly be prayed for'. Significantly, he brought the accounts to a halt at a point just prior to Richard Haddon's wardenship. Later accounts were transcribed, entered in fuller form but an inferior hand; not Haddon's account, though. Similarly, the benefaction lists were up-dated to reflect later donors and donations, but Haddon was never properly reinstated, even though the censures that his name once attracted were not reinvoked. In summary then, even discounting the jottings at its end, the Book had a complex evolution. It certainly provides a digest of some materials compiled long before. Its second and third sections seem to have been gathered together in the late 1460s. Its first section took longer to crystallise, but was written down initially in the 1480s, when apparently the second and third sections were also rendered into fair copy, with some pointed exclusions, in the form that we now have them. Thereafter materials were appended to the first section until the early sixteenth century, and some attempt was made to add a few more recent accounts, and the end-papers were used (in a fairly desultory fashion) to note down certain information. Sir John Thomas failed to complete the enterprise. In the long-run the use of a large, even cumbersome volume for everyday matters may well have proved impractical. What we have is a Book compiled for a purpose. In this context, Haddon's fate should give pause: just as material might be

[13] In his will, made and proved in 1503 and recorded in the Prerogative Court of Canterbury Registers, 29 Blamyrs (fo. 244–244v), Thomas refers to John Chestre as his kinsman. He had clearly inherited property, or the duty of guarding property, from John Chestre and in his will devises this to one Johanne Hervey. He also names Humphrey Hervey his executor. It is to be noted that John Chestre's widow, Ann, had married Humphrey Hervey after John's death. That Ann's child, Johanne, and second husband played so prominent a part in Sir John Thomas' plans suggests a close link between the respective families.

[14] Referred to on page 153 of the Book.

intentionally excised, so contrivance and calculation might determine precisely what was included. I will return to consider the implications of the Book's contents after a summary of them.

The contents of the All Saints' Church Book

It is not my intention to describe the contents of the Book in any detail. They are easily read and to offer what amounts to a paraphrase can be no substitute for the reader's careful scrutiny.

a. Constitutions and Ordinances

The first section of the Book, pages 3 to 6, following a contents page, expounds rules made (we are told on the contents page) by vicar and parishioners to guide parish business and behaviour. The pages record ten or so ordinances, some relating to the parish clerk's sustenance and behaviour, others to the audit of the parish accounts, to the appointment of churchwardens and to the limits on their behaviour and powers of expenditure. These ordinances were surely only part of the apparatus in place to determine parish procedures: quite why they are included, to the exclusion of others, is not clear. One ordinance is dated to 1488, which would match the most recent material, concerning the Chestres, in the first redaction of the benefaction list. The other ordinances, too, may have been decided or confirmed at just about the same time. But this is speculation. What is more certain is that an urban parish community such as All Saints' had the wherewithal to formulate and impose upon itself sophisticated rules to guide conduct in as fair and firm a way as possible, paying surprising heed to the interests of poorer householders, to the extent, indeed, of incorporating 'the meaner sort' into the processes both of assessing householders' liability for the rate supporting the parish clerk and of choosing churchwardens.

b. The benefaction list

The benefaction list was initially compiled in the late 1480s and then added to for the next twenty years or so. In essence it resembles a bede-roll, a list which could be 'showed and declared' in church to prompt parishioners to pray for those who had given the church its livelode, that is its endowments, and who had equipped and embellished it. It was to be read out on Sundays at High Mass, but with special reverence on the Sunday before Ash Wednesday prefatory to the General Mind for all benefactors celebrated on the following Thursday and Friday. Perhaps the most remarkable aspect of the benefaction list is the preamble on page 68 of the Book, which any interested in late medieval piety will read with profit. The preamble provides a clear statement of the motives behind and benefits accruing from generosity. The parish undertook to rehearse the names of benefactors to ensure that they 'should not be forgotten but had in remembrance and prayed for of all this parish that be now and all of them that be to come'. The spiritual benefits were considerable, particularly for those whose wealth and worldly success might prove a spiritual impediment. Apart from the merit attached to the good work (which, significantly, is hardly mentioned), the preamble emphasizes that guaranteed, reciprocal intercession would hasten the salvation of the soul. What we are dealing with, stated in the preamble and manifest in the benefaction list that follows, no less than in the later list of churchwardens and their achievements, are the palpable effects of the doctrine of Purgatory as it had come to operate in a late medieval urban parish.[15] Suffice to say that this doctrine elicited a truly prodigious response as individuals, particularly the wealthy, sought to do as much as possible to benefit their souls. The poor, whose prayers were powerful, were probably the main beneficiaries as the wealthy sought both present and posthumous assistance.[16] But the parish was the next most obvious beneficiary, a prime focus for generosity with both clergy and the body of parishioners able to remember and pray for benefactors, and, by the fifteenth century, with the administrative experience to organise and guarantee this response for long periods of time. The All Saints' Church Book records the generosity of wealthier parishioners; it also registers the official response. A list was compiled committing the names to corporate memory. This could certainly be quarried for names to be recited in appropriate liturgical circumstances stimulating the required intercession. Contemporary wills and church building, to name but two sources, are eloquent as to the generosity with which individuals and communities responded to church teaching; the All Saints' benefaction list and its preamble together comprise a rare and invaluable testimony to the orchestrated institutional response. Reciprocal intercession was promised and, if parish accounts are anything to go by, an annual General Mind for all benefactors was faithfully kept. The benefaction list, too, is tangible evidence that benefactors were commemorated, although whether this was the bede-roll that was read out must be a point for debate. As it stands, with its record of who had given what, it is long; perhaps a pithier list was

---

[15] On the evolution of Purgatory, see J. Le Goff, *La Naissance du Purgatoire* (Paris, 1981), subsequently published in English as *The Birth of Purgatory* (London, 1984); for a stimulating review of the same, see R.W. Southern, 'Between Heaven and Hell', *Times Literary Supplement*, 18 June 1982, pp. 651–2. On Purgatory and related beliefs, see E. Duffy, *The Stripping of the Altars: Traditional Religion in England, c.1400–c.1580.* (New Haven and London, 1992), chapter 10; for aspects of the doctrine's impact on parish life, see my '"A fond thing vainly invented": an Essay on Purgatory and Pious Motive in later medieval England', ed. S. Wright, *Parish, Church and People, Local Studies in Lay Religion 1350–1750* (London, 1988), pp. 59–70.

[16] P.H. Cullum and P.J.P. Goldberg, 'Charitable Provision in late medieval York: "To the Praise of God and the Use of the Poor"', *Northern History* xxix (1993), 24–39; a recent appraisal which explores charity to the poor and emphasizes its importance.

actually used for recitation. The shorter, early sixteenth-century list (found on pages 162 to 167 of the Book) may more satisfactorily have fitted the bill in this respect.

The benefaction list is in three parts. The first itemizes the real property and revenues that benefactors had given. The most valuable was the Green Lattice, a property in the High Street, near the church, given by Alice Hayle in the thirteenth century and which by the later fifteenth century was a hostelry commanding a rent in the region of £5 per annum. This was much the most generous benefaction that the church had received, but there were other endowments like the property on Baldwin Street which William Newbery had given in the early fifteenth century which contributed some 12s annually to the parish coffers, or by the later fifteenth century the tenement in the High Street which Agnes Fyler had devised to the parish which, if it can correctly be identified as the property occupied by John Snygge and later by his widow Alice, yielded an annual income of £3 6s 8d. It should be noted, however, that both Newbery and the Fylers were to benefit from anniversaries provided from the incomes accruing from their endowments, an annual charge of 6s 1d in the case of Newbery, but a proportionately less onerous 12s in the case of the Fylers. By the fifteenth century no such commemoration was provided for Alice Hayle's soul. The list also itemizes a number of quit-rents and rents of assize, small sums accruing annually from a number of properties or arrangements given or made in parish and town usually long before.[17] Most were worth only a shilling or two, and by the later fifteenth century the parish was having difficulties collecting them. Two town worthies, William Canynges and John Shipward, both men of notable piety in other circumstances, reneged on such obligations to the intense chagrin of the parish. Such rights seem by the late fifteenth century to have been almost more trouble than they were worth; but it is notable that while earlier endowments and rights are recorded in the list, later benefactions, like those made by the Chestres and Bakers, both families devising property endowments in the period when the list was being compiled or added to, are less fulsomely recorded. The impulse to give was strong but the list as it stands reflects earlier rather than current generosity. This is curious. It may, however, be the result of the compiler's reliance on the work of earlier churchwardens, Aschton and Torner, who, as mentioned earlier, compiled in 1391 a list of benefactors who gave livelode.[18]

The second and third parts of the benefaction list itemize the movable goods that named clergy and parishioners had given to All Saints'. As Bristol was a mercantile community, it comes as no surprise that the movables given to the church should in some respects be more

---

[17] A quit-rent was a small rent paid by a freeholder or copyholder in lieu of services which might be required; a rent of assize was a fixed rent. See *Littleton's Tenures*, ed. E. Warnbaugh (Washington D.C., 1903).

[18] Above, note 9.

impressive than the real property. Nevertheless, given that testamentary survival is patchy and that many individuals made their bequests before death, the information in the Book is invaluable: it not only confirms that many men and women were very generous to their parish, but emphasizes once and for all that wills reveal part only of what individuals might give. These are lessons to be borne in mind if any attempt is made to treat testamentary benefaction as an index of the intensity of late medieval piety; and, as we have so few non-testamentary sources shedding light on donation, the lists in the Book are of great importance. If anything, though, it is the second of the lists which proves the most salutary. It itemizes the movable goods that a number of the parish clergy, including the priests maintained by the fraternity of Kalendars, had given to the parish. Many priests were generous, some decidedly so. In the absence of the list, the scale of clerical generosity, particularly that displayed by one incumbent after another, would never have been predicted. Clearly, the clergy, too, sought intercession, from their successors and from the parish community as a whole. They bequeathed their material possessions to secure it, and some had a good deal to give.

The third part of the benefaction list records what the parishioners of All Saints' gave. Just as the clerical section has a rough chronological order, so here the items towards the beginning of the list had the earliest provenance. But acquaintance with the material reveals that the textual composition of the lay benefaction list is complex. It falls in point of fact into four different sections, the first, third and fourth of which impose a rough chronological order on the donations mentioned. While there is a good deal of overlap between the sections, all differ as to what precisely is described and which period of activity is covered. The four sections should be briefly outlined. The first, on pages 133 to 145, is the longest and devotes perhaps more detail than any other section to a number of fourteenth- and earlier fifteenth-century donations. It is the section of the list written for the most part in the hand which may be taken to be Sir John Thomas's and its coverage extends to the late 1480s, but there are at its end on pages 144 and 145 a number of later additions in different hands. The second section, which has been scored, is concerned with the donations made by Thomas Spicer *alias* Baker, who died in 1492, and his widow Maud. It seems in the main to have been written in 1496 when Maud was still very much alive and when, we are told, she had given the parish a sumptuous suit of vestments. It also appears to have been written, up to and including the entry describing the gift of the vestments, by Sir John Thomas in a relatively infirm hand. One or two additional donations which Maud made later are also described, but these entries were apparently entered at the time when the gift was made and are in differing hands. The third section, which is to be found on pages 150 to 160, itemizes benefactions made to the parish in the 1490s and in the very early sixteenth century. There are a number of scribes at work, different ones recording the activities of Wilteshire and Snygge and Jenkyns, for instance, and a distinctive and elegant hand records the generosity of the Spicer *alias* Baker family and of other worthies. This particular material seems to have been compiled after Maud Spicer *alias* Baker's death in 1503 since it makes prominent mention of this date, and it is notable that a number of donors at about that time gave sums to All Saints' conduit, never before mentioned but apparently a new 'good cause' in the first decade or so of the century. The fourth section, on pages 161 to 167, is written neatly in a small hand and is a redaction, essentially, of the fourteenth- and fifteenth-century donations previously mentioned in both clerical and lay lists, but as far as the laity was concerned abbreviating and conflating the first and third versions of the list. This final draft may represent a rendition of the material into a form which could actually have been used as a bede-roll, but there are problems: perplexingly it makes no reference to the Spicer *alias* Bakers nor to other donors, like Thomas Pernanunt, referred to by the scribe with the elegant handwriting in the previous section, although other benefactors from the 1490s and early-1500s are included. There is then a good deal of repetition in the lay list, but descriptions of the same donors and donations vary and new information emerges even in the abbreviated versions of the material.

Like the clergy, some parishioners were very generous. But it is to be emphasized that only a small proportion of All Saints' parishioners were ever benefactors. The great majority must either have been too poor, or had other commitments, particularly children, whose claims took priority. Clement Wilteshire, several times a churchwarden of All Saints' and mayor of Bristol, who died in 1492 during his office as mayor, may be briefly mentioned in this context. Clearly he was wealthy but left less to the parish than may have been expected. The obvious reason for this, as his will discloses, is that he had four sons and two daughters all of whom had yet to reach maturity when his will was made in 1488.[19] Their claims pre-empted the parish's. But more simply, if benefactors made a donation of a few shillings, and if this had been done long before the composition of the benefaction list and not thoroughly recorded, then trace of the gift might be lost. The memory of generous benefactors was properly maintained for long periods, as demonstrated, for instance, by the examples of Roger le Gurdeler's gift in 1303 of a chalice, cup and cross and the Goldsmiths' pre-1395 gift of a gold and silver tabernacle, the two donations at the head of the lay benefaction list.[20] Small-scale benefactors, particularly if they gave money, could by contrast easily be forgotten. It is, however, likely that most of the more noteworthy benefactions made by parishioners in the 1480s and 1490s are recorded in one section or another of the list and that, therefore, we have a fairly full impression of giving for perhaps as much as a thirty-year period spanning the last two decades of the

---

[19] Great Orphan Book, fos. 244v–245.

[20] Gurdeler's gift can be dated from documentation in the parish deed collection (Deed NA 1, 24 December 1303); the Goldsmiths' benefaction is recorded in the earlier of the two inventories, compiled in 1395.

fifteenth and the first of the sixteenth century. It should be noted, though, that benefactors and their benefactions might 'fade' with time. Consider the Halleways who had died in the 1450s, some thirty years or more before the lists were compiled.[21] They were rich and generous: among their accomplishments for the parish was the foundation of a perpetual chantry which functioned until the Dissolution, the only perpetual chantry successfully established in All Saints' in the fifteenth century. The record of the Halleways' benefactions admittedly fills the side of a page in the Book, but, by the standards of the first section of the benefaction list, it is a terse record, less fulsome for instance than that entered for the Leynells, late fifteenth-century parish benefactors who were certainly less generous. Similarly, the Chestres are given pride of place in the first version of the lay benefaction list; in the fourth version, written perhaps twenty years later, and which is admittedly abbreviated, their contribution is quite brusquely recorded. Time altered perspectives as one set of benefactors succeeded another; it is no surprise that recent, or even current, benefactors commanded the detailed coverage, although it is puzzling that the Spicer *alias* Baker benefactions, described in fitting detail in the second and third sections of the list, should be omitted from the fourth.

This is not the place for extended analysis of the material in the livelode and clerical and lay benefaction lists. It is in general self-explanatory and a glossary has been provided at the end of this introduction which, it is hoped, will elucidate specific words and terms. One or two explanations may, however, prove useful. We are told, for instance, that John Haddon, vintner (Richard Haddon's father), 'let make the story of the doom in the cross aisle and paid for the same £8'. This presumably refers to the commission of a painting, presumably a mural, of the Last Judgement in the south aisle of the church. Its exact site within the aisle remains a matter for conjecture. William Wytteney, similarly, is said to have commissioned 'the Dance of Pauls' at his own cost, no lesser sum than £18. Quite what this was may best be explained by reference to John Stow's *Survey of London*: 'There was also one great cloister on the north side of this church [St Paul's Cathedral], invironing a plot of ground, of old time called Pardon churchyard . . . About this cloister was artificially and richly painted the Dance of *Machabray*, or dance of death, commonly called the Dance of Pauls.'[22]

---

[21] E.G.C. Atchley, 'The Halleway Chantry at the Parish Church of All Saints', Bristol, and the Halleway Family', *T.B.G.A.S.*, xxiv (1901), 74–125 is a useful quarry on the Halleways.

[22] J. Stow, *A Survey of London*, ed. C.L. Kingsford (2 vols, Oxford, 1908), i, 327. John, or Jenken, Carpenter, town clerk of London, is said to have paid for the painting in the north cloister of St Paul's 'with great expences'; Stow also tells us (vol i, 109) that it was 'painted upon board . . . a monument of death, leading all estates, with the speeches of death, and answer of every estate.' These verses were translated from French into English by Lydgate.

Wytteney's donation, which cannot be accurately dated but which was probably made in the mid fifteenth century, was a *danse macabre*, a painting of a Dance of Death. The parish accounts reveal that this was put up and taken down again usually twice a year, at St James's tide in high summer, and at All Hallows' tide in the autumn. It must then have been painted on board or probably on canvas to form a banner. It was expensive, costing over twice as much as Haddon's doom, and, one assumes, large or long. Wytteney's reported motives are particularly telling: the painting was to be 'a memorial that every man should remember his own death'. Haddon's intentions in commissioning a Doom would presumably have been much the same. It is of great interest that, in addition to the parish benefaction list or bede-roll, All Saints' clearly had a number of other, in this case visual means of concentrating the minds of its parishioners on what would happen to them. All must make preparation because all would need services, either by clergy or surviving laity. An awareness of death and what was required underpinned the doctrine of Purgatory and the responses it prompted. This had a profound impact on parishes such as All Saints', and indeed the benefaction list is hard evidence of the generosity elicited from the wealthier element to procure intercession. Haddon's and Wytteney's choice of decorative scheme is fascinating evidence of the system, as it were, reinforcing itself as a result of lay benefaction.[23]

c. The inventories and the list of churchwardens

If the first section of the All Saints' Church Book reveals quite how much the parish derived from gifts, particularly from the wealthy prompted by the requirements of Purgatory, then the second section of the Book – in two parts, two inventories on pages 315 to 358, and the list of churchwardens on pages 375 to 382 – demonstrates the part played by parish authorities both in maintaining equipment and, by acting on behalf of the collectivity, adding to possessions and improving fixtures and fittings. Together the two parts of the second section emphasize the importance of the role of conventional collective acquisition and maintenance, the day-to-day management of this role being very much in the hands of churchwardens. The benefaction lists afford a rare and vivid insight into the part played by individual generosity in benefiting a parish. The inventories and churchwardens' list (the first quite common survivals, the second very unusual), if at first less striking, are of no less importance. Indeed, with time and reflection, their significance increases. The second and third sections of the Book, that is inventories, churchwardens' list and accounts, balance the first section with its emphasis on individual generosity. Together they emphasize the contribution made by churchwardens towards the

---

[23] Cf. Duffy, *The Stripping of the Altars*, pp. 302ff.

embellishment and smooth running of the church — the contribution, in other words, of conventional parish provision and management. The second section encapsulates the commitment and achievement of successive sets of churchwardens, both by the summaries of the contributions made by different pairs, and also by the two inventories. Whether or not their juxtaposition was intentional, comparisons are unavoidable because, quite simply, compiled some seventy years after the first, the second inventory is very much fuller. It provides eloquent testimony to the powers of acquisition and maintenance exercised by parish management.

The first of the two inventories was compiled or commissioned by William Lenche and Stephen Knyght who were wardens in 1395; the second by Richard Haddon and John Schoppe in 1469. That the first of these had been recovered to be written down at the same time as the second is suggested by the fact that each is in the same handwriting. This matches the basic hand in much of the rest of the text, taken to be that of scribe and vicar, Sir John Thomas. It is worth pointing out that there are additions in parts of the second inventory reporting new acquisitions made after 1469. Some of these may well have been added by Thomas as an old man; indeed on page 338 is an addition itemising the gift of a collectory, a liturgical book, with noted anthems, epistles and gospels given by Sir John Thomas in 1496. The entry is in an infirm version of the basic hand, matching for instance that describing Maud Spicer *alias* Baker's gift of a sumptuous suit of vestments in the same year on page 148 of the text. These would certainly seem to have been additions by an elderly Sir John Thomas, an assumption strengthened by the monogram JT in the margin by the entry referring to the collectory. Clearly Thomas made some effort to keep different parts of the book up to date, particularly if they reflected well on his generosity or powers of advocacy, although it must be reiterated that large tracts of the volume were never completed. By the same token, while there is no guarantee that the first inventory is necessarily a full description of what was in the church in the late fourteenth century, the second is obviously much more comprehensive; some of its sections, however, have been left blank. Where direct comparisons are possible, for instance between the vestments or books in possession of the church at the two different dates, the inescapable conclusion is just how much more the parish had in the later fifteenth century. For instance in 1395 the parish had only two Mass books and, apart from miscellaneous chasubles and copes, two suits of vestments (a suit, it should be noted, was sufficient to robe priest, deacon and sub-deacon at High Mass); the lists of books and vestments in the second inventory, on pages 333 to 339 and 342 to 343 are at least three or four times fuller in virtually every category. Starting with books and vestments, the first inventory continues to list cloths, towels and mantles, then equipment for church and liturgy, then jewels, comprising cups, chalices, censers and the like, and concludes with a short section mainly of wooden goods including desks, candlesticks and ladders. The second inventory starts with wooden goods, moves on to curtains and curtain rails, and cloths to drape images during Lent and to cover altars throughout the year. The first inventory mentioned very few candlesticks, surprisingly enough; in the second, on page 329, there is a much better collection, as indeed on the following page there is of stained cloths for various altars and for various hangings. As mentioned, the book list is much longer in the second inventory and just as, earlier, the exact dimensions of altar cloths had been given, presumably for reasons of security, so with the books care is taken to itemize the first and last phrases in every volume.[24] There follows a list of the parish's vestments and banners which, interestingly, is perhaps the most added-to section of the inventory, presumably reflecting the fact that fabrics were particularly perishable, both because of their intrinsic fragility and because of wear and tear with time; it may also reflect the fact that parishioners were keen to give such items both because they were used at times of moment in the liturgy and because they could be made to be distinctive, identifying donor with garment in the eyes of successive parishioners.[25] Two pages listing jewels and chalices comprise the last section of the inventory. After a few blank pages there is then, on pages 353 to 358, a section which has no equivalent in the first inventory but which is of considerable interest. An attempt was made to list the evidence that the church had confirming ownership of and rights over various endowments. The list is incomplete, a good many gaps occurring, but there can be no doubt that parish authorities were aware of the importance of documentary evidence in strengthening interests and withstanding predators. It also underlines the fact that the defence of property at law, for which such evidence was essential, was an integral aspect of the churchwardens' responsibilities. Sorted muniments would greatly have eased their task on these occasions. This section may indeed confirm the supposition that that one reason at least which explains why the parish moved to compile the materials comprising the Book was as a response to insecurities experienced after coping either with predatory parishioners or with legal frustration in the 1460s and early 1470s.

One item should be singled out, however, partly in explanation but also to demonstrate just how much more sophisticated the parish was by the later fifteenth century. Although significantly there is no detailed reference to specific equipment, the first inventory mentions two stained cloths for the sepulchre 'with four knights and Mary Magdalene'. This refers to the Easter sepulchre, customarily positioned to the north side of the chancel: here, at the conclusion of the liturgy on Good Friday, the parish priest 'buried' a pyx containing the third Host consecrated on the

[24] Books could go missing: the primer given to All Saints' by William Wytteney was twice stolen, as reported on page 136 of the book.

[25] Sir Maurice Hardwick, the Chesters and the Spice *alias* Bakers, for instance, all gave cloths, equipment or vestments embroidered either with their initials or symbols associated with them, as described on pages 84, 141 and 148 of the Book.

previous day, as well as the cross which had been kissed by the congregation.[26] The sepulchre might consist of a box on a frame draped with cloths, which would seem to have been the case in All Saints', or it could be more substantial. Continuous watch was kept over the sepulchre until the service early on Easter morning when the Host was removed to hang in its pyx above the high altar and the cross was also 'raised' to be carried in procession around the church. The empty sepulchre would remain an object of devotion throughout the following week. Quite what All Saints' used for its sepulchre in the late fourteenth century is unclear, but both the accounts and churchwardens' list reveal that All Saints' built anew in 1422–3, and the second inventory discloses aspects of the more substantial sepulchre certainly in use by the later fifteenth century. The inventory mentions one sepulchre, five gilded battlements, two gilded crucifixes for the two ends of the sepulchre, four bolts of iron with two battlements of red and one crown with four angels of painted wood; later, in the section devoted to cloths, there is a reference to one cloth of Mary Magdalene with four knights for the sepulchre (whether this was the same cloth or a replacement is not clear); also 'for the sepulchre' was one cloth of stained work powdered with birds of gold and another stained cloth powdered with flowers of gold. Many churches built elaborate sepulchres in the course of the fifteenth century. All Saints' spent 47s 2d on constructing, painting and carving a sepulchre in 1422–3, but by the latter part of the century it would, with its red and gold paint and its fine draperies, have appeared opulent. Both the equipment and hangings may be taken as an index for changes wrought within All Saints' in the fifteenth century: it is not just that there was much more in the church, what was there was more impressive.

In many respects providing the key to the second and third sections of the Book, the list of churchwardens and their achievements merits close consideration.[27] It provides an epitome of the accounts to be found in the third section, singling out and celebrating the achievements of successive pairs of wardens, with some gaps, from c. 1410 to 1469. Two entries, one concerning William Lenche and Stephen Knyght and the other concerning John Aschton and John Torner, are intrusions, being late-fourteenth century in provenance. The remainder follow the order of the accounts copied into the Book later on. The most consistent feature of these epitomes is to record the surplus that each pair of wardens managed to secure of income over

[26] Duffy, *The Stripping of the Altars*, pp. 29–37, and n. 52 for bibliography.

[27] Although I have yet to see any which exactly resembles the epitomes of churchwardens' activities in the second section of the All Saints' Church Book, epitomes of accounts can occasionally be found: they exist, for instance, in the fifteenth-century 'Miscellany' surviving for St Mary at Hill, London (Guildhall Library, London, MS 1239/2); moreover, in the archives of St Mary Redcliffe, Bristol, a seventeenth-century ledger entitled 'Account Book 7 & The Great Ledger of Benefactions' (BRO: P/StMR/ChW/1(g)) contains, in addition to much else, epitomes of the parish's financial transactions by year. I am grateful to Sheila Lang in the Bristol Record Office for drawing my attention to this example.

expenditure in their year of office. Almost all made a profit. Some managed an excess of £5 or more; others much less, William Raynes and Thomas Chestre, for instance, brought only 7d clearly to the church, but they had made the Easter sepulchre. In some cases expenditure exceeded income, as with Thomas Halleway and John Gosselynge; and Richard Brewer and John Coke still owed the parish £5 17s 4½d, presumably having refused to hand over this surplus or having embezzled it. The standard exhortation that God should have mercy on their souls is conspicuously absent in the latter pair's case. But the question arises that if the parish was generally running a healthy surplus, what happened to it? What was it used for? Sets of wardens seem to have paid for their achievements without recourse to the surplus. The one obvious exception to this occurs on page 380 where William Peyntour and Robert Walshe 'brought in on All Hallows' eve the best suit, *p'c* – £100'. Surely this would have mopped up the surplus. But a later entry suggests that the figure of £100 is an error. William Boxe and John Schoppe are said to have paid John Leynell £7 1s 2d in part payment of £20 for the best suit. These sums seem much more realistic. Moreover, rather than tapping a reserve, wardens seem to have arranged their finances to repay debts with surpluses from subsequent years. What the accumulated surplus was used for remains unresolved, but both the general health of parish finances and most wardens' competence are beyond dispute.

The churchwardens' list bears witness to more than this. Admittedly some wardens are credited with nothing other than a financial surplus, but most did something else. Many acquired equipment, be it bells or vestments, or, like Peyntour and Walshe, they procured the organ, or, like William Ward and William Baten, they purchased latten candlesticks and bowls. Ward and Baten had in fact refurbished and redecorated the rood loft where the candlesticks and bowls were to stand; others, like William Raynes and Thomas Chestre improved equipment, the Easter sepulchre in their case, while others like Thomas Fyler and William Haytfield rebound the church books. John Baker and John William erected the cross in the churchyard, while Roger Abyndon and Richard Andrew rebuilt the churchyard wall. The achievements credited to others pertain more to the repair of church fabric and to bolstering parish income. Several sets of wardens are said to have carried out repairs to the parish's endowments, like Richard Andrew and Richard Abyndon (wardens for three consecutive years) who restored Martin Layfyll's house and William Ward's house, as well as repairing the church steeple, or Roger Abyndon and Robert Core who are said in their day to have made great repairs both in the church and on the tenements. Ill fortune is also recorded, such as the fire in the two houses adjacent to the steeple which occurred in the wardenship of Clement Wilteshire and Howell apRees; if nothing else subsequent repairs would greatly have increased the wardens' work-load, and the successors, William Boxe and John Schoppe, are said to have rebuilt part of this property. Problems with endowment and finance are also recorded, such as Shipward's refusal to pay the quit-rent due from the property in Marsh Street, or, on several occasions, the law suits to which wardens had recourse in their attempt to maintain the parish's holdings. These may not always have been successful, as with the loss of John Pers's house in the 1430s, but the work which wardens like William Raynes and John Taylor put in to fight such a case is certainly remembered with gratitude, no less than William Rowley and John Compton's more successful case against Fyler in the 1460s.

A phrase used in the preamble to each inventory sheds light on the role that the second section of the Book was presumably intended to play. Each was intended to be 'a memorial and a remembrance to all manner of people that come after us', and before the second inventory, it may be noted, there is the extra information that it was commissioned also 'for the great worship and love of God and to profit the said church'. Whether the scribe who wrote the lists down deliberately inserted and repeated 'a memorial and a remembrance' is ultimately an imponderable; nor, as mentioned, can we ever be sure whether juxtaposition and comparison, with its inevitable conclusion, was also intentional. Neither is unlikely. Even if, for the time being, each inventory is treated discretely, both stand as testimony to the generosity of parishioners and to the assiduity of parish management. This was worth commemorating. But comparison surely is inevitable, and this serves to emphasize the cumulative achievement of gathering, maintaining and embellishing goods and equipment. The point of including the first inventory in a volume written, after all, almost a century later must surely have been to emphasize quite how far the parish had come in the variety and quality of its possessions. This is testimony to its churchwardens' collective achievement. It deserved a memorial, which is what the two inventories provide; it also deserves to be remembered, to benefit the churchwardens' souls. The churchwardens' list enlarges on this process in an altogether pithier manner. In contrast to an emphasis on the general and the cumulative, the list emphasizes individual achievements in a wider arena. As mentioned the information was extracted from the surviving churchwardens' accounts with the intention of providing snap-shots of what each pair had done to improve or embellish equipment, decoration and fabric, or to invest in and defend the property comprising the parish's endowments. As well as being more personalized, the impression is more comprehensive. What emerges, generally from the inventories and more specifically from the list, is that the churchwardens' contribution was essential if the parish were to flourish, and, no less importantly, that management was a good work. In this fashion, as intimated earlier, the second section, emphasizing corporate achievement as ordered by churchwardens, can be set against the impression of individual generosity conveyed by the benefaction lists. Inventories and list celebrate the churchwardens' collective and individual donation, fixing the names and contribution of these otherwise unsung benefactors into the parish memory. They too must be remembered. It should be noted that only a few wardens found inclusion in the benefaction lists; had there been no churchwardens' list, they and their contributions would have proved ephemeral. The point of 'a memorial and a remembrance' becomes clear and is accomplished as a result of this material.

d. The accounts

These start on page 437 of the Book, with the undated account of John Derby and William Backe. It is likely that this was compiled at some point in the first decade of the fifteenth century, with the second account, compiled by Laurence Brocke and William Baten, securely dated to 10 Henry IV, that is 1408–09. Although there are chronological gaps in the run, particularly in the reign of Henry V, the surviving accounts are written in the same hand, identified with that of Sir John Thomas, and some forty accounts are presented in a reasonably uniform fashion on successive pages. There are no breaks in the text to mark lost accounts. This continues until page 551, with the account of Martin Symonson and John Branfeld for 1467–68. Recommencing on page 553, with Clement Wilteshire and John Chestre's account for 1472–73, the format is changed. The handwriting is inferior; the ink a different colour; the accounts much fuller. Some ten survive for successive years in this final section, the account of Clement Wilteshire and Thomas Pernaunt for 1481–82 being the last, ending on page 597. So, in total, fifty fifteenth-century accounts are preserved in the All Saints' Church Book. There are duplicates for some in the latter part of the run which survive in the unbound accounts for All Saints'. There is also by very good fortune one account surviving from the late 1420s preserved in the collection of the Bristol antiquary F.F. Fox; this differs markedly from the later unbound accounts. It is in Latin, is on one large sheet of parchment, and the entries in the account are not tabulated like those in the Book or in the unbound accounts.[28] It is a document both more perishable than the folded quires of the unbound accounts and more awkward to use. That it is a sole survivor gives no occasion for surprise. There can be no doubt that the cache recorded in the Book represents a very considerable repository of otherwise lost information concerning the parish in the earlier decades of the century. As it is intended that the second volume of All Saints' material to be published in the Bristol Record Series should be devoted to parish accounts, specifically the unbound accounts, the introduction to that volume will be a more suitable place for proper discussion of the contents of the surviving All Saints' accounts. Only the briefest of surveys is needed here.[29]

---

[28] Above, note 7.

[29] C. Drew, *Early Parochial Organization in England* (St Anthony's Hall Publications, vii, 1954) provides a clear and useful discussion both of the evolution of the office and of the duties discharged by churchwardens.

Churchwardens were charged with responsibility for maintaining the fabric of the parish church, specifically nave and tower, and with acquiring and maintaining the equipment necessary for the proper discharge of the services and sacraments within the parish church. They were responsible for collecting the rents accruing from parish endowments and for collecting the offerings and dues which parishioners were, respectively, urged to make and obliged to pay. They spent this income on the fabric of the church, on equipment and on maintaining the endowment. Their brief, then, had its limitations, and it is to be emphasized that churchwardens' accounts give us only the bare bones of parish financial affairs, not a full picture. They contain nothing about tithe, for instance; nor do the All Saints' accounts deal with the charges levied to support the parish clerk, even though there is no doubt that the parish maintained an auxiliary. The All Saints' wardens were not responsible for the vicar's salary; if they were responsible for the clerk's stipend, they administered it separately, only occasionally 'borrowing' from the main account to correct a shortfall. The accounts that survive were audited in the presence of the vicar, whose presence appears mandatory, and also, by the end of the fifteenth century, before all parishioners – although it may be safer to assume that for the century generally, the 'worshipful', the more eminent among them, would have been most likely to attend the audit.[30] The accounts invariably deal first with income, derived both from rents and from collections and dues levied from and on parishioners. Expenditure on fabric and equipment, commonly on preservation and mending and sometimes on building afresh or buying anew, constitutes the second and usually lengthier part of the account. The accounts in the Book are, with the slight exception of the ten accounts at the end of the run, very neat. The important point to consider here is why these accounts were tidied up and written into a Book decades after the affairs and personnel with which and whom they deal had had their day, and it is to consider the intended use of the accounts as they now exist that I turn.

An obvious priority is to establish the extent to which the accounts, or at least the first forty of them, were trimmed. Confining ourselves, for the present, to the material printed in the present volume, a start may be made comparing the surviving, apparently authentic account presently preserved in the Fox manuscripts with the version of the same account which, by very good fortune, is written into the Book.[31] The comparison is salutary. Not only has presentation been adapted to match that in the accounts as they were compiled, to judge from the unbound survivals,

---

[30] The ordinances towards the beginning of the All Saints' Church Book, on page 4, give unequivocal indication that a parish clerk was maintained by the late fifteenth century. The ordinances on page 5 reveal that a decision was taken in 1488 which stipulated that all parishioners were to attend to the audit; indeed, parishioners were to be fined if absent without a good reason.

[31] Printed below on pp. 139–41 and pp. 58–9 respectively.

from at least the mid fifteenth century, but other alterations have been made. Although there is a possibility that the scribe who copied the version into the the Book may have had another prototype than that surviving in the Fox collection, the dates as given in the Book do not tally with the original. The year is a mismatch and the day of audit, said to be the feast of *sci Mathee apli*, that is the feast either of St Matthew, 21 September, or possibly St Mathias, 24 February, in the Fox manuscript, is given as the last day of March in the Book. The scribe seems to have been guided by concern to match his version of proceedings with, what for him, was current practice. Scrutinizing the accounts proper, two points are to be made: first, that the authentic version is much more detailed; and second, that when condensing the material for the Book, the scribe conveys the gist of the material reasonably well but was not unduly concerned with accuracy. Look, for instance, at the section devoted to income: whereas the Fox manuscript mentions the sums collected at Easter and other miscellaneous donations, these are simply lumped together as Easter receipts, and the total is given incorrectly. The income from seats and burials and torches is similarly slightly inaccurate, as is the rent that Nicholas Hoper paid for the tenement in Baldwin Street. And whereas the addition for the rents in the Book is correct as it stands, making the necessary adjustment given the alteration in Hoper's rent, the overall total is hopelessly inaccurate. Generally, simplification is the watchword. Admittedly, the section on book repair, a fairly unusual entry, is copied faithfully; elsewhere details are elided to shorten the account. For instance, a short section on Ash Wednesday is reduced to one line 'for the General Mind', very probably an anachronistic soubriquet; similarly, where the original itemizes payments of '4d for straw at All Saints" and '5d for straw at Christmas', the version in the Book combines the two as '9d for straw at Christmas'. The version in the Book is a digest. It conveys a fairly full impression of what the wardens were doing. But it is not entirely reliable. It is for show, not audit: a troubling conclusion as far as the historian of the parish in concerned. This, however, makes some sense of the surprising admission in the receipts on page 522 of the Book (for 1453–54): 'Item of William Peynter, 'y wote ner wher for' – 2s 6d'.[32] The scribe could hardly suppress the entry but, presumably, whatever record he was working from did not fully reveal why Peynter had given the sum.

The accounts as written into the All Saints' Church Book are, then, a digest processing and representing all that could be found of earlier fifteenth-century records by the 1480s, or thereabouts. This explains the neatness of presentation and the fact that gaps in the sequence necessitate no break in the transcript. It also explains why the chronology as given in the accounts is so slipshod. The originals were apparently dated by regnal years only; the scribe's attempt to render these into Anno Domini, which he does intermittently, is unhappy: witness the mistake on page 531 where Henry VI's last year, correctly

---

[32] Below, p. 133.

said to be his thirty-ninth, and Edward IV's first, is given as 1459.[33] It should have been 1461. That the scribe misattributed the date of a significant and really quite recent event gives pause: clearly precise chronology did not exercise him unduly. It was simply not the point. So what was his purpose in trawling and processing the past? Why did he devote so much time, energy and paper to the exercise?

The answer is obvious if the accounts, the third section of the Book, are considered as an adjunct of the second. Just as the inventories and churchwardens' list celebrate, first, the sustained achievement of management and, second, amplify specific improvements made by different sets of wardens, so the accounts give an exhaustive impression of the unremitting effort which underpinned both gradual accumulation and more notable achievements. The accounts make a subtle point well: even the day-to-day running of the church took a great deal of work. Wardens deserved to be remembered for this, first and foremost, rather than for specific achievements, and this is what the accounts convey. Overall, there can be no real doubt that the second and third sections were meant to be taken together. As asserted earlier, the churchwardens' list is very much the accounts reduced to a series of epitomes, graphically demonstrated for instance in the first account where marginal notes precisely match the main points in the first of the churchwardens' summary. Or, to turn this point about-face in recognition of the order in which material is presented in the Book, the accounts inevitably expand on the epitomes emphasizing the detailed work, worry and commitment that any set of wardens, whether or not they made a profit on the year, inevitably had to invest to ensure the good running of the parish. By definition, the accounts contain and convey minutiae, whether of collecting monies, dues and rents, or the details of myriad expenditures on equipment, on fixtures and fittings, on the fabric of church and on parish endowments, all too often down to the last lath or nail. The onerous nature of wardenship is vividly conveyed as, more subtly, is the finesse of judgement that was needed to keep in credit and the tenacity required to defend parish property and interests against predators. To write up the accounts was a striking act of piety to former generations of churchwardens, celebrating their achievement. The accounts may not be entirely accurate, but they serve their purpose, celebrating the contribution which successive pairs had made, acting again both as 'a memorial and a remembrance.' To continue an earlier theme, if far from obvious initially, the second and third sections of the Book offer a fascinating complement to the first. They balance the tangible donations of the benefaction lists with the often intangible but absolutely vital contributions, of time, expertise and sustained commitment which churchwardens consistently made. It should be added that benefactors would not have been inclined to

---

[33] Below, p. 138.

generosity in the first place had they not been convinced that their donations would be properly maintained and the church properly managed, each of which depended on wardens doing their duty. The Book becomes a celebration of successful wardenship, a proof that memory could be sustained, and thus it advocates that present and future generations should be as generous as those preceding because all might rest in confidence that their interests would be served.

e. Memoranda and jottings

Towards the end of the volume there are three discrete, short sections of material, all indifferently presented and appearing to be either unfinished or simply notes in progress. While consideration of this material proves useful, the most striking conclusion to emerge is an appreciation of the value of the rest of the Book: incomplete it may be, but for so much material to be preserved in both tidy and detailed form emerges, by comparison, as all the more remarkable. The first of the final pieces is a single side, page 997 to be precise, containing material on parish anniversaries. The composite services and costs of the anniversaries of Sir Thomas Marshall, vicar, celebrated on 7 and 8 January, and that of the Chestres, celebrated on 13 and 14 February, are itemized. The intention would appear to have been an ordered listing of all the anniversaries celebrated in All Saints' through the year, but the compiler managed only the first two. Two points should be made. The first is to note that although other information matches and confirms the details of the Chestres' requirements, in the absence of Marshall's will it is particularly useful to have information concerning his wishes. Marshall had built or refurbished the vicarage and the anniversary was the return apparently specified for this benefaction.[34] He had died in 1434, and it is pleasing to have some confirmation that his service was apparently still being kept some fifty years on. It should be noted, too, that detail on the services kept for clergy is rare; this service, though, would seem to have been entirely conventional. Second, even though the list is obviously very incomplete, there is enough to remind us that wardens rightly took the correct discharge of the requisite services seriously. Perpetual anniversaries were almost invariably the liturgical return that a benefactor expected from devising an endowment; the parish's continued tenure and enjoyment of any profit accruing depended on the full discharge of a relatively complex ritual. A memorandum would clearly have been

---

[34] Marshall's generosity is mentioned in the clerical benefaction list on pages 78 and 79 of the Book. A problem emerges, though, comparing the information in the benefaction list with that in the jottings at the end of the volume: in the first Marshall is said to have died on 7 June 1434; his anniversary was to be celebrated on 7 January. Given that day of death and subsequent anniversary date usually coincided, and given also that Marshall's anniversary is itemized in the jottings before the Chestres' February anniversary, then a January death looks the more likely. On anniversaries in Bristol, see my 'A service for the dead: the form and function of the Anniversary in late medieval Bristol', *T.B.G.A.S.*, cv (1987), 183–211, and on the reciprocal aspect of anniversaries particularly pp. 199–203.

useful and at least some effort was made to enter one, possibly a copy of a now lost loose-paper version, in the Book.

The second piece is to be found on pages 1055 to 1057 of the Book and consists, in the main, of rough accounts for the Jesus Guild in All Saints' from the first half of the 1480s. They are not full accounts as they only itemize income, sometimes simply entering the total received. Nevertheless, given the scarcity of guild accounts, not only for Bristol but for the country at large, these are of significance. A weekly Jesus Mass, celebrated on Fridays, was established in All Saints' by the Chestres and, as they are said to have done this jointly, the endowment may well have predated Henry's death in 1470. Whether the foundation of this service stimulated the formation of a fraternity of Jesus, or whether the Chestres were moved by an existing devotion within the church is unclear. But it could well have been the former, and it may well have been the stimulus responsible for the change in the name of the north aisle towards the end of the century, Our Lady's aisle becoming the Jesus aisle. It should also be noted that the ordinances at the beginning of the volume reveal that just as anyone elected churchwarden who refused to serve was to be fined 6s 8d, so too any chosen to be a proctor of Jesus who refused to serve was to pay the 'treasury of Jesus 3s 4d'. The Kalendars apart, who were in any case supervised by their own prior, the Jesus Guild seems to have been the only parish confraternity with any particular profile,[35] and certainly seems to have been an adjunct of the parish under the supervision of parish officials. The income of the guild was generally small, in the region of half a mark per annum, but, given that the Chestres' largesse paid for the weekly celebrations, it is not quite clear what the income was intended to find. The accounts reveal that a surplus was accumulating and that it was managed by some of the more eminent parishioners. It is tempting, considering the names of the guild wardens, names like Chestre, Spicer *alias* Baker, Pernaunt and Wilteshire, to speculate whether the Jesus guild was for the parish elite. No proof can be adduced, but the characters who managed the parish as churchwardens were also often guild wardens. The evidence is also insufficient to determine whether or not the same pairs of men who had served as wardens for either parish or guild served the other organization after a set interval. Again, two points arise. First, the references in the guild accounts that they were audited both before the vicar, as were parish accounts, but also 'before divers of the parish beside' or 'before the vicar and the parishioners' are significant. The ordinances at the very beginning of the Book stipulate that all parishioners were to attend the parish audit; in the absence of detail in the main parish accounts, references here confirm that parishioners did indeed attend audits. Similarly, just as the ordinances

---

[35] There is a reference to a chalice belonging to the Fraternity of Carpenters on page 319 of the Book in the earlier of the two inventories; there would, however, seem to be no trace of this Fraternity in All Saints' fifteenth-century records.

suggest that clergy and parishioners together took decisions, information in these accounts reveals that it was 'ordained by the vicar and the parishioners' that monies for the guild were to be put into a coffer. Mention of the coffer leads to a second point of interest. There is a memorandum dated 7 April 1491 almost at the end of the section containing the Jesus Guild details noting the sums of money contained in the respective coffers in the church. In the 'purse of Jesus', so called, there was £5 12s 4d; in the parish treasure coffer £42 0s 8 1/2d; in the Halleway chantry coffer £33 19s 1d. Such information is rare, and given the detail that survives for other aspects of parish income and expenditure, it is pleasing to be told quite what All Saints', a small but apparently reasonably well-heeled urban parish, had in reserve at a given moment. As intimated earlier, the accounts themselves make no reference to accumulated surpluses, although quite how the money was managed, and whether it could be used for anything other than crises, is still not clear. What perhaps is more striking, with a surplus not much less than the parish's, is the reserve for the Halleways' chantry. It provides another reminder of quite why a parish might value and even cherish a perpetual chantry foundation, and why anger might greet its loss: even if ordinarily kept separately, its monies significantly bolstered parish reserves.

The third and final piece, on page 1090 and following, is also concerned with the parish coffers and who was entrusted with keys. Again, to judge from names, the material was compiled in the 1480s. There is little here of any value, but the attempt to keep up-to-the-minute information teaches an important lesson. The section is, to put it mildly, a mess. It clearly proved impossible to chart different wardens having different keys year by year, with some dying and their key being handed on, while others lived and kept their key. The material is so scrappy and untidy that it fails to serve any useful purpose. If confirmation were needed, the slipshod appearance of these few pages, and indeed of all the miscellanea towards the end of the volume, underlines the fact that the All Saints Church Book was a formal, perhaps even a ceremonial compilation. It was not, never could have been a volume concerned with the day-to-day, present management of the parish and parish activities. Rendering such activities in the tidy and consistent manner which characterises the great majority of the Book would have been well nigh impossible. It is significant that the only untidy section, apart from the miscellanea, is that attempting to keep the benefaction lists current. The final entries emphasize that the Book, as a whole, provided a backward look, away from the day-to-day; essentially it was compiled to commemorate past activity and generosity.

The implications of the All Saints' Church Book

While it is undoubtedly tempting to seize on and quarry the materials preserved in the All Saints' Church Book, caution is essential. It was a volume compiled for distinct purposes which quite possibly colour the presentation and selection of its contents; it was also produced in human circumstances which, if uncertain, definitely shaped what was ultimately produced. To treat briefly with the second of these, it is worth remembering the role of Haddon and Schoppe in compiling the second and perhaps the third sections of the Book: these were perhaps the men who first started to celebrate and commemorate the role of the churchwarden, and they may well have done so in collaboration with the vicar, Sir Maurice Hardwick. Haddon subsequently fell from grace; his role as benefactor could be minimised, but his collaboration with Schoppe meant that this contribution could not be obliterated without slighting Schoppe. It is, however, interesting to note that Haddon acted as supervisor to Agnes Fyler's will; and, given the generosity of the Fylers' benefaction, interesting also to ponder this family's relative obscurity in the benefaction list. Agnes Fyler is commemorated, but her son's activities can have done little to predispose parish celebration of the family. With the eventual disgrace of both Fyler junior and Haddon junior, two families previously prominent in parish life and who had perhaps been closely associated one with another, could justifiably be displaced in the parish pantheon and other role models substituted. This motive probably played at least some part in Sir John Thomas's objectives in, apparently, compiling and writing-up the Book in its basic form. His relatives, the Chestres, could be brought to the fore, along with other contemporaries like the Spicer *alias* Baker family, who provided much better role models. Local rivalries and family politics aside, a vicar and the parish authorities had very good reason to commit some to relative oblivion and set others up for emulation, given that so much depended on good will and generosity. It is in passing worth speculating, too, whether changing the name of the north aisle, built by Richard Haddon remember, from Our Lady's aisle to the Jesus aisle was done with something of the same motive in mind, both the Chestre family and the Spicer *alias* Bakers exhibiting noteworthy devotion to the cult of Jesus.[36] So, as far as the creation of the Book is concerned, it is important to emphasize that both laity and clergy collaborated in an ambitious endeavour, but that rivalries and undercurrents appear influential in fashioning the final product.

Turning to consider the wider purposes that the Book was to serve, of the references to the process of compilation which occur in the text that relating to Hardwick's role offers the best understanding of what was intended: 'Item he laboured to compile and make this book for to be a memorial and remembrance for ever for the curates and the

---

[36] This is not to deny that both Alice Chestre and Maud Spicer *alias* Baker also exhibited notable devotion to the Blessed Virgin, but what with the former engaging a priest to celebrate the weekly Jesus Mass and the latter providing candles to burn at this Mass, as well as a vestment decorated 'with five wounds in the cross' and, among other things, a table of the Transfiguration to 'move and excite people unto devotion', the two widows certainly seem well abreast of devotional developments; see R.W. Pfaff, *New Liturgical Feasts in late Medieval England* (Oxford, 1970).

churchwardens that shall be for the time, that every man to put yearly his account for one evidence of the livelode of the church, and for to put in names of the good doers and the names of the wardens of the church and what good they did in their days that they must yearly be prayed for.' Memorial and remembrance are emphasized, particularly in enabling parish authorities to discharge their responsibilities fully. It is also to be noted that good doers and wardens, the beneficiaries of memorial and remembrance, are assigned equal prominence. If Hardwick inaugurated this enterprise, another priest, it has been argued, played the major part in compiling the volume which was to accomplish these purposes. However much he was aided and abetted by parishioners, Sir John Thomas's achievement is striking, subtly exploiting the parish archives – translating and piecing together old accounts, records and inventories – to commemorate benefactors and managers more fulsomely than had previously been possible. This was done by a priest to benefit the whole parish; it was done to urge fidelity, particularly in the aftermath of Fyler and Haddon; it was done to urge participation, the promise of commemoration undoubtedly acting as a powerful incentive on contemporaries to involve themselves in parish management. Indeed, compiling a Book over half of which celebrated churchwardens' achievements could really only have been contemplated with a very definite intention of encouraging busy individuals to emulate earlier wardens in what may otherwise have been an unattractive task, running the parish. Consider: in a Book almost totally devoted to the past rather than the present, the one relatively substantial section which occupies itself with practicalities is the section recording parish ordinances. If at first sight odd, the section does in part concern itself with the activities of wardens. On page 5 the one dated section in the ordinances reveals that in 1488, seemingly when the Book was compiled, 'in the time of Sir John Thomas being vicar, and Richard Stevyns and Thomas Pernaunt proctors's agreement was reached with the whole parish being present about proper conduct on the day of audit and, note, about the procedure for selecting wardens. The penalty for refusing to serve, a fine of 6s 8d, seems feeble given the work involved in being a warden. It could hardly have been a deterrent for the 'worshipful'. A much more effective deterrent would have been exclusion from the chance of commemoration. This, perhaps, is why the Book was needed. It is not a bede-roll as such, and even the benefaction lists as they survive could hardly have been read out; but the Book was clearly a book of memory in which achievements could be formally recorded and preserved. Its existance prompted the possibility of exclusion, of being excluded from the good and the great, and from commemoration. The Book, I would argue, was compiled to stimulate participation, where fines and financial deterrents may have fallen short. The past could be harnessed to serve the here and now; the Book facilitated the process.

In conclusion, two points must be made. First, that immersion in the practices and values of late medieval piety naturally reveals the otherness of that world. One of the most striking divergences which emerges is that the dead were hardly less of a presence in life than the living, a conclusion reinforced by consideration of the contents and purposes of the All Saints' Church Book. Strict chronological accuracy may not have been an imperative; nor was computational accuracy. The guiding objective of the Book was a general commemoration and celebration of past achievement by the named dead. As such the Book is striking testimony to the values of the time. It was not a work-a-day compilation slavishly entering inventories, lists and accounts. It was a Book of memory, an accolade of past achievers, and was compiled to urge, or perhaps to manipulate, present and future parishioners to sustain the endeavour. Second, familarity and some understanding of the material preserved in the All Saints' Church Book gives pause. So often starved of evidence and understandably anxious to process the information that is available, the historian of the late medieval parish needs carefully to consider quite what has been preserved and why. Why should a parish keep formal accounts once a year's financial transactions had been checked and approved by the appropriate authorities and witnessed by parishioners? And in those cases where accounts have been tidily written up in large and impressive books, why did the parish go to the expense and bother involved? Was it simply to ensure that later generations could consult them for guidance? Was it done for protection against queries which might arise as to the proper collection and disbursement of funds, for protection in other words against charges of laxity and fraud? Or was it done to commemorate churchwardens' achievements, and to preserve and celebrate a substantial, if relatively intangible good work? All were possibilities, and were probably intertwining motives. But if the commemorative, as opposed to the purely fiscal, motive is taken seriously, which heretofore it has not, then questions of presentation, selection and even glorification must at least be borne in mind: how far did formal accounts differ from working accounts? how much was omitted? do wardens tend to emerge with undue credit, in order to encourage others to discharge an otherwise relatively unattractive task? when so little generally survives, how can we discern between the practical and the commemorative? The material in the All Saints' Church Book certainly suggests that these are questions which should be taken seriously when considering survivals from a period when the need for intercession fostered certain activities and very distinct intensities.

Editorial technique

The text of the All Saints' Church Book is almost entirely in English. My brief in transcribing and rendering the material for publication has been to make the text as accessible as possible, easy both to read and

understand. I have modernized spelling and, in the absence of
punctuation in the original, inserted what seemed necessary to resolve
confusion and bring out the sense of the material in a clear and
uncomplicated manner. Nevertheless, it is as well to admit that the
version of the All Saints' Church Book presented here falls between
two stools: it is neither a verbatim edition, nor is it a calendar. Where
necessary the language has been slightly changed, word orders altered
and repetitions ironed out. Equally, nothing of any substance has been
jettisoned. Indeed, a great deal has been left as it is, if spelt differently.
At risk of sounding consciously archaic at times, I have preserved
some original phrasing in order to convey the 'feel' of the text. To
take one example, I decided to preserve a commonly used
construction, as found in 'John Haddon let make the story of the
doom', or 'William Wytteney let ordain and let make at his own cost a
memorial', or 'Alice [Chestre] . . . has let made to be carved at her
own cost a new front to an altar' and so on; given that the original is
certainly intelligible, rendering these phrases with a verb like
'commissioned' simply seemed too insipid. It should be noted,
however, that one section of text did need fairly rigorous reordering to
achieve something like lucidity, and I'm aware that it is still opaque
but would blame the frustrating illegibility of the manuscript. I refer to
the entry describing John and Agnes Jenkyns' gift of a nut, a black
cup, on page 153 of the Book. It should moreover be noted that I made
the decision to leave the term *p'c* as it is. It stands for *precium*, but
whether this should be translated as 'price' or as 'value' is not always
clear, and may well have been used with intentional ambiguity by
scribe or scribes. In one or two instances one of the scribes did
actually use the word 'pryce', as on page 150 of the original text, and
these I have simply modernised to 'price'.

The great majority of numbers in the original text are in roman
numerals; I have replaced these with arabic numerals. It has also
proved preferable, both in terms of keeping some consistency with the
original and also to maintain some internal consistency, to render
number as used in the prose of the text in arabic numerals rather than
spelling the word in full. Consistency generally has been the biggest
problem that I have encountered in preparing this work for
publication. Names, in particular, exist in a distracting variety of
forms. There seemed to be a need for some attempt at standardization
particularly for names which occur frequently. I have rendered the
names of prominent parishioners in a consistent form, but the names
of minor players have by and large been left as they are. I have also
standardized the name of the parish in the text as All Hallows', despite
again a myriad of forms and despite All Hallons probably being its
most frequent coinage. Having made a decision I have attempted to be
consistent (somewhat against the grain of the original!); I can only
hope that my decisions seem sensible and that I have been thorough
without being bludgeoning.

For the most part the original text is easy to read but inevitably there are some sections which either bristle with additions in different hands or which present difficulties. I have tried to indicate, by descriptions in square brackets, where different scribes have made additions to the original. I have kept these to what seemed to be a useful minimum. There are nevertheless some parts of the benefaction lists which are even more complex than I have indicated, but I doubt whether a welter of 'stage directions' in square brackets could lucidly convey complexity and so have preferred simplicity to obfuscation. I have also used descriptions in square brackets to indicate whether an addition is superscript or in the margin. There are, of course, words in the text which are either illegible or of doubtful meaning. If I have been unable to make any sense of a word or phrase, I have left a gap and inserted a question mark in the text; if, however, I have guessed at the likely meaning then I have appended a question mark to the word or phrase about which I am not wholly certain. Occasionally I have kept a phrase or word which seems worth having even if its meaning is perhaps opaque or difficult; in these circumstances I have put a rendition in square bracklets immediately following the word or phrase. Occasionally, too, I have kept a Latin tag or phrase, but in these cases have also inserted the translation in square brackets. Once or twice the scribe has made mistakes; I have left these as they are but indicated, again in square brackets also containing the tag 'recte:', what the word or date should in fact be. In general, where the scribe has used regnal years to date events or accounts I have inserted the A.D. equivalent in square brackets; and where these fail to tally with the A.D. date that the scribe has himself given, I have pointed this out. There are dates pencilled or inked into the margins at certain points in the text. As these insertions are both relatively recent and frequently wrong, I have made no attempt to reproduce them in the text as published here. For instance, at the beginning of the accounts the date 1407 is pencilled into the margin. The provenance and hence the accuracy of this date is by no means clear and it is best ignored. I have, however, been careful to indicate the pagination of the Book, also made at some stage after its initial compilation, and have inserted the page numbers in round brackets through the text. A jump in these numbers of course indicates a run of blank pages in the original.

It is perhaps also worth adding that the text as it appears on the printed page, where I have at times injected a consistency of presentation into the material which the original may lack, is almost misleadingly neat when compared to what actually survives.

Finally I offer two apologies. The first is for the index. Given the welter of repetitive detail about liturgical equipment and building materials in the accounts, selectivity seemed essential in these areas. It will hardly take the reader any longer simply to light on one account and find the references to surplices, or baldrics, or candles, or sand and lime, or laths and nails, than to go through the process of using an index for the same. Names are treated carefully, as are items necessitating out of the ordinary expenditure; but the index is, perforce, selective. Second, it ought to be admitted that the following text contains a very considerable quantity of often repetitive and detailed information. Although I have made every effort to be accurate there are doubtless errors in my transcription and for these I offer my apologies.

GLOSSARY

1. Service Books.

Antiphonal: Contained not only the music for antiphons – or anthems – which began and ended the psalms sung at the canonical hours, but also other musical portions of the divine office, such as the invitatories, hymns, responses and little chapters. Content could, therefore, vary. Increasingly, however, antiphonals included music for the canonical hours. Antiphonals were occasionally divided: the *antiphonale sanctorum*, gave music for the feasts of saints; the *antiphonale temporalis*, gave that for Sundays and weekdays throughout the year, including festivals such as Christmas, Easter and Whitsun, around which the temporal cycle was structured.

Breviary, or portifory: Not prescribed by canon law, the breviary or portifory was a convenience rather than a necessity. It brought together in one volume the antiphonal, lesson book (usually in abbreviated form) and all the other service books necessary for the celebration of the canonical office. Often a large and imposing volume, it might also include music for the offices.

Grail, or gradual: The book containing all the music sung by the choir during the celebration of Mass. Usually a church needed at least two grails or graduals – one for each side of the choir.

Lesson book, or legendary: Usually found in two volumes – the *legendum sanctorum* and *legendum temporalis* – the book contained the lessons read at mattins. The lessons consisted of readings from the Bible, homilies, the sermons of the doctors and fathers of the Church, and also lives of the saints to be read on their festival days. There was an increasing tendency for lessons to be read in two distinct forms or recensions: the shorter form was given in the breviary or portifory, often more for private use; the longer recension was included in the lesson book or legendary and was for use in the choir.

Manual: A portable volume containing the order of administering the sacraments and sacramentals. It generally contained the offices of baptism, matrimony, the churching of women, the order of visiting the sick, extreme unction, of burying the dead, and miscellaneous other blessings and ceremonies. Contents might vary considerably.

Martyrology: This book, divided into sections corresponding to each day of the year, contained short accounts of the lives and sufferings of the saints and martyrs commemorated on each day. These were read aloud daily after the office of prime.

Mass book: Contained everything necessary for the priest at the altar when saying or singing Mass. It was usually a single volume, not bound with other texts; nevertheless, Mass books varied greatly in size and quality. Some belonged to special altars.

Ordinal: Bishop Frere refers to this as 'a guide book to the rest of the service books'. It was the volume to which the clergy turned when they wished to discover the order of service prescribed for any particular day. The ordinal contained a list, embracing the entire year, of their cues of each portion of the service together with the rubrics controlling its performance. Further, the ordinal served as a perpetual guide and directory to the movable feasts which depended on the ever-changing date of Easter. In larger churches it was customary to chain the ordinal to a desk in the choir so that all who took part in the service could consult it.

Processional: Contained the music for the responsories and anthems sung in processions made before Mass on Sundays and festivals and Rogation days. Not usually a large book since, of necessity, it was to be portable.

Psalter: The liturgical psalter consisted of the 150 psalms arranged in the order in which they occurred in the course of the weekly office; it also contained certain canticles sung in the divine office and frequently the anthems before and after each psalm or group of psalms. Generally a slim volume, it was often bound together with other service books.

2. Vestments

a) Mass Vestments

NB At High Mass the celebrating priest is assisted by deacon and sub-seacon. The officiating priest wears amice, alb, girdle, stole, maniple and chasuble. The deacon wears a dalmatic in place of a chasuble, and the sub-deacon a tunic in place of the chasuble and stole. At Low Mass the single celebrating priest is vested as at High Mass. So a complete suit of vestments for High Mass includes three amices, three albs, three girdles, three maniples, two stoles, a chasuble, a dalmatic and a tunic. A suit of vestments generally referred to a whole outfit of High Mass vestments. The individual garments can be considered in more detail.

Alb: A white linen garment with narrow sleeves covering the whole figure down to the ground. Like the amice, the alb was decorated with apparels – these often matched.

Amices: Pieces of white linen worn over the head in the manner of a hood and secured by tapes or strings passing over the shoulders. During the greater part of the service the amice was lowered behind the head on the shoulders. An amice usually had an apparel, a strip of coloured material attached to the front edge of the hood and usually matching the orphrey.

Chasuble: A large conical garment covering the whole figure from the neck to below the knees. To cover the seams down the middle and at the back of the garment (necessary in so broad a garment) strips of stouter stuff called orphreys were superimposed. Orphreys became an integral part of the vestment and were usually fashioned in a richer material of contrasting colour, or decorated with embroidery. Orphreys became increasingly broad and served as a background for images, often of the saints or Christ on the cross.

Dalmatic: Worn by the deacon at High Mass. A tunic with wide sleeves, reaching below the knees and of the same colour and material as the priest's chasuble. The dalmatic usually had two vertical strips at back and front; these were called orphreys although, strictly, they did not originate as seam coverings but were residual aspects of the ancient garment from which the dalmatic was derived. By the late middle ages these strips were treated just like the orphreys of the chasuble in design, material and decoration.

Girdle: The girdle, made either of twisted cord (coloured or white) or else in the form of a narrow sash, gathered the folds of the alb around the waist and served to keep the stoles of deacon and priest in position.

Maniple: A narrow double strip of coloured material worn on the left arm and reaching to the kness. Colour and material almost always matched the chasuble or dalmatic, or that of the orphreys – possibly more frequently the orphreys.

Stole: A narrow strip of coloured material worn by the deacon over the left shoulder and crossed under the right arm, and by the priest behind the neck and crossed below the breast. (The sub-deacon did not wear a stole.) Colour and material were identical with the maniple.

Tunic: Worn by the sub-deacon at High Mass. Closely resembling the dalmatic, though often of simpler decoration and narrower sleeves.

b) Other vestments

Cope: Closely connected with the High Mass suit and frequently forming part of it (although not strictly required). Identical to the chasuble save that the semi-circle of material was not joined at the front and therefore hung in cloak-like fashion over the shoulders. It also had a hood at the back, although the cope hood was tending to become merely a ground for embroidered decoration; the amice fitted into it as one hood inside another. The opening in front was decorated by orphreys on either side: increasingly these were widened to form the background for more extensive ornamentation and embroidery. The sides of the cope were secured at the breast by a morse or clasp.

The cope was worn by the priest when presiding at much of the office in the choir. It was also worn for processions, for reading the bidding prayers, and all ceremonial acts not directly connected with the celebration of the Mass.

Mantle: A loose, sleeveless cloak of varying length.

Rochet: Similar to the surplice but with no sleeves; it was substituted for the surplice when the sleeves of the latter proved an encumbrance.

Surplice: The medieval surplice was usually of linen and reached right down to the feet, had very large sleeves cut so that the openings hung down vertically, and was of ample material gathered in at the neck. It was in practice worn by the priest, deacon and sub-deacon under the alb at High Mass. A church, therefore, had to possess at least three.

3. Equipment and practice

Bier: Provision of a bier for the dead was included among the parishioners' obligations, and Bishop Cantilupe of Worcester had stipulated that the use of the parish bier should be free to all. On the wooded bier the corpse lay covered with a funeral pall through the dirige and Requiem, and the corpse was carried on it from church to grave.

Censer: Incense was used at High Mass, at Lauds and Evensong for censing the altar during the Benedictus or Magnificat, during certain processions, certain solemn blessings and during the office of the dead. By the 14th century a censer was much the same as today's: it was made of metal with a lid that could be raised or lowered on a chain.

Cloth for crucifix or covering cloth: On the first Monday in Lent, according to the Sarum Use, all the crucifixes, especially the great rood over the chancel arch, were veiled.

Corporas case: At Mass time, a large double linen cloth was spread by the deacon in the middle of the altar. On this cloth – or corporal – the sacred elements were placed, covered by the upper part of the corporal folded over them from behind. When not in use, these corporals were kept in a small, either linen or silk, case or burse.

Cruets: Vessels containing wine and water for Mass; usually of metal and with lids.

Cushion or pillow: The missal on the altar was put upon a cushion; an altar may have had more than one for this purpose.

Desk: A sloping board, or lectern, on which books and texts used in the service were laid (and under or in which they may have been stowed).

Eagle: Presumably a brass or wooden lectern made to resemble an eagle on a pedestal, the wings supporting the book covers.

Lych bell: A hand bell rung before the corpse.

Mazer: A bowl, drinking cup or goblet without a foot, originally made of mazer wood, often richly carved or ornamented and mounted with silver or gold or other metal. The term could also be applied to bowls made entirely of metal.

Monstrance: An open or transparent vessel of precious metal in which the Host is exposed.

Nut: A cup originally made from the shell of a coconut, mounted in metal.

Paschal candlestick and judas: The paschal candlestick was usually of brass and had seven branches, the seventh or middle one of which was a tall, thick piece of wood shaped like a candle, called the judas of the paschal, on top of which the wax paschal candle was placed at Eastertide.

Paxbread: A small plate (round or oblong) usually of metal or of painted wood. It commonly bore on its face a representation of the crucifixion and had a handle behind for convenience of holding.
Up to the middle of the 13th century, the kiss of peace at the Mass had been the direct kiss of ancient liturgical practice; from c. 1250, however, the custom was introduced of substituting a sacred object which was kissed first by the priest at the altar, after the Agnus Dei, and then offered by the clerk to all members of the clergy and congregation in turn.

Pece: A cup.

Reserving the Eucharist: Reserved either for the sick or, increasingly, in order to facilitate a particular reverence for the Sacrament. There were three ways of reserving the Sacrament: first, in an aumbrey, or sacrament-house, away from the altar; second, in a tabernacle or closed coffer on the altar; third, in a pyx or silver box suspended above the altar. The third of these was the most common in England, and the pyx was usually of silver gilt or of ivory and was hung, locked over the high altar under a small canopy, possibly being lowered and raised by a small windlass.

Riddels: The side curtains of the altar. (The iron riddel was the bar on which the curtain hung).

Ship: The incense itself was usually kept in a small boat-shaped box, from which it was spooned into the censer.

4. Materials

1) Metals

Latten: A mixed metal of yellow colour, either identical with or closely resembling brass.

2) Fabrics

Baudkin: Closely allied to cloth of gold, baudkin was rich stuff of silk woven with gold thread.

Diaper: A linen fabric woven with a small and simple pattern consisting of lines crossing diamond-wise and formed by different directions of the thread, with different reflections of light from its surface.

Twilly: A woven fabric characterised by parallel diagonal ridges or ribs.

5. Miscellaneous

Groundsel: A timber serving as a foundation to carry a super-structure, especially a wooden building; the lowest member of a wooden framework. Occasionally the lower framing timber of a door; a door-sill or threshold.

Morrow Mass: The first Mass of the day.

Seme: A horse-load, the weight of which varied with the commodity (and the locality). A seme of glass was in the region of 120 lbs; a seme of grain was 8 bushels; a seme of sand was 6–8 pecks; a seme of apples was 9 pecks. In practice the phrase was often used to signify a cart-load.

TEXT

(1)
A kalendar for the guiding of this book

In primis constitutions and ordinances made by the vicar and the parishioners

Item names of conducts and what they receive in their keeping

Names of debtors that owe good to the church

Names of them that have keys of the treasury or of evidences of the church or of the chantry

Names of good doers that have given any livelode unto the church and how many evidences pertaining to every tenantry

Names of vicars and priests that have been good doers giving or doing any benefit unto the said church

Names of parishioners and of other places secular men and women that have been benefactors and good doers unto the said church of All Hallows'

Evidences of bonding of all the livelode of the church

Inventories of jewels, books, vestments and of all other goods of the church by order

(3)
Constitutions and Ordinances

Item that none of the parish from henceforward lend out no manner book out of the church to no manner of use under the pain of 12d *tociens quociens* [as often as necessary].

(4)
Constitutions and Ordinances for the Clerk's finding

It is ordained and assigned by the agreement of the parishioners that 7
of them [are] to find the clerk's board one whole year and 7 another
year, and so yearly to be found by the assignment of the proctors; and
every man of the parish to pay to his wages quarterly as they shall be set
and stended[assessed] by such 3 as shall be chosen by the parish, that is
to say 1 of the worshipful and 2 of the mean of the said parish; and he
that shall disobey from henceforward to pay and content the clerk for
the time being after the stenting and setting of such 3 men so chosen,
when by the proctors or the clerk it is asked of them, then it shall be
lawful for the proctors to content the clerk of the church money as much
as can not be levied unto the feast of Easter. And then they so
disobeying and withholding against this ordinance be compelled to
abstain from their housel until such debts before expressed be paid and
to the church restored.

The Clerk's charge

In primis he [is] to be true and profitable unto the church unto his power
as in keeping and guarding the vestments and books, jewels and all
other ornaments belonging to the said church, and to see that the church
doors be opened and shut in due times, and by him surely searched or
by some other man of true and sad disposition.

Item he to be lovingly attendant unto the vicar in time of divine service
and in visiting the sick and to be obedient unto him in all things that is
lawful concerning the laud of God and of the church, and truly to yield
unto the vicar all manner oblations and all manner of things that is lost
within the church that come to his hand that true enquiry might be had
to whom it belongs unto.

Moreover that he to bear no tales between the vicar and his brethren,
nor between him and his parishioners, nor between neighbour and
neighbour, whereby any occasion of strife or debate should grow in time
come.

And so to see the church kept clean in roofs, windows, pillars, walls and
the ground stalls, seats and especially the altars.

(5)
Consitutions and Ordinances of old time ordained to be kept for the
wealth of the church under divers pains as follows

In primis, in the year of our lord 1488, in the time of Sir John Thomas
being vicar, Richard Stevyns and Thomas Pernaunt proctors, it is
ordained, agreed and assented by the whole parish that every man from
henceforward that come not to the accounts of the church after 3

knellings of the great bell, the knowledging of the day [having been] had and assigned by the vicar the Sunday before, whosoever he be having no reasonable excuse, if he be of the council to pay to the church 1 lb wax, and every other man not of the council, so failing, to pay ½ lb wax, and this ordinance ever to be continued.

Item it is ordained, agreed and assented by the said parishioners and forever to be continued that whosoever he be that is chosen proctor by the most voice of the parishioners if he refuse he that is so chosen shall pay unto this said church of All Hallows' to be put into the treasury coffer in money without pardon or release of the whole or of part, 6s 8d; and at every time after that year [that] he shall be chosen again, likewise afore rehearsed to fall into the said pain as oft as he shall refuse it, unless his excuse by the parish may be found the more reasonable.

Item he that shall refuse to be proctor of Jesus after he is chosen as oft as he so do without any favour, as it is rehearsed above, to pay to the Treasury of Jesus, 3s 4d.

(6)
Constitutions and Ordinances

Item, it is agreed and assented that from henceforward no proctor set [lease] out any house for years, nor abate any rent of any house, without the advice and consent of the substance of the parishioners, under the pain of £20.

Item, likewise it is agreed and assented that from henceforward the costs of the General Mind for the good doers exceed not the sum of 13s 4d, and if it do the residue that comes over shall be at the charge of the older proctor in office and not at the charge of the church; the which General Mind shall be kept yearly after Ash Wednesday, that is to say the Thursday the dirige and the Friday the mass.

Item, where it has been yearly used before this time that on Corpus Christi day on the church cost the proctors gave a dinner unto the vicar and the priests and the clerks, it is now agreed and ordained that from henceforward the dinner to be left and the vicar, the priests and the clerk for the time being [and] to come on that day shall have of the proctors money, that is to say the vicar to have 8d, every priest of the church 4d, and to the clerk 2d.

(7)
These be the names of the conducts that have books, vestments and chalices of the said Church
[Blank, and subsequent pages headed with the phrase Names of conducts]

(37)
Debtors that owe good to the said church
[Blank, and subsequent pages headed with the phrase For debts of the church]

(53)
For keys of the treasury
[Blank, and subsequent pages headed with the phrase For keys of the treasury]

(68)
Names of good doers as follows
The names of good doers and wellwillers by whom livelode, tenements and other goods have been given unto the church of All Hallows' in Bristol, unto the honour and worship of all mighty God and increasing of divine service, to be showed and declared unto the parishioners on the Sunday before Ash Wednesday and at high mass and yearly to be continued as follows.

Where it has been of a laudable custom of long continuance used, that on this day, that is to say the Sunday before Ash Wednesday, the names of good doers and wellwillers by whom livelode – tenements, buildings, jewels, books, chalices, vestments and with divers other ornaments and goods, as follows – has been given unto the church unto the honour and worship of almighty God and increasing of divine service, to be rehearsed and shown yearly unto you by name, both man and woman, and what benefits they did for themselves and for their friends and for others by their lifetimes, and what they left for them to be done after their days that they shall not be forgotten but be had in remembrance and be prayed for of all this parish that be now and all of them that be to come, and also for an example to all you that be now living that you may likewise to do for yourself and for your friends while they be in this world, that after the transitory life you may be had in the number of good doers rehearsed by name and in the special prayers of Christian people in time coming that by the infinite mercy of almighty God, by the intercession of our blessed lady and of all blessed saints of heaven, in whose honour and worship this church is dedicated, you may come to the everlasting bliss and joy that our blessed lord has redeemed you unto AMEN.
And the anniversaries of these good doers to be held and kept in this church yearly, that is to say on Thursday shall be their dirige and on Friday next their mass.

(69)
These be the names of the good doers that have given livelode and tenements to the church of All Hallows' of Bristol
Baldwin Street
In primis William Newbery gave 12s rent assize in Baldwin street, in the which dwells John Albyrton merchant [margin: and since others].

And thereto belong 12 evidences under authentic seals, and his obit to be held yearly the 10th day of May. God have mercy on his soul.

Lewins Mead
Item Martin Draper gave 12d in Lewins Mead of 1 house that John Sybyll holds of Richard Erle [margin: and since others], to the finding of the lamp before the cross altar. God have mercy on his soul. And thereto belongs 2 evidences under 7 seals with 1 copy of a testament over-sealed.

The Corner House in Corn Street
John le Gate gave 4s to the church of All Hallows' of the corner house next to the conduit to find 5 tapers before Our Lady altar and to this belongs 1 evidence with 2 seals. God have mercy on his soul.

(70)
Names of the good doers that gave livelode
Green Lattice in the High Street
Item Alice Hayle gave to the said church £5 6s 8d going out of the tenement called the Green Lattice in the High Street, and there belongs to to said tenement 9 evidences under diverse seals with 1 testament under the Dean's seal, and obit 10th day July Anno Domini 1241. God have mercy on her soul.

For the Baste door in the churchyard
Item Joce Regny gave to the said church 2s 6d for 1 easement of 1 baste door going out of John Branfeld cook's house in the churchyard before the south door of the church and thereto belongs 1 evidence with 1 seal. God have mercy on his soul.

For the Gutter going out of John Branfeld cook's house under the Beer House
In the ninth year of Henry V after the Conquest, Sir Thomas Marshall vicar of the said church, Thomas Halleway and William Temple wardens of the said church, with the assent of all the parishioners, gave 1 easement of 1 gutter going out of the said house through the churchyard to Harry Harsfeld, Thomas Busschope, Thomas Holme [and] William Pyall, chantry priests of Everard Frensche, as for the term of 49 years, and they for to pay for the said term 5s, the which was laid down and received to the works of the church. And so the state is passed.

(71)
Skadspyll Street now Marsh Street
Item Sir William Selke, vicar of the parish church of All Hallows', gave to the said church 2s rent assize going out of one house in Skadspyll Street, now called Marsh Street, in the which late dwelled Nycoll Stoke, mariner, and out of mind has been paid, save for the second year of the reign of King Edward IV. And thereto belong 7 evidences under divers

seals. God have mercy on his soul. The which 2s John Shipward the elder withdrew, God amend him. [Added: And hath do long, but since that is to say the 19 day of January 1484, John Shipward the younger, to have his father's [and] his mother's soul and his soul to be prayed for amongst all other good doers, has delivered us to our old possession of that 2s rent assize again.]

Redland
Item Nicholas Scherston gave to the said church 12½d of one acre of land in Redland there to belongs 1 evidence with 1 seal. God have mercy on his soul.

The Almshouse next to Abyndon's Inn
Item Stephen Gnowsale gave to the said church 12d going out of 1 tenement next Abyndon's Inn and thereto belongs 2 evidences under authentic seals. God have mercy on his soul. Now called the Almshouse.

(72)
Names of good doers that gave livelode
Saint Peter's Street
Lawrance Mercer gave unto the said church 6d rent assize going out of one tenement of William Canynges, the which John Steyner holds [added: held] in St Peter's parish and thereto belong 2 evidences. God have mercy on his soul.

Le Barres
Richard Mangottesfeld, mayor of Bristol, gave unto the said church 12d rent assize of one tenement at the Barres and thereto belongs one evidence under the common seal of Bristol. God have mercy on his soul.

Venny Lane otherwise All Hallows' lane
Geffrey Cornmonger gave to the said church 2s of rent assize. God have mercy on his soul.

(73)
Baldwin Street
Robert Pykard gave unto the said church 12d rent assize in Baldwin Street and by the same evidence 12d unto the house of Kalendars under 2 seals. God have mercy on his soul. 1 evidence.

The house between Thomas Aden and Martin Bardman in the which dwells Margery Manymoney. [Added: before the counter viz A.D. 1414] Unto the said house belongs 2 evidences that is to say 1 evidence with 3 seals under the mayor and the dean and 1 evidence of 1 plea for the said house between Sir William Rodberd vicar of the said church and the parishioners of the 1 party and Sir Roger Asshton knight of the other part; by the law both tenements were given unto the said church, that is to say the house that the said Martin dwells in and where that late John Leynell dwelled in, and that other tenement [which] Margery Manymoney dwells in [added: and since many others]. God have mercy on their souls.

(74)
Names of the good doers that gave livelode
Wine Street
Harry Muellard [recte: Suellard] gave to Sir William Mooche [recte: Scoche] vicar of the said church and to his assigns 1 house in Wine Street and thereto belongs 1 evidence and seal. God have mercy on his soul.

The High Street
Thomas Fyler and Agnes Fyler gave unto the said church 1 tenement in the High Street in the which some time she dwelt in and now John Roger, mercer, otherwise Pynner, dwells in [added: and since John Snygge], and they yearly to have their obit kept by the vicar and the proctors of the said church the 20th day of November after the tenor of their testament. God have mercy on their souls. Amen.

[In different ink:]The which tenor here follows and to be spent yearly about it 12s.
In primis to 8 priests to every of them 4d – sum 2s 8d.
Item to poor people in bread to be dealt – 5s.
Item to the clerk for the ringing of the bells – 12d.
Item for his dirige – 2d.
Item to the bellman of the town, otherwise bedeman – 2d.
Item to the vicar of the church for the time being for his wax at dirige and mass burning – 12d.
Item to the said vicar to oversee this being done and to recommend the souls of the foresaid Thomas and Agnes every Sunday – 12d.
Item to the 2 proctors for their diligent labour – 12d.
Sum – 12s.

(78)
These are the names of the vicars and priests that have been good doers unto the said church
In primis Sir Walter Isgar vicar of the said church, died the 1st day of the month of December Anno Domini 1321.
In primis he gave half one breviary of the *temporall* and *sanctorum*.
Item he gave 1 ordinal to the said Church.
Item he laboured [for] the confirmation of all the indulgences of the house of the Kalendars.

Sir William Selke.
Item Anno Domini 1270 11th kal junii Sir William Selke vicar of the said church gave 1 red mass book.

Item 1 grail with 1 processional.

[Scored:] Item 1 eagle of tree [wood].

[Scored:] Item 1 little candlestick of brass that was of Saint Thomas of Canterbury.

[Scored:] Item of the skull that was of Saint Thomas of Canterbury.

Item 2 processional crosses.

Item 1 psalter.

Item 1 manual with one ?hymner with other observance and with many other good deeds as showed by his testament.

Item 2s rent assize in Skadpull Street now called Marsh Street.

God have mercy on his soul. Amen.

Sir Thomas Marshall

In primis Anno Domini 1434, 7th die Junii [sic; cf page 997] obiit Sir Thomas Marshall, vicar of the said church, did the good deeds following

In primis he gave 1 great mass book unto the said church, *p'c* – 13 marks 6s 8d.

(79)

Item the said Thomas gave 1 antiphonal with 1 psalter.

Item 1 processional.

Item he paid for the glazing of 2 windows in the cross aisle, the 1 window of the 7 works of mercy and the other window of the 7 sacraments.

Item the said Sir Thomas gave unto the treasury of the said church – £10.

Item to be distributed among the poor parishioners – £10.

Item of his own cost he made 1 gable window for ease of light to be had in the choir in the south side over the presbytery.

Item 1 pair of sad green vestments with orfreys of gold of red.

Item 1 pair of blue vestments with garters.

Item he made as a perpetual alm for all his successors, a vicarage as for an habitation, and his obit is to be kept yearly by the vicar that shall be for the time. God have mercy on his soul. And after his day he found 1 priest 10 years.

Sir Richard Parkhouse

Qm obiit Anno Domini 1436, 8th die Augusti

In primis he gave unto the said church 1 pair of light green vestments of cloth of gold, *p'c* – £3.

Item 2 torches to the high altar, *p'c* – 8s.

Item 10 lbs of wax.

God have mercy on his soul. Amen.

(80)

Good doers of the vicars and priests

Sir William Rodberd

Qm obiit 6th die mens Junii 1453

In primis to one suit of vestments – £20.

Item to the ?ceiling of the ?back of the church – £6 13s 4d.
Item 1 pair of cruets of silver of 6 ozs.
Item 1 coverlet of red to lie before the high altar.
Item he found 1 priest in the said church 10 years.
God have mercy on his soul. Amen.

Sir Harry Colas, fellow of the Kalendars
In primis he gave unto the said church 1 processional with 7 psalms and
the litany in the end.
God have mercy on his soul. Amen.

Sir John Gyllarde, Prior of the Kalendars
Qm obiit 28th die mens Junii Anno Domini 1451, gave unto the said
church
In primis 1 paxbread of silver weighing 9 ¼ ozs.
Item 1 pair processionals.
Item he let made the 4 seats in the cross aisle – £3.
Item the said Sir John and Richard Haddon let made one tabernacle of
gold and silver of Saint Saviour at the high altar – £20.
(81)
Item the said Sir John and Richard let made at their own free will the
chapel of Our Lady in the north side of the church and worshipfully
glazed it with 1 story of *Te deum laudamus* for the souls of John
Haddon, vintner, and Christine his wife; and where the said John and
Christine ordained but 20 marks for the repair of the said chapel, the
said Sir John and Richard, for the laud and worship of God, built anew
out of the ground, that cost £227.
Item the said Sir John and Richard lent unto Sir William Rodberd and
the parish of All Hallows' for [re]building a house of the said church
called the Green Lattice, £100 in money.
Item the said Sir John and Richard let made 1 house for the Kalendars
over the said chapel of Our Lady for an Easement unto the prior and his
bretheren, and they to repair the gutter next the street side. [Margin:
Nota for the gutter of the Kalendars going to the library]
Item the said Sir John and Richard, where John Haddon and Christine
had ordained by testament for 1 priest to sing in the said church but 12
years, they [a]mortised 20 marks of livelode for 1 priest to sing in
perpetuity at Our Lady altar in the said church, as it appears by 4 copies
of the same mortifications. [Margin: And since has been embezzled as
follows & sufficit ut sequit] And as for the mortifications, my lord John
Carpenter Bishop of Worcester delivered them in one coffer locked and
sealed to Sir Thomas Sutton, Abbot of Saint Augustine's, and he
delivered them to Richard Haddon and the said Richard delivered them
(82) to John Hawkys, and so without the grace of God the chantry is
destroyed. God amend them.

Sir Maurice Hardwick vicar of the said church in his first coming in,
that is to say Anno 1455, gave unto the making of 1 pair of clasps for

the best suit 5 ozs of silver, and paid to Richard Baten, goldsmith, for fashioning and gilding of one clasp – 6s 8d.

Item the said Maurice gave to the buying of 1 pair organs, the same time – 6s 8d.

Item to the ?ceiling of the roof in the back of the said church – 6s 8d.

He let made 1 image of Saint Ursula in wood to excite people to devotion, *p'c* – 5s.

Item he let made 1 pair of altar cloths of red with 1 crucifix, *p'c* – 15s.

Item he let made 1 pair of white altar cloths with the Coronation of Our Lady, *p'c* – 26s 8d.

Item he let made 1 pair of altar cloths of Saint Ursula, *p'c* – 18s.

Item he gave to the high altar 2 fine corporas with 1 green case of needle work.

Item he paid for gilding the image of All Hallows' in ?burnished gold, *p'c* – £3.

Item he paid for gilding the crucifix with the sun, *p'c* – 23s 4d.

(83)

Item the said Sir Maurice let set out the tabernacle at the high altar at principle feasts unto the more laud and worship of almighty God.

Item he laboured to compile and make this book for to be a memorial and a remembrance for ever for the curates and the churchwardens that shall be for the time, that every man to put yearly his account for one evidence of the livelode of the church, and for to put in names of the good doers and the names of the wardens of the church and what good they did in their days that they must yearly be prayed for.

[Added: And Sir John Thomas helped too and wrote this book up.]

Item he let make 1 coffer with lock and key to put in the evidence of the livelode of the church, where before they lay abroad likely to be embezzled and mischiefed; now they have been set under four keys, the vicar to have 1 key and the 2 proctors 2 keys and the most worshipful man of the parish the 4th key. God have mercy on his soul. Amen.

Item he gave 1 pair vestments of red ?dymysay. [Margin: Sufficit with other good deeds]

Item he procured, moved and stirred Agnes Fyler to give her said house in the which she dwelt in the High Street, on the south side of the Green Lattice. And where that Thomas her son would have broken her last will and alyenyd [alienated] the house to his own use, [and] promised the said Sir Maurice great good to assist him. The said Sir Maurice and William Rowley and John Compton, churchwardens, by plea withstood him as it appears in their said account.

(84)

Names of the vicars and priests

Item the said Sir Maurice Hardwick, vicar of the said church, the 4th day of April Anno Domini 1471, gave to the foresaid church, Thomas Abingdon and Richard Alen being proctors at that time, a cloth of red velvet embroidered with 10 flowers of gold with scriptures in the foot of the flowers *Hymnus omnibus sanctis* with 2 letters of gold in the said cloth, M & H, the which cloth is of breadth a yard save the nail, and of deepness three quarters of a yard and a half save an inch, the which cloth he gave to the intent that at every principal feast it be hung behind All Hallows' head.

Item the same day the said Sir Maurice gave unto the said church a frontal of cloth of gold to hang over All Hallows' head at every principal feast, the which frontal is of length a yard and five eighths, and of deepness a quarter save an inch.

Item the said Sir Maurice gave to the said church 4 stained cloths of red and yellow with wreaths, and the arms of the passion in the middle of the wreaths, and a scripture in the middle of the arms *Dulcis est illo amor meus*, the total length of the cloths is 13 yards and three quarters, and of deepness a yard and a quarter, the which cloths he ordained to be hung about the choir at principal feasts.

Item the said Sir Maurice ordained and let made the same year on his own cost 3 quires of velum in the new antiphonal which lies before the vicar, and at his cost he paid for all the chapters and collects for the year both for the *temporall* and the *sanctorum* and the common to be written in the said 3 quires in order, and at the end of the said quires is written all the benisons for the year. And the said quires are set at the end of the book, in the which there was never chapter, collect, nor benisons written before.

God have mercy on his soul. Amen.

[Added: And John Chestre gave the stuff of it that is to say the velum.]

(85)
Sir William Howe, vicar of the said church in the second year of his coming in, that is to say anno domini 1474, gave a corporas case of cloth of gold. God have mercy on his soul.

Sir William Warens chantry priest gave unto his chantry, that is to say Halleway's chantry, a pair of red baudkin vestments to be sung in on holy days. God have mercy on his soul.

Qm obiit in die conversionis Sti Pauli Anno Domini 1482.

Item the said Sir William Warens gave to the said church to the laud of almighty God and the increase of divine service, 4 books of pricksong.

Item the said Sir William gave to the said church a breviary to be chained in the church to the ease of all manner priests to say their service when they have not their own books with them, and also paid for the chaining. God have mercy on his soul. Amen.

The said book is chained to a pillar in the south side of the church within the enterclose before the rood altar.

Sir Thomas Haxby, a brother of the Kalendars qm obiit 19 die mens junii 1484, gave unto this church to be remembered amongst its good doers – 20s.

Item to the high altar to be set in things necessary to be had – 6s 8d.

And besides he was a well willed man in all his days and profitable unto this church, especially when he was common servant in this parish, that is to say parish clerk, and that 28 years together. No clerk in this town [was] like unto him in cleanliness and in attending in those days; and he was as profitable unto the Kalendars as for his time there being and full worshipfully left to that place at his departing to be prayed for.

God have mercy on his soul. Amen.

(86)

Names of vicars and priests

[Different hand] Master John Herlow, some time prior of the Kalendars and parson of Saint Stephens q' obiit 6th die mens December anno 1486

In primis he let made a book to the organs for matins and evensong for all the year.

Item to the lighting and garnishing of the high altar he gave 75 flowers of gold that cost him – 53s 4d.

[Different hand] Sir Thomas Furber, brother and fellow of the Kalendars, gave to the gilding of the rood loft – £5, and he also caused a priest to sing in this church 1 year.

[Different hand] Sir John Thomas, vicar of this church, from his own goods caused the roof of the choir to be sealed.

[The pages following are headed with the phrase Names of vicars and priests, until:]

(133)

These are the Names of all the good doers and benefactors unto the said church [Added: *viz parochianus et de aliis parochibus* [parishioners and those from other parishes].]

Roger le Gurdeler

In primis he gave unto the said church unto the worship of the precious and glorious sacrament to be borne in, 1 bowl of silver gilded within and without, with 1 cover and 1 crucifix over the head, with precious stones worshipfully endowed, and 1 little cup and 1 spoon both gilded, weighing 45 ozs. And that this said bowl, cup and spoon be not alienated, sold nor broken, under pain of cursing us as it appears by writing under the dean's seal.

God have mercy on his soul. Amen.

Goldsmiths dwelling in the Goldsmiths Row now called Cook Row

The said Goldsmiths unto the worship of almighty God and all the saints let made at their own costs for the high altar 1 tabernacle with gold, silver and precious stones of the Coronation of Our Lady with 1 ruby imperial all over the head, *p'c* – £20.

God have mercy on their souls.

John Pers, mercer
Qm obiit 22 die January Anno Domini 1431, gave unto the said church
1 cope of black baudkin with the sypyll [?chasuble] and 2 tunicles with
orfreys of green, and had purchased unto the said church in fee of John
Suthfolke, weaver, as it appears by 12 evidences.
God have mercy on his soul.

(134)
Names of the good doers
Item the said John Pers found 1 priest in the said church 8 years and
gave to the building of the cross aisle in the south side of the church –
20 marks.

Item Emott Chylcombe gave to the said church 1 chalice of 13 ¾ozs.
God have mercy on her soul.

Roger Gurdeler gave to the said church 1 bowl of silver and gilt, [and] £3
to the censers and to the making of the gable window in the west end.

John Forges, cook, gave to the said church for the censers and the said
gable window – £3.
Item he gave to the building of the cross aisle – £5 6s 8d.

Richard Ake gave to the use of the vicar for the time being 1 antiphonal,
p'c – £10, in order to be prayed for among the benefactors of the
church. God have mercy on his soul.

(135)
John Haddon, vintner, let make the story of the doom in the cross aisle
and paid for the same – £8.
Item the said John gave to the building of Our Lady chapel – £13 6s 8d,
but the executors of the said John built the said chapel anew, and the
costs drew unto the sum of – £227.
Item the executors of the said John let make the second part of the
tabernacle of the high altar.
Item the said executors amortised and founded 1 priest in perpetuity for
the said John and Christine his wife, and endowed the said chantry with
1 mass book, worth £18, and with 4 pairs of vestments. And Sir John
Gyllard, prior of the Kalendars, gave by testament to the said chantry 1
chalice, *p'c* – £7 6s 8d. God have mercy on their souls.

Julian Papnam gave to the church 1 chalice and 1 paten of 24 ozs. And
John Carpenter, Bishop of Worcester, has given 40 days Indulgence [at]
every principal feast when the said chalice is sung with. God have
mercy on their souls.

(136)
Names of the good doers

William Wytteney let ordain and let made at his own cost a memorial that every man should remember his own death, that is to say the Dance of Pauls the which cost £18. God have mercy on his soul. Amen.

Item he gave 1 primer with 7 psalms, litany, dirige and commendations, psalms and the passion, with many other devotions, the which stood in the grate at Saint Christopher's foot, and the said book was stolen and found at Saint James in Galicia and brought home and returned to the grate and has since been stolen again.

John Whytsyd, notary, and Joan Selwode, widow, gave unto the said church 75 ozs of silver to make 1 pair of candlesticks for the high altar. God have mercy on their souls.

William Newbery bequeathed to the said church – 20s.
Item he gave rent assize in Baldwin Street – 12s.
God have mercy on his soul.

John Wellys gave to the said church 1 mazer, price – 17s 10d.
God have mercy on his soul.

Walter Perkyn, barber, gave to the said church 1 standing pece with 1 cover, *p'c* – 46s 8d.
God have mercy on his soul.

(137)
Thomas Halleway, that died 13 day of December Anno Domini 1454, and Joan his wife, that died the first day of March Anno Domini 1455, both lie buried by the Cross altar under the great stone joined to the ?Greese.

In primis they founded 1 chantry in the said church in perpetuity [added: as it appears by the mortifications expressed and by their composition there ordered.]

Item they gave forever to find the lamp before the precious sacrament in the choir – 8s.

Item they gave forever for 1 chamber that the said priest dwelled in, the which they built in the churchyard at their own cost – 6s 8d.

Item they gave unto the said church 1 worshipful jewel with 2 angels called a monstrance to bear the precious sacrament with divers relics [en]closed in the same, of 57 ¼ ozs.

Item they gave 1 mass book to the high altar.

Item they ordained 1 bell to be rung daily to mass, and hung him and enclosed the rope in one case of lead for all manner ?wedryngs.

Item they gave to the best suit of vestments – £20.

Item they gave to the building of the Cross Aisle – £20.

Item moreover most well willed to all good works of the church to oversee the repairs of the church 4 times a year going in his coat. [Added: Mayor and after he was mayor.]

Item they made the seats in the church before St Dunstan's altar, *p'c* – £3.
God have mercy on their souls.

(138)
Names of the good doers .
William Rayne, Isabell and Joan gave to the said church 1 ship of silver.
Item they gave to a new suit of vestments – £3.

Thomas Fyler and Agnes gave to the said church 1 tenement that they dwelt in.
Item they found in the church a priest 3 years.
Item they gave the roof to cover the south aisle.

[Different hand] William Palmer of London, goldsmith, gave to this said church in money to be prayed for – 40s.

Robert Derkyn of London, mercer, gave to this said church in money to be prayed for – 20s.

[Different pen] Martin Symondson of this parish, hardwareman, qm obiit in festo Cathedere Sci Petri AD. 1482, gave to this said church in money to be prayed for – 20s.

(139)
Henry Chestre and Alice his wife.
In primis they have ordained at their proper costs to find a priest to sing in this church for 12 years to the laud and the loving of almighty God and augmenting of divine service, for every year 9 marks sum – £72.
Item moreover in the worship of Jesus, to the foundation of a Mass of Jesus by note to be kept and continued every Friday in this church and likewise an anthem, the said Harry and Alice have given to this church a tenement in Broad Street where William Rowe, brewer, once dwelt in. To this intent, that they be prayed for every Friday at that Mass by name, and also that an obit be kept for them yearly for ever on Saint Valentine's day, on the which day the said Harry deceased in the year of Our Lord 1470, and the costs of this obit should approach the sum of 7s 1d; and so that this is done and certain rents of assize paid, this church shall have yearly of that house 4 marks as the rent goes now. And this house sometime was mortised to the chantry of this church which Richard Haddon alienated and sold for £60, delivering the remaining livelode with the mortifications to John Hawkys, and so wrongfully he kept it, as is more plainly rehearsed above. Almighty God send him grace to make amends to this church ere he depart out of this world. Amen.
Also the said Alice, executrix to the said Harry, has let made in carved work a tabernacle with a Trinity in the middle over the image of Jesus, and also at her own cost had it gilded full worshipfully, with a cloth hanging before to be drawn at certain times when it shall please the vicar and the parishioners.
Also the said Alice has let gild at her own cost Our Lady altar [ad]joining the said image of Jesus, and let made a stained cloth to hang

before with imagery of Our Lady, Saint Katherine and Saint Margaret.

Also the said Alice has let carve at her own cost another tabernacle to the north side of the said altar with 3 stories of Our Lady: one, of the stories of Our Lady of Pity; the second, of the Salutation of Our Lady; and the third, of the Assumption of Our Lady.

(140)

Names of good doers

Also the said Alice, to the worship of almighty God and his church, and to have both their souls prayed for specially amongst all other good doers, has let made to be carved at her own cost a new front to an altar in the south aisle of the church, called the rood altar, with 5 principal images: one of Saint Anne, the second of Mary Magdalen, the third of Saint Giles, the fourth of Saint Erasmus, the fifth of Saint Antony. And in addition, a crucifix with Mary and John over a door by the altar; and also she has gilded all that front full worshipfully as it appears, with a cloth of the passion of Our Lord before the altar to be drawn at certain times after the pleasure of the vicar and the parishioners.

Also they have given a towel of diaper to be kept in the church to the use of the parish while they ben a comenyng [are at communion], that is to say y howselyd [houselled] on Easter day.

Also they have given to the high altar for principal feasts an altar cloth of diaper and a towel of other small cloth, and to the rood altar for the said feasts an altar cloth and a towel and to Our Lady altar another altar cloth and a towel.

Also to Our Lady altar 2 stained cloths for the over part and for the nether, where in the over cloth is a picture of Our Lord rising out of the sepulchre and in the nether [blank] and 2 curtains to the same of ?1 work.

Item a large cloth of twilly with streaks of blue to cover the best cope when it is laid open.

Item moreover a great latten basin to wash relics on Relic Sunday.

(141)

Also the said Alice, considering and understanding that the church had never a cross for Sunday processions except that they should occupy every Sunday the best cross, gave to the said church to be prayed for a cross of silver gilded and enamelled with Mary and John enjoined to the same cross in one work, the whole weighing 60 ozs, and costing her £20.

[Margin: She gave the second best cross of silver, *p'c* – £20.]

Moreover the said Alice, 2 years before her decease, being in good prosperity and health of body, considering the rood loft of this church was but single and no thing [of] beauty, according to the parish entente [intent], she, taking to her counsel the worshipful of this parish with others having best understanding and [in]sights in carving, to the honour and worship of almighty God and his saints, and of her special devotion unto this church, has let to be made a new rood loft in carved work filled with ?22 images, at her own proper cost; of the which images, three are principal – a Trinity in the middle, a Christopher in the north side, and a Michael in the south side; and besides this, each of the 2 pillars bearing up the loft has 4 houses there set on in carved work, with an image in each house. [Margin: In sentence, she let made the rood loft.]

Also the said Alice, considering that there was no hearse cloth in the church of any reputation in value, saving only an hearse cloth that Thomas Halleway ordained for his own anniversary, for the love and honour that she had unto almighty God and to all Christian souls, and for the ease and succour of all this parish unto whom she owed her good will and love in her day as it appears in this church as it is afore expressed and rehearsed, she has given an hearse cloth of black worsted with letters of gold of H & C & A & C and a scripture in gold '*Orate pro animabus Henricus Chestre et Alicie uxoris eius*', and the cloth is of length [blank]. [Margin: She gave the hearse cloth of black worsted.]

(142) Names of good doers

Also besides the finding a priest for 12 years above mentioned, the said Alice has found a priest to maintain God's service for the space of 5 years; and on the day of O Sapientia, that is to say the 16th day of December the year of our lord God 1485, the soul of this blessed woman departed out of this world, the which soul almighty God of his infinite grace take his mercy, and reward her for her good deeds.

Moreover besides all this, for the common weal of this town and for the saving of merchants' goods, both of the town and of strangers, the tenth year before her death she let made at her own costs and charges a crane upon the Back by the Marsh Gate, where was never none before that time; the which cost her £41 and odd money, and of the crane a fair rent comes and rests yearly unto the Common Chamber of this town.

Item to certain churches of this town and to the four orders full largely departed two years before her death, we all that are now and they that are to come are bound to pray for her.

Also you shall pray for the soul of her son John Chestre that deceased on Vig Natlis [?Christmas Eve] Anno Domini 1488, the which in all this business of his mother above expressed was a special well willer, who moved and stirred her unto the same full wholesomely and by whose advice and counsel and comfort many of these good deeds were done and performed. And not only in this, but in all other business concerning the weal of the church was full ready unto his power at all time both in word and in deed, and he has let ordained a priest to sing in this church for two years.

(143)

John Leynell and Katherine his wife.

In primis they have ordained at their own proper costs to find a priest to sing in this church 10 years to the worship of almighty God and augmenting of divine service, every year 9 marks, sum – £59 6s 8d.

Item, moreover his anniversary to be held in this church 10 years following.

Item they have given to this church a mass book, *p'c* – 10 marks.

Item a chalice double gilt weighing 25 ozs, at 6s the ounce, sum – £7 13s 4d.

[Scored: Item a pair of vestments of blue velvet with flowers of gold, price £5.] [Margin: & as it follows after she has according to the same ordained a suit.]

Item a pair of cruets of silver weighing 7 ½ ozs – 26s 8d.

Item a corporas of fine cloth.

Item a corporas case of blue velvet embroidered with gold – 5s.

Item more, they have given a great pair of latten candlesticks, called standards, for the choir; where before we had but 2, now we have 4, and also where we were wont to borrow in time of necessity and now, blessed be God and them, we have no need as for such stuff. The which candlesticks weigh 94 lbs and cost 4 marks. [Margin: price 4 marks ut sequor also the best blue vestments for priest, deacon and subdeacon with 2 copes to the same, price £25.]

Item moreover where our second suit of vestments were of baudkin and no thing of fineness unto to the best suit, the said Katherine, considering this, ordained and has given to the honour of almighty God and of All Hallows unto this church a finer suit of blue velvet with flowers, otherwise branches, of gold with orfreys of red velvet and eagles of gold, that is to say a chasuble, 2 tunicles with their albs and amices and their apparels and 2 copes according to the same, and it cost £25.

(144)

Names of good doers

Item moreover the said Katherine of her own devotion by her days and at her own proper cost, found a priest to sing in this church in addition to the 10 years before rehearsed that she was bound unto, that is to say 2 years.

Item besides all this, she left in money at her decease to find a priest to sing in this church for the space of 3 years, for every year 9 marks, and her dirige was full worshipfully kept for the whole month and that by note, [different hand: as other worshipful folk have used [to do] before times and likewise since her departing.]

[Different hand] John Pynke the younger, merchant of this parish, that deceased the [blank] of the month of September Anno Domini 149[blank] gave unto this church by testament 4 measures of good woad, delivered by Alison Pynke to the proctors of the said church, Richard Sutton and John Baten.

Item besides this, he has ordained a priest to be found to sing in this church 2 years.

Item delivered to the vicar [an]other 4 measures of woad.

Hugh Forster has given a mazer with band and ?prent gilt after the decease of Joan his wife, and it weighs [blank].

Item the said Joan has promised after her days a pece of silver, weighing [blank].

(145)
Memorandum Agnes the wife of John Cogan, of the parish of Saint Nicholas, at her decease gave unto the parish church in money – 20s.

Memorandum Agnes Bartlett, of the almshouse in All Hallows' Lane, at her decease gave unto the church a silver spoon weighing ?1 ounce the which is set about with stones under the figure of Jesus.

[Different ink] William Rowley, merchant of the parish of Saint Ewen, qm obiit 6th die mens Septembri anno domini 1488, gave to the church by testament, and delivered by Margaret his wife, that is to say a quarter of woad.

[Different hand] Robert Mattson, sometime apprentice with Thomas Pernaunt, bequeathed unto this church at his decease – 3s 4d.

Clement Wilteshire of this parish, merchant, that deceased during his mayoralty, gave unto this church in money the sum of 20s. And besides this he ordained to find a priest to sing in this church 3 years. And ever in his days a well willing man and a loving unto the church and to the parish, he lies before Saint John's altar.

[Different hand] Item since his departing of this world his wife Joan Wilteshire alias Baten has given a pair of vestments of blue satin with flowers ?embroidered of gold – 28s 4d.

Item a ?pagent with a rose in the bottom gilded, with 6 candlesticks of latten, price – 26s 8d.

(146)
[This page and the two following are in an inferior hand to those preceding and have all been scored; there is a note to the effect that the material is better presented below.]
Names of good doers
Thomas Spicer & Maud his wife, and afterward a lady most devout and charitable.

Thomas Spicer alias Baker of this parish, grocer, died on the morrow of St Valentine viz 15th day February 1492, gave to this church as follows.

In primis he ordained a priest to sing in this church 6 years, 9 marks per annum – £36 13s 4d.
Item he bequeathed to the church and paid – 40s.
Item his obit to be kept in this church 10 years.
Item he has bequeathed to the church a pax of silver and gilt, with a crucifix with Mary and John, weighing 5 ½ ozs at 5s the ounce, sum – 27s 6d.
God have mercy on his soul. Amen.

Moreover since his decease my lady Maud Spicer, wife to the said Thomas, for the weal of their souls both, unto the worship of almighty God, Our Blessed Lady and All Hallows' has given unto this church as follows.

In primis a chalice well gilded, weighing 24ozs, at 5s 6d the ounce, sum – £6 13s.

Item 2 cruets of silver, weighing 11 ozs, at 4s the ounce, sum – 44s.

Item 2 candlesticks of silver part gilt, weighing both in whole 80 ozs at 4s 6d the ounce, sum total – £10.

Item a mass book in prent [print] work – 15s.

Item a light blue vestment of damask with five wounds in the cross, with its apparel – 48s ½d.

Item a vestment of cloth of gold, £6 6s 8d, of red, with all its apparel.

So that all this afore expressed be at my lady's commandment during her life and after her decease to be delivered unto this church of All Hallows' in Bristol for ever more. Almighty God preserve her long. Amen.

[Entries to page foot in different hand] To the gilding of the rood loft – 6s 8d.

A goodly censer of silver.

A priest to sing for her by space of 12 years, and to have every year 9 marks.

(147)

Item beside all this that we have in possession for the profit of the church, the said lady has given hangings for the high altar, for the over part and the lower part, 11 yards of satin of Bruges with flowers and a crucifix of gold there set out on the same, with 2 frontals of black velvet with crowned emmys [ie 'M's] of gold, and Jhc [ie the holy monogram], and the lower part of the frontal there fringed with silk of changeable colour, and 2 curtains of blue pattern with fringes of silk of divers colour, which in all came to the sum of – £7 18s 7½d.

Item more an eagle of latten for the gospel to be read upon, weighing 2 ¼ hundredweights, *p'c* – £8

Item a table of the Transfiguration of Our Lord Jesus Christ to move and excite people unto devotion – 40s.

Item for the painting of 2 stories on 2 pillars of the lower part of the church, the one story over the font of the baptising of Our Lord Jesus Christ, and on that other pillar of the other part of the church a figure otherwise an image of Saint Christopher, that cost her – 30s.

Item 2 latten candlesticks that stand on Saint Thomas's altar for 2 tapers, that my said lady has ordained at every mass celebrated there to be lit and that of good substance full worshipfully unto the honour of almighty God, *p'c* – 4s 6d.

(148)

Names of good doers

Moreover in the vigil of the Assumption of Our Lady AD 1496, the foresaid Dame Maud Spicer in the honour and worship of Almighty God and Our Blessed Lady has given unto the church forever an honourable suit of vestments of white damask with flowers of gold and

all the orfreys of the suit of cloth of gold, the which suit contains a
chasuble, 2 tunicles with their apparels belonging, and 2 copes of the
same with shells of silver enamelled with the arms of Grocers, that cost
unto her – £27.
[Different hand: My said lady has given a principal censer of silver and part
gilt, weighing 40 ozs, at 4s 10d the ounce, sum the whole – £9 13s 4d.]
[Different hand: The said honourable lady ordained that a priest should
sing in this church after her death by the space of 12 years, to the
honour of God and augmenting of divine service *pro salute anime sue*;
every year he is to have for his salary 9 marks at the least. And by her
lifetime she had a chaplain singing in the said church by the space of 5
years, besides the years of her husband aforesaid.
Also she gave to the gilding of the rood loft – 6s 8d.
Item she provided 3 tapers of wax before the image of Jesus, there to
burn at the Jesus Mass on Fridays and at the anthem at night and at
other times convenient, so to be continued as long as any of her
executors shall continue this present life.]

(150)
Names of good doers
[Inferior hand] Clement Wilteshire deceasing mayor gave 20s in money.
Item caused a priest to sing in this church 3 years.
Joan wife to the said Clement gave 20s in money.
Item one pair of vestments of blue satin with branches and flowers, *p'c*
– 28s 4d.
Item 3 fine altar cloths of diaper.
Item 6 candlesticks of latten, *p'c* – 26s 8d.
[Different ink: Item his obit to be kept in this church for 4 years, 40s to
be distributed at every obit.]

[Different hand: Alys Pynke widow[:erased] gave 2 measures of woad.]

(151)
[Another hand] John Snygge, qm obit 17th die mens Septembri AD
1490, at his departing he bequeathed unto this church in money £5 *ac
remanet in manibz filii Sur Thomas Snygge junior*. [To which is added a
note to the effect that the proctors finally received this money in 1525].
Item [he] ordained that a priest be found in this church for 3 years – £18.
Item since his wife Alison has since paid for a pair of vestments for the
said priest to sing in, and afterwards to the church, *p'c* – 16s.
Item 2 tapers of 3 pounds and a torch to be maintained the said 3 years.
Item a pair of latten candlesticks weighing [blank] *p'c* [blank].
Item the said Alison of her devotion has given a censer of silver party
gilt, weighing [blank], sum – £8.

(153)
Names of good doers
Thomas Abyndon, innholder, at his decease gave unto this church in

money as a good doer – 40s.
Item Joan Abyndon, wife of the said Thomas, has given unto this church at her departing – 20s.

John Jenkyns *alias* Steyner, innholder, has at his own cost paid for the gilding of a shrine in the which to bear the blessed sacrament in and holy relics on certain days of the year in procession, that cost – 33s 4d.
[Different pen] Item the said John and Agnes his wife, longing to be prayed for, ordained with our assent to this church by testament a standing nut with a cover well gilt, with a black shell, weighing 37 ozs, to be given after their days; the which testament, according to their wills, was written by the vicar of this church, John Thomas then being ghostly father to them both, being sore sick and in peril of death. And the said John Steynour *alias* Jenkin outliving the said Agnes, his wife, when it again pleased almighty God to visit him with sickness, he desired the said vicar to read the said testament before him and his brother Thomas, being his executor, and Master John Davidson notary, and was well content that the said nut after his days should remain to this church for ever. How be it, after such persons that gave him counsel according to his desire, the same vicar delivered unto him in the said testament in keeping not to be ?provided? unto this church, in so much [as] the Easter following, the foresaid John Jenkins moved the said vicar, as his trust was in him, that he should so order in this book, the Register of good doers, that this nut should never be alienated nor sold, but was to remain in the treasure coffer, to the behoof and pleasure of the parishioners in the day of the General Mind of good doers.

(154)
Jesus Mercy
Names of good doers
[Distinctive hand, to foot of p.159]
Thomas Spicer otherwise Baker
and Maud his wife, and afterwards lady by profession to the mantle and the ring.
This said Thomas, departing to God the 15th day of February A.D. 1492, gave to this church 40s in money.
Item a pax of silver and gilt with the crucifix, Mary and John, weighing 5 ½ ozs, at 5s the ounce, sum – 27s 6d.
Item he ordained a priest to sing for him in this church by the space of 6 years, every year to have for his wages 9 marks and a noble. The whole sum is – £37 13s 4d.
Item he ordained his anniversary to be kept for him in this church 10 years. Jesus have mercy on his soul. Amen.

(155)
The reverent and gracious lady Dame Maud Spicer otherwise Baker, singular benefactrix to this church, deceasing to God A.D. 1503, provided and gave to this church as follows.

First she caused a priest to sing by her life in this church by the space of 5 years to the honour of God and augmenting of divine service, in addition to the 6 years aforesaid for her husband, Thomas Spicer.

Also the said good lady caused a priest to sing in this church after her blessed departing by the space of 12 years. Every year to have for his salary – £6.

Item the said honourable lady gave a good chalice, substantially gilt, weighing 24 ozs, at 5s the ounce, the whole sum – £6 12s.

Item 2 cruets of silver, weighing 11 ozs, at 4s the ounce, sum – 44s.

Item a pax of silver.

Item 2 candlesticks of silver, weighing 80 ozs, at 4s 6d the ounce – £18.

Item a principal censer of silver and parcel gilt, weighing 40 ozs, at 4s 10d the ounce, sum total – £9 13s 4d.

Item the said charitable lady gave a sole vestment of red cloth of gold, price – £6 6s 8d.

(156)

Names of good doers

Item a sole light blue vestment of damask with five wounds in the cross, price – 48s.

Item a mass book of print, *p'c* – 15s.

Item she gave a goodly suit of vestments of white damask with flowers of gold, and all the ofreys of the suit cloth of gold, which suit contained 2 copes and vestments for the priest, deacon and subdeacon, the price of the whole suit – £27.

Item she gave apparel for the high altar, both for the over part and the nether, which is satin of Bruges with flowers and a crucifix of gold. Also to the same, 2 curtains of blue satin. The price of the whole was – £7 18s 7d.

Item she gave an eagle of latten for the gospel to be read upon, the price – £8.

Item a table of the Transfiguration of Jesus, which cost – 40s.

Item the said devout lady has provided for a yearly obit to be kept in this church for the wealth of her soul and all Christian souls, as it appears in the composition of the same.

Item 2 latten candlesticks to stand continuously upon Saint Thomas's altar, price – 4s 6d.

Item to the gilding of the rood loft – 6s 8d.

Jesus have mercy on her soul.

(157)

Maud Woddington, mother to the said good lady, gave a good and fine towel of twilly.

Thomas Spicer the younger, otherwise Baker, gave in money – £4.

Item he paid for the repairing and mending of the books of the church, the which cost – 26s 8d.

Item he gave to All Hallows' conduit – 20s.

[Scored: Paul James gave in money – 40s.]

(158)
Names of good doers
Thomas Parnaunt gave unto the church – 40s.
Item he had a priest to sing in this church by a year [scored: the which had for his salary.]
Item he gave also to All Hallows' conduit – 40s.
Item a banner of silk with the image of the Trinity.
Item he gave a mitre for Saint Nicholas bishop.
Jesus have mercy on his soul.

[Different hand] Thomas apHowell gave a table of alabaster that stands upon the morrow mass altar.

(159)
Richard Myell, bookseller, gave his best gown, *p'c* – 16s.

John Lard gave to the church – 20s.
Item to the gilding of the front at the high altar – 10s.
Item a candlestick of latten with 3 branches before the image of Our Lady in Jesus' guild, *p'c* – 5s 4d.
Item to the gilding of the rood loft – 3s 4d.
Item to All Hallows' conduit – 5s.

[Scored: Richard Wale gave unto the church, [blank].]
[Scored: Item he gave unto All Hallows' conduit, [blank].]

William Like of Lichfield gave unto the gilding of the high altar – 10s.

[Different hand] John Watson, fishmonger late deceased, gave to the maintaining of the church – 20s.
Jesus have mercy on his soul.

(161)
[From here to page 168 in same, small script with a few additions and scorings]
Names of good doers
Fundator domus Kalendarum

William Newbery gave a rent of assize of 12s by the year going out of a house in Baldwin Street to have an obit yearly, and he gave 20s in money.

Martin Draper gave a rent assize of 12d in Lewins Mead to find a lamp before the cross altar.

John le Gowe [gave] 4s yearly out of the corner house next to All Hallows' conduit, to find 5 tapers before Our Lady's altar and the Jesus altar.

Alice Hayly, special benefactrix, gave the house in the High Street, called the Green Lattice, going then at £5 6s 8d the year.

?James Regny gave 2s 6d for a baste door of the house that [added: Rawlyn Webbe] John Watson now dwells in.

Sir William Sylke, sometime vicar of the church, gave 2s rent assize in Marsh Street.

Nicholas Sherston gave 12 ½d yearly of an acre of land in ?Tridland.

[Scored: Stephen Grocesale gave 12d yearly going out of a tenement next to Abynton's Inn.]

Lawrance Mercer gave 6d rent assize in Saint Peter's parish.

Richard Mangottesfold gave 12d yearly of rent assize at the Barres.

[Scored: Geffrey Cornmonger gave 2s rent assize [illegible].]

Robert Picard gave 12d of rent of assize in ?Baldwin Street, and [an]other 12d to the Kalendars.

Thomas Fyler and Agnes his wife gave a tenement in the High Street, in the which John [scored: Snygge] Hoper now dwells, to have a perpetual obit costing 12s.

Humfrey Hervy and Anne his wife gave a tenement in the High Street in which John Roper grocer now dwells, and a garden in the old market place.

(162)
Names of good doers.
Sir Walter Isgar, sometime vicar of the church, gave a portewse [breviary] of *Temporal* and *Sanctorum* and an ordinal. [Scored: Item he gave the confirmation of all Indulgences belonging to to the Kalendars and special benefactors.]

Sir William Sylke sometime vicar of the Church gave a red mass book, a grail with a processional, a little candlestick of brass [scored: which was saint Thomas of Canterbury's], a psalter, a manual, with many other gifts as it appears in his testament.

Sir Thomas Marshall, vicar, gave the best mass book, price – 13 marks 6s 8d, 1 antiphonal with a psalter, a processional. [He provided for] the glazing of two widows in the rood [scored: cross] aisle, one of the 7 works of mercy and the other of the 7 sacraments. [He gave] to the treasure of the church – £10, and to be distributed among the poor parishioners – £10, [also] a great gable window in the choir, a pair of green vestments with orfreys of gold, a pair of blue vestments with garters. He built the vicarage and found a priest to sing for his soul in this church 10 years.

Sir Richard Parkhouse, vicar, gave a pair of light green vestments with orfreys of cloth of gold, *p'c* – £3, 2 torches and 10 lbs of wax.

Sir William Rodberd, vicar, gave a suit of vestments, p'c – £20. To the ?ceiling of the roof of the church – £6 13s 4d. A pair of cruets of silver weighing 6 ozs. A priest to pray for his soul in this church, 10 years.

Sir Harry Collas, sometime a fellow of the Kalendars, gave a processional with 7 psalms and litanies in the end of this same book.

Sir John Gillard, sometime prior and master of the Kalendars, gave a paxbread of silver of 9 ¼ ozs, a fair processional, and he let make 4 seats in the rood [scored: cross] aisle, *p'c* – £3. Item this same Sir John and Richard Haddon let make a tabernacle of gold and silver of Saint Saviour that stands at high feasts upon the high altar, *p'c* – £20.
Item they caused to be made the aisle of Jesus with the library above with the goods of John Haddon and Christine his wife, which aisle with the glasing cost them 11 score and 7 pounds. The house of Kalendars to keep the repairs of the gutter next to the street. [Next sentence scored:] Also as some say, they amortised 20 marks worth of livelode (163) to find a priest for evermore videnda est illa ?materi. Item the said John Haddon gave a massbook to his said chantry, price – £18, with 4 pairs of vestments, and the said Sir John Gillard gave to the chantry a chalice, *p'c* – £7 6s 8d.

Sir Maurice Hardwick, sometime vicar of this church, paid for the clasps of the best copes. To the buying of a pair of organs he gave – 6s 8d. To the ?ceiling of the roof of this church – 6s 8d. He let make the image of Saint Ursula, [and gave] a couple of altar cloths with a crucifix, *p'c* – 15s. Item he gave a couple of altar cloths, painted with the Coronation of Our Lady, *p'c* – 26s 8d; a couple of altar cloths of Saint Ursula, *p'c* – 18s. To the high altar, 2 fine corporas [cloths] with a green case of needlework. He let gilt the image of All Hallows, *p'c* – £3. He let gilt the crucifix – 23s 4d. He caused the book of good doers to be made. He gave a pair of red vestments of ?dimysary. He gave the cloth of velvet with flowers of gold that were wont to hang behind the image of All Hallows in the principal feasts, with the frontal to the same. Also he gave 4 stained cloths pictured with the arms of the passion of our saviour, Christ, to hang in the choir [at] principal feasts.

Sir William Howe, vicar, gave a corporas case of cloth of gold.

Sir William Warens, chantry priest of Halleway's chantry, gave a pair of red baudkin vestments to sing in on holy days, and a breviary to be chained in the church.

Sir Thomas Haxby, fellow of the Kalendars, gave to the church – 26s 8d; and ever a well willing and a tendable man to the church. Jesus reward his soul.

Master John Harlow, sometime prior of the Kalendars and parson of Saint Stephen's, gave a book for the organs and as many flowers for the high altar as cost him – 53s 4d.

Sir Thomas Furber, sometime fellow of the Kalendars, gave to the gilding of the rood loft – £5. He found a priest to sing for him in this church for a year. He gave a psalter book to be chained in the church. [Margin: a pair of vestments of white damask]

Master John Thomas, sometime vicar, let seal the roof of the ?choir.

(164)
Names of good doers
Roger Gurdeler gave the pyx wherein the blessed sacrament is borne in visitations, with the cup and spoon, all silver and gilt, weighing 45ozs.

The Goldsmiths let make at the high altar a tabernacle of the Coronation of Our Lady, being of gold, silver and precious stones with a ruby, *p'c* all – £20.

John Pers, mercer, gave a cope of black baudkin, a chasuble with two tunicles with orfreys of green, and certain land as it appears by twelve evidences, and he found a priest in the church 8 years, and gave 20 marks to the building of the [scored: cross] rood aisle in the south side of the church.

Emote Chilcombe gave a chalice weighing 13 ¼ ozs.

John Forges, cook, gave towards a pair of censers – £3, and to the building of the cross aisle – £5 6s 8d.

Richard Ake gave the antiphonal that lies before the vicar, *p'c* – £10.

Julian Papnam gave a chalice of 24 ozs, and bishop Carpenter sometime bishop of Worcester has given 40 days of pardon to everyone hearing the mass said with the same chalice on principal feasts.

William Wytney let make the Dance of Powles, which cost him – £18.

John Whiteside, notary, and Joan Helwood [ie Selwood?], widow, gave 75 ozs of silver towards a pair of silver candlesticks.

John Wells gave a mazer, *p'c* – 17s 10d.

?Walter Parken gave a standing pece of silver with a cover, *p'c* – 46s 8d.

Thomas Halleway and Joan his wife founded a perpetual chantry in this church. Item 8s yearly to have the lamp continually burn before the high altar. Item the monstrance with 2 angels and relics to bear the blessed sacrament in on Corpus Christi day, weighing 57 ¼ ozs. Item a mass book to the high altar. Item the morrow mass bell with the hanging of the same. Item £20 toward the best suit of vestments. Item £20 towards the building of (165) the [scored: cross] rood aisle. Item he let make all the seats or pews before Saint Dunstan's altar, which is the morrow mass altar. Item many other things to the said chantry, such as books, vestments, chalice, cruets of silver, and divers other things as it appears in his compositions [scored: which things should be in the custody of his chantry priest].

William Raynes [scored: Isabel and Jane] gave a ship of silver. Item to the best suit of vestments – £3.

Thomas Fyler and Agnes his wife found a priest in this church by the space of 3 years, in addition to his said tenement.

William Palmer of London, goldsmith, gave 40s in money.

Robert Derkyn of London, mercer, gave 20s in money.

Martin Syson gave 20s in money.

Harry Chestre and Alice his wife found a priest in this church by the space of 12 years giving 9 marks by the year, sum – £67. Also they were special benefactors and the main founders of the Jesus Mass and Jesus anthem kept in this church on Fridays. Item the same Alice Chestre, after the decease of her husband, let make the tabernacle over the image of Jesus, and the tabernacle [insert: with the images of Our Lady] on the other side of the same altar, and had them both gilded along with the whole front and story of the same altar and also provided for stained cloths to cover the same. Item she let make and gilded the front and story of the altar in the south aisle, providing stained cloths to the same. Item she let make the rood loft with all the images belonging to the same. Item she gave the second best cross, weighing 40 ozs, which cost her £20. Item she and her husband gave a long towel of diaper for the parishioners to be communioned or houselled withal at Easter. Item to the high altar, a fine altar cloth and a towel. Item to the rood altar, an altar cloth and a towel. Item to the Jesus altar, an altar cloth and a towel. Item to the same altar of Jesus, 2 stained cloths, 1 for the lower part and another for the over part, 1 with the picture of Jesus rising out of the sepulchre. Item 2 curtains to the same. Item a large cloth of twilly, with streak of blue to cover the best cope when it is laid forth. Item a hearse cloth of black worsted with letters of gold, and is written in the same

Orate pro animabus Henrici Chestre et Alicie uxoris eius. Item a great basin [scored: to wash relics in on Relic Sunday] Item she founded a priest in this church 5 years beside the 12 years before rehearsed. [Next sentence underlined:] Item she departed to God the 16th day of December the year of our lord God 1485, on whose soul Jesus have mercy.

(166)
Names of good doers
John Chestre son to Harry Chestre and Alice, found a priest in this church by space of 2 years, and he was very benevolent in exhorting his father and mother to their good deeds.

John Leynell and Katherine his wife found a priest in this church 12 years and they have a mass book, *p'c* – 10 marks. Item a chalice double gilt weighing 20 ozs, at 6s per ounce. Item a pair of cruets of silver, weighing 7 ozs. Item a corporas of fine cloth with a case of blue velvet. Item a great pair of latten candlesticks called standards before the high altar, price – 4 marks. Item the 2 best blue copes and all the vestments of the same for the priest, deacon and subdeacon, *p'c* – £25.

John Pynke the younger found a priest in this church 2 years, and he gave 4 measures of good woad.

Hugh Forster gave a mazer [scored: to be delivered after the decease of Joan his wife.]

Agnes, the wife of John Cogan of Saint Nicholas parish, gave 20s in money.

William Rowley, merchant of Saint Ewen's parish, gave a quarter of woad.

Robert Matson gave 3s 4d.

Clement Wilteshire gave 20s in money and caused a priest to sing in this church 3 years.

Joan Wilteshire, wife to the said Clement, gave 20s in money. Item a pair of vestments of blue satin with branches and flowers, p'c – 28s 4d. Item 4 fine altar cloths of diaper. Item a branch in the [scored: cross] rood aisle with 6 candlesticks, p'c – 26s 8d.

Alice Pynke gave 2 measures of woad.

(167)
John Snygge gave £5 in money [scored: *ad huc remanibz filii sui*] and found a priest to sing in the church by the space of 3 years.

Alice Snygge gave a pair of vestments, *p'c* – 16s. Item a pair of latten candlesticks. Item a good censer of silver, *p'c* – £8. To All Hallows' conduit – 40s.

Thomas Abyndon gave 40s in money.
Item Joan, his wife, gave 20s in money.

John Jenkins alias Stainer gilded the shrine to bear the blessed sacrament in on Corpus Christi day which cost – 33s 4d. Item a nut with a cover, gilt with a black shell, to be occupied at the obit or mind of the good doers.

Anne Hervy gave 3 altar cloths.

Paul James gave 40s in money.

Richard Stephens gave 10s in money.

Joan Stephens, widow, gave 3s 4d to this church and 3s 4d to the chantry. Item a spice dish of silver and gilt of 7 ozs. Item a priest to sing in this church 1 year. Item a large towel of diaper.

?David Cogan gave 20s to the church and 20s to the conduit.

Master Doctor Harper let make the great press in the choir for the copes and vestments, price 40s.

Alice apHowel gave an altar cloth of diaper.

[Different hand] John Watson, fishmonger late deceased, gave to the maintaining of the church, 20s.

[Different hand] Master Thomas White gave 20s yearly to the continual repair of All Hallows pipe to be had out of his 5 houses in Broad Street, which he gave to the chamber of Bristol.

[Subsequent pages are blank, but for heading Names of good doers]

*   *   *

(225)
In Evidence abounding of all the livelode of the Church
John Asshton John Torner
[Page blank, and following pages headed with Evidence for bonding for livelode]

*   *   *

(312)
A transcribed Latin decree, dated 16 July 1493, the original of which was said to be written under the bishop's seal and kept in a round box in a coffer among the evidences of the church. The decree records that

John Hawley, rector of St Mary le Port, Bristol, acting on behalf of Robert Bishop of Worcester, has visited All Saints' and confirmed that the Abbot of St Augustine's, in return for tithes and various payments, has the responsibility for maintaining the chancel of All Saints' church; he confirms the feasibility of withholding the tithes and payments in a situation where building work needs to be done to the chancel.

(313)
A.D. 1518
Memorandum that at about All Hallows' tide in the 10th year of the reign of Henry VIII, my lord the Abbot of St Augustine's at his own cost and charge did repair the roof of the chancel and the gutters of the same as well with tiles and soldering. John Howse and John Mawnell, grocers, at that time being proctors; William Thorn, being servant to my said lord, was overseer of the same work; and one called Maurice Tiler was workman. Through me John Flock, then vicar.

                    *   *   *

(315)
This inventory[1] was made on the 5th day of March in the year of Our Lord 1395 by William Lenche and Stephen Knyght, wardens of the parish church of All Hallows' of Bristol, before Sir William Lynch, vicar of the said church; and the parishioners by indenture delivered the goods that follow to Reynold Taverner and John Lente, wardens of the said church for the year following, for to be a memorial and a remembrance to all the manner of people that come after us, to understand what goods they receive and what they deliver so that that the goods of the church be not wasted, lost nor destroyed. God have mercy on their souls. AMEN.

In primis, 1 red mass book, *p'c* – 40s.
Item 1 old mass book without boards, *p'c* – 13s 4d.
Item 1 grail with bosses, *p'c* – 53s 4d.
Item 1 grail, *p'c* – 40s.
Item 1 white grail, *p'c* – 53s 4d.
Item 1 little grail to serve Our Lady Mass, *p'c* – 6s 8d.
Item 1 little grail, abridged, *p'c* – 10s.
Item 1 old grail, *p'c* – 12d.
Item 2 manuals, *p'c* – 10s.
Item 1 martyrology, *p'c* – 10s.
[Different hand: Item 2 new antiphonals, *p'c* – [blank].]

(316)
Stephen Knyght William Lench Inventory.
Item 1 breviary, *p'c* – 40s.
Item ½ white breviary with a psalter – 20s.

---

[1] A Latin version of this inventory is printed by E. Atchley, *Archaeological Journal* (1901), 152.

Item 1 old breviary, *p'c* – 13s 4d.
Item ½ old breviary with psalter – 10s.
Item 1 antiphonal, *p'c* – 6s 8d.
Item 1 little antiphonal, – 3s 4d.
Item 1 ordinal, *p'c* – 20s.
Item 1 white psalter, *p'c* – 10s.
Item 1 psalter of Thomas Norton's gift – 10s.
Item 1 psalter, *p'c* – 2s.
Item 1 psalter, *p'c* – 2s.
Item 1 legendary *temporalis*, *p'c* – 40s.
Item 1 legendary *sanctorum*, *p'c* – 13s 4d.
Item 6 new quires for the legendary *temporalis* – 16s 8d.
Item 1 processional, *p'c* – 13s 4d.

Inventory of Vestments
In primis 1 blue cope with 1 chasuble and tunicle, *p'c* – £4.
Item 1 green cope with 1 chasuble and 2 tunicles with orfreys of ray velvet, *p'c* – £6 13s 4d.
Item 1 cope of blue, *p'c* – 13s 4d.
Item 1 chasuble with 2 tunicles, *p'c* – 30s.
Item 1 cope, *p'c* – 20s.
Item 1 black vestment, *p'c* – 13s 4d.
Item 1 red vestment with griffons, *p'c* – 20s.
Item 1 red vestment, *p'c* – 6s 8d.
Item 1 white vestment, *p'c* – 6s 8d.

(317)
Stephen Knyght William Lenche Inventarium.
Item 1 chasuble with birds, *p'c* – 6s 8d
Item 1 chasuble of white and black diaper, *p'c* – 5s.
Item 1 red chasuble of satin, *p'c* – 20d.
Item 1 yellow chasuble, *p'c* – 20d.
Item 1 chasuble, *p'c* – 6s 8d.
Item 2 albs, *p'c* – 3s 4d.
Item 1 green corporas case with flowers – 3s 4d.
Item 1 stained cloth for the high altar with 1 figure of the Trinity and 2 curtains with angels and 1 stained cloth with the Coronation of Our Lady – 30s.
Item 6 pillows of silk, *p'c* – 6s 8d.
Item 2 tables and 2 paxbreads, *p'c* – 6s 8d.
Item 1 Lent cloth of white, *p'c* – 12d.
Item 1 red amice powdered with ?perth, *p'c* – 3s 4d.
Item 1 pectoral of copper overgilt, *p'c* – 3s 4d.
Item 1 veil of black velvet for the cup – 3s 4d.
Item 2 ?pawtnerys of needlework, *p'c* – 3s 4d.
Item 1 cloth for the crucifix, *p'c* – 3s 4d.
Item 3 Lent cloths for the altars, *p'c* – 5s.
Item 12 towels and 2 frontals of red silk – 6s 8d.

Item 3 surplices.
Item 2 mantles of red satin for Our Lady.
Item 2 mantles of red satin for St Anne.
Item 1 mantle of checker velvet.
Item 1 mantle of red satin for Our Lady in the pillar.
Item 4 towels and 2 frontals.

(318)
Stephen Knyght William Lench Inventory.
Item 2 candlesticks of pewter.
Item 1 red ray vestment of satin and 6 kerchiefs of silk.
Item 3 ropes of 60 fethym[?fathom], *p'c* – 11s 10 ½d.
Item 1 great bucket, *p'c* – 20d.
Item 5 little buckets, *p'c* – 2s 7d.
Item 1 double pulley, *p'c* – 10d.
Item 2 banners of stained work, *p'c* – 18s 6d.
Item 2 painted banner staves.
Item 1 pair of tin cruets for the high altar – 6d.
Item 1 cross of gilded wood, *p'c* – 24s.
Item 2 painted cross staves.
Item 1 paxbread of gilded copper.
Item 2 stained cloths for the sepulchre with 4 knights and Mary Magdalene.
Item 1 stained cloth of the Passion of Christ for the high altar in Lent.

Inventory of Jewels
In primis 1 cowpe [bowl] of silver gilt of 34 ozs and 7 ha'pennyweight.
Item 1 little cup of silver gilt weighing 1 ½ ozs and 4 pennyweight.
Item 1 oil-fat of silver weighing 8 ozs.
Item 1 tabernacle of silver and gilt of the Coronation of Our Lady with 1 ruby imperial standing in the middle of the high altar, *p'c* – £20.

(319)
Stephen Knyght William Lench Inventory
Item 1 chalice, weighing – 21 ½ ozs.
Item 1 chalice weighing – 13 ¾ ozs and 2 ½ pennyweight.
Item 1 box of ivory bound with silver.
Item 1 chalice weighing 13 ½ ozs and 2 ½ pennyweight.
Item 1 chalice weighing 15 ½ ozs.
Item 1 chalice of the Fraternity of the Carpenters.
Item 1 chalice weighing 13 ozs and 5 pennyweight.
Item 2 cruets of silver weighing 5 ½ ozs.
Item 4 lych bells weighing 17 lbs.
Item 1 censer of latten, *p'c* – 6s 8d.
Item 2 ships of latten.
Item 2 pairs of pewter candlesticks, *p'c* – 12s.
Item 1 eagle of gilded wood, *p'c* – 6s 8d.
Item 1 desk, *p'c* – 2s.

Item 1 desk for the high altar – [blank].
Item 1 latten bell for the high altar, *p'c* – 12d.
Item 1 little bell, *p'c* – 4d.
Item 1 iron candlestick weighing 12 lbs.
Item 2 wooden candlesticks, *p'c* – [blank].
Item 3 wheels for the bells.
Item 2 ladders, 1 of 8 rungs and the other of 26 rungs.
Item 1 wooden box bound with iron, *p'c* – 16d.
Item 1 cross of silver and gilt, weighing 220 ozs.

[Latin: Here ends the inventory of William Lenche and Stephen Knyght, wardens of the said church.]

(320)
In the name of God. Amen. This inventory was made on the 1st day of March the year of Our Lord 1469, and the 9th year of the reign of Edward IV. Richard Haddon and John Schoppe, churchwardens of the parish of All Hallows' of Bristol, before Sir Maurice Hardwick vicar of the said church and the parishioners, received divers goods and money without any inventory, indenture or any other writing, which in time to come could have been greatly to the prejudice, hurt and hindering of the said church. Wherefore, the said wardens, for the great worship and love of God and to profit the said church, let make this said inventory to be a memorial and a remembrance to all people that come after us [as to] what goods we found in the said church and what goods they shall receive that come after us, and so yearly to make deliverance before the vicar and the parishioners, that the goods of the said church be neither wasted, lost nor destroyed. God have mercy on their souls. Amen.

(321)
Richard Haddon & John Schoppe
In primis 2 lych bells weighing [blank].
Item 4 candlesticks of wood, *p'c* – [blank].
Item 1 checker for the holy loaf, *p'c* – [blank].
Item [space] clappers [for] all Judas bells, *p'c* – [blank].
Item 1 Judas for the candles the 3 nights before Easter.
Item 1 sepulchre.
Item 5 gilded battlements.
Item 2 gilded crucifixes for the 2 ends of the sepulchre.
Item 4 bolts of iron with 2 battlements of red.
Item 1 crown with 4 angels of painted wood.
Item 3 painted cross staves, *p'c* – [blank].
Item 1 board with 2 trestles for obits.
Item 2 painted crucifixes of wood.
Item 2 berys [?beirs].
Item [blank] buckets of wood.
Item 2 great ladders.

Item 1 little ladder behind the high altar.
Item 1 reredos to set jewels on at the high altar.
Item 1 gilded eagle of wood.
Item 1 bowl of wood for the pascal.
Item 1 desk of carved wood with 1 crucifix.
Item 1 plank to lay wax on.
Item 3 chairs for the choir.
Item 1 little stool for the organs.

(322)
Richard Haddon & John Schoppe Inventory
Item 1 little desk for the organs.
Item 1 desk for the high altar.
Item 1 carved desk with 1 crucifix for Our Lady's altar.
Item 1 carved desk for Saint Thomas' altar.
Item 1 desk for the singers at Our Lady's altar.
Item 2 banners with staves.
Item 1 spear.
Item 1 foot for the cross painted with Mary and John.
Item 1 foot painted for the monstrance.

(323)
Richard Haddon & John Schoppe Inventory
Item 1 bar of iron at the high altar for stained cloths.
Item 2 riddels with flowers de luse [fleurs-de-lis] at the high altar for curtains.
Item 2 iron riddels at Our Lady's altar.
Item 2 iron riddels at the Cross altar.
Item 3 iron riddels at Saint Thomas' altar.
Item 3 iron riddels at Saint John's altar.

(324)
Richard Haddon & John Schoppe
Inventory of coffers and almerys [?aumbries] for conducts of the said church
In primis [blank]

(325)
Richard Haddon & John Schoppe
Inventory of Lent cloths
In primis 1 cloth of Our Lady of Pity, *p'c* – 40s.
Item the Lent veil, *p'c* – [blank].
Item 1 stained cloth with the signs of the Passion for the rood.
Item 1 stained cloth with 1 crucifix before Saint Dunstan.
Item 1 cloth of blue and white before Saint Saviour.
Item 1 cloth of blue and white before Saint Thomas.
Item 1 stained cloth of Jesus in the pillar for the high altar.
Item 2 cloths for Our Lady's altar.

Item 1 cloth of silk of ray for Our Lady in the pillar.
Item 1 cloth of silk of ray for Saint Anne.
Item 1 stained cloth with dolphins.
Item 1 black cloth of silk for Saint Ursula.
Item 1 vernicle wrought in silk at Our Lady's altar.

(326)
Richard Haddon & John Schoppe
Inventory of altar cloths
In primis an altar cloth of diaper, 5⅜ yards long and a yard and a nail broad.
Item an altar cloth of diaper 4 yards long and a yard and a nail broad.
Item an altar cloth of diaper 3 ⅝ yards long and ¾ broad with crosses on.
Item an altar cloth of twilly 4 ½ yards long and ⅞ broad.
Item an altar cloth of twilly 4 ½ yards long and ¾ broad.
Item an altar cloth of twilly 2 ⅝ yards long and 1 ⅛ broad.
Item an altar cloth of twilly 3 yards long and 1 broad.
Item an altar cloth of plain work a skant 4 ½ yards long and a yard save a nail broad.
Item an altar cloth of plain 2 ½ yards long and a yard and the nail broad.
Item an altar cloth of plain 3 ¾ yards long and a yard broad.
Item an altar cloth of plain 4 ⅜ yards long and a yard save the nail broad.
Item an altar cloth of plain a scant 3 ¾ yards long and 1 ⅛ yards broad.
Item an altar cloth of plain with crosses 3 yards long and 1 ⅛ yards broad.
Item a ?covering of canvas for the high altar 3 ⅜ yard long and a yard broad.
Item a ?covering of canvas for Our Lady's altar 3 ⅜ yards long and a yard broad.

(327)
Richard Haddon & John Schoppe
Inventory of altar cloths and towels
Item a towel of diaper 9 ⅝ yards long and ½ a yard and a nail broad.
Item a towel of twilly 3 ¾ yards long and ⅜ broad.
Item a towel of plain 8 ⅜ yards long and ½ a yard broad.

(328)
Richard Haddon & John Schoppe
Inventory of bankers and coverlets for the high altar
In primis [blank]

(329)
Richard Haddon & John Schoppe
Inventory of candlesticks and bowls of latten and pewter.
In primis 2 great candlesticks of latten, *p'c* – 51s 8d.

Item 2 candlesticks of latten for the high altar.
Item 2 processional candlesticks of latten.
Item 13 bowls of latten for the rood loft, *p'c* – 33s 4d.
Item 6 bowls of pewter, weighing [blank].
Item 2 candlesticks of iron standing at the Cross altar.
Item 2 ships of latten.
Item 1 bell of latten for the high altar, *p'c* – 12d.
[Different ink] Item 2 great standard candlesticks of latten of the gift of Katherine Leynell previously rehearsed, that weigh 94 lbs and cost 4 marks.

(330)
Richard Haddon & John Schoppe
Inventory of stained cloths
In primis 1 stained cloth of the Coronation of Our Lady.
Item 1 cloth with popinjays and scriptures.
Item 2 cloths of red and damask work with 1 crucifix with Mary and John, *p'c* – 16s 8d.
Item 2 white cloths with the Coronation of Our Lady with other imagery work, *p'c* – 26s 8d.
Item 2 cloths of blue damask work for Our Lady's altar, *p'c* – 13s 4d.
Item 2 cloths of blue damask work for Saint Thomas' altar, *p'c* – 15s.
Item 2 cloths of blue damask work for the Cross altar, *p'c* – 20s.
Item 1 cloth with popinjays and scriptures for Our Lady's altar.
Item 1 cloth with popinjays and scriptures for Saint Thomas' altar.
Item 1 cloth with popinjays and scriptures for Saint John's altar.
Item 1 cloth with popinjays and scriptures for the Cross altar.
Item 4 cloths of the said work for the choir.
Item 2 blue cloths for the Cross altar.

(331)
Richard Haddon and John Schoppe
For the altars and the sepulchre
Item 1 cloth of Mary Magdalene and 4 knights for the sepulchre.
Item 1 cloth of stained work powdered with birds of gold for the same.
Item 1 stained cloth powdered with flowers of gold for the same.
Item 1 black cloth of stained work for obits with 1 crucifix of white with 1 scripture of Jesus.
Item 2 cloths of stained work of the Nativity and the Passion of Christ for Saint Dunstan's altar.
Item 1 stained cloth of white with 1 image of Saint John the Baptist for the said altar.
[Different hand] Item 4 stained cloths of red and yellow with wreaths and the arms of the Passion, and in the middle of the arms *Dulcis est Jhc amor meus*, the which cloth is 13 ¾ yards long and 1 ¼ yards deep. And it is ordained that the said cloth is to be hung about the choir at every high feast. Given by Sir Maurice Hardwick.
[Different hand] Item a cloth of black worsted for the obits of the

parish, given by Alice Chester with letters of gold H & C & A & C with a scripture of gold *Orate pro animabus Henrici Chestre et Alicie uxoris eius*, with a stained cloth across-wise with a crucifix.

(332)
Richard Haddon and John Schoppe
Inventory of curtains for the high altar and the nether altars
In primis 2 curtains of white and purple silk for the high altar.
Item 2 of stained work powdered with gold.
Item 2 of stained work with popinjays.
Item 1 stained curtain with 1 angel.
Item 2 curtains of blue and green silk for Our Lady's altar
Item 3 stained curtains of blue damask work at Our Lady's altar.
Item 2 stained curtains of blue damask work at Saint Thomas' altar.
Item 2 stained curtains of the Passion at Saint John's altar.
Item 2 stained curtains of blue damask work at the Cross altar.

(333)
Richard Haddon and John Schoppe
Inventory of antiphonals
In primis 1 great antiphonal embossed lying before the vicar, beginning the third leaf *Septrum Juda* and ending the last leaf *dixit domino*.
Item 1 antiphonal, beginning the third leaf *Nat be me* and ending the last leaf save one *Fides sue*.
Item 1 antiphonal, beginning the third leaf *Bit tibi* and ending the last leaf save one *de cuius*.

(334)
Richard Haddon and John Schoppe
Inventory of breviaries
In primis 1 black breviary, beginning the third leaf *Nomen eius Emanuel* and ending the last leaf save one *pro disposicione cantoris*.
Item 1 half breviary with 1 psalter, beginning the third leaf of the breviary *Erat ante* and ending the last leaf save one *dimiserunt prepter*.

[Lower on page] Item 1 psalter, beginning the third leaf *laboram* and ending the last leaf save one *aiabus pris*.
Item 1 psalter, beginning the third leaf *Fac propter* and ending the last leaf save one *In magna*.
[Different hand] Item a book for the organs.
Item a quire with new ?feasts.

(335)
Richard Haddon and John Schoppe
Inventory of legendaries
In primis 1 new legendary *sanctorum*, beginning the third leaf *Natale templi* and ending the last leaf save one *Non gravant*.

Item 1 legendary *temporalis*, beginning the third leaf *Christo hospicm* and ending the last leaf save one *viz nomine*.

Item 1 legendary *temporalis* from the beginning of Advent unto Easter, beginning the third leaf *Significat* and ending the last leaf save one *Et arma co*.

(336)
Richard Haddon and John Schoppe
Inventory of processionals.

In primis 1 processional, beginning the third leaf *satam Joseph* and ending the last leaf save one *Regem ad*.

Item 1 processional, beginning the third leaf *Agm ee* and ending the last leaf save one *unius honor*.

Item 1 processional, beginning the third leaf *Ecce radix* and ending the last leaf save one *Alleluya*.

Item 1 processional, beginning the third leaf *Ecce radix* and ending the last leaf save one *jungitur Ec*.

Item 1 red processional, beginning the third leaf *Diebus eius* and ending the last leaf save one *Nostra ut pu*.

Item 1 processional contained in 1 grail, beginning the third leaf *Na regentem* and ending the last leaf save one *Sampson*.

[Different hand] Item 2 abbreviated processionals.

(337)
Richard Haddon and John Schoppe
Inventory of grails.

In primis 1 grail, beginning the third leaf *dutur orum* and ending the last leaf save one *Agnus dei qui*[erased; different hand:] *Miserat nobis*.

Item 1 grail, beginning the third leaf *Na regnate* and ending the last leaf save one *Pu nostri forma*.

Item 1 grail, beginning the third leaf *?zons da'm* and ending the last leaf save one *Aromatu virga*[erased; different hand:]*Cibo dulci*.

Item 1 embossed grail, beginning the third leaf *Eccliam confiteor* and ending the last leaf save one *Ceci surdi*.

Item 1 abbreviated grail, beginning the third leaf [blank].

Item 1 grail for the Lent season, beginning the third leaf *Justicie indutu* and ending the last leaf save one *Tamen inequali*.

[Different hand] Item a grail, beginning the third leaf *quem onant* and ending the last leaf save one *Peccata unum*.

(338)
Richard Haddon and John Schoppe.
Inventory of ordinals and manuals [different hand: with hymnal and martyrology also a collectory with epistles and gospels]

In primis 1 ordinal, beginning the third leaf *Socis suo* and ending the last leaf save one *Crastina die ?et nobis*.

Item 1 ordinal, beginning the third leaf *domine deus virtutum* and ending the last leaf save one *Deffesto loci*.

Item 1 manual, beginning the third leaf *didue sce* and ending the last leaf save one *Suorum vem*.

Item 1 manual, beginning the third leaf *datorum tuorum* and ending the last leaf save one *Repellit domi*.

[Next two entries in different ink] Item a noted hymnal, beginning the third leaf *Stmencia ipi* and ending the last leaf save one *respnens*.

Item a martyrology, beginning the third leaf *apud* and ending the last leaf save one *dampnicam*.

[Monogram JT in margin; infirm hand] Item a collectory with noted anthems, also with epistles and gospels of the *temporalis* and *sanctorum*, beginning the third leaf *qm auderat mi . . . sict* and ending the last leaf save one *supplicit patunius ut a malis*, of the gift of John Thomas vicar in vig Nicho dm Anno domini 1496 as it is written before [in] the kalendar.

(339)
Richard Haddon and John Schoppe
Inventory of mass books
In primis 1 great mass book, beginning the third leaf *menta sua* and ending the last leaf save one *Et in valitudine*.

Item 1 mass book, beginning the third leaf *unum baptisma* and ending the last leaf save one *per enndm dmn*.

Item 1 little old mass book, beginning the third leaf *dnica p'ma in adve'tum dm* and ending the last leaf save one *Justificaccem nram*.

Item 1 old mass book without boards, beginning the third leaf *Dixit aliquando* and ending the last leaf save one *& zefri*.

Item the Chantry book, beginning the third leaf *Concede quesmius* and ending the last leaf save one *Delic*.

[Different hand]Item an abreviated mass book, beginning the third leaf *sed ad locum* and ending the last leaf save one ?*Genitce ma* and of the gift of William Cornowe, bowyer.

(340)
Richard Haddon and John Schoppe
Inventory of all other books not occupied
[Blank].

(342)
Richard Haddon and John Schoppe
Inventory of all manner suits of vestments
In primis 1 pair of vestments of light green of cloth of gold baudkin with the orfreys of purple baudkin.

Item 1 pair of sad green with orfreys of cloth of gold.

Item 1 pair of sad blue with garters and red orfreys.

Item 1 pair of black with stars of gold and with orfreys of white powdered with lilies.

Item 1 pair of red dimisay with orfreys of yellow dimisay.

Item 1 pair of sad purple with old orfreys of cloth of gold. [Margin: Changed for children.]

Item 1 pair of old cloth of gold with orfreys of yellow ribbon.

Item a pair of old cloth of gold with orfreys of fustian ?Napulo.

Item 1 pair of white vestments for lent.

[Different hand] Item 1 pair of green ?tartern vestments with red orfreys and peacock feathers, of Thomas Cogan's gift.

Item a pair of black with ?borys and the orfreys of green skin ?leaves.

[Different hand] Item a suit of vestments of cloth of gold tissue, that is to say copes, chasuble and 2 tunicles with their albs and parcells and stoles.

Item a suit of blue velvet vestments with branches of gold that is to say 2 copes, chasuble, and 2 tunicles with their albs and parcels and stoles, and of the gift of John Leynell and Katherine his wife.

Item a vestment of Mistress Wilteshire of blue satin with flowers of gold and red orfreys.

[Different hand] Item 1 pair of vestments of green ?dornex with yellow dornex to the orfreys, of the gift of Mistress Alice Snygge.

(343)

[Page in infirm hand] Item a vestment of blue with scorpions with small orfreys of purple of a ?trail of flowers, that is to say for priest and deacon with a cope.

Item a suit of blue baudkin with white flowers, the orfreys of green satin and stars of gold, with 3 copes.

Item a black suit of worsted with orfreys of green powdered with red and one cope with branched damask.

[Scored: Item a suit of cloth of gold of tisssue with 2 copes, 1 couched with pearl *ut a prescribitm in solis pcadent.*]

[Scored: Item a suit of blue velvet with orfreys of red with splayed eagles, and thereto belong 2 copes of Katherine Leynell.]

Item a suit of white damask with flowers of gold and the orfreys of cloth of tissue, of the gift of my lady Spicer.

(344)

Richard Haddon and John Schoppe

Inventory of fringes and banners

In primis 1 frontal of black velvet powdered with stars.

Item 1 black frontal of silk powdered with stars of gold.

Item 1 frontal of green and black silk for the sepulchre.

Item 1 frontal of red and black buckram for the sepulchre.

Item 1 frontal of cloth of silver for the high altar.

[Different pen] Item a frontel of cloth of gold over All Hallows' head, the which is a yard and five eigths in length, and a quarter save an inch broad.

Item a cloth of red velvet embroidered with 10 flowers of gold with scriptures in the foot *O hymnus omnibus sanctis*, with 2 letters of gold in the said cloth M & H, the which cloth is a yard save the nail in breadth [sic] and in deepness three quarters of a yard and a half save an inch.[The preceding 2 items are said in the margin to be Hardwick's gift.]

[Original pen] Item 2 banners of stained work of All Hallows and the Ascension.

Item 1 banner of cloth of silver with lions.

Item 4 pensels of paper for the paschal.
Item 1 banner of blue silk with 1 figure of All Hallows of gold for the cross.
[Different hand] Item a banner of blue sarsnett with flowers of gold and the image of All Hallows with 2 letters, that is T & P which was of the gift of Thomas Parnaunt.

(345)
Richard Haddon and John Schoppe
Inventory of jewels
In primis 1 cross of gold and silver weighing 220 ozs.
Item in the middle of the high altar 1 tabernacle of gold and silver of the Coronation of Our Lady with 1 ruby imperial, *p'c* – £20.
Item the said altar 1 tabernacle of gold and silver with 1 figure of Saint Saviour and 2 figures of John Haddon and Christine with angels, *p'c* – £20.
Item 1 monstrance of gold and silver with 2 angels and 2 stones of crystal weighing 57 ¼ ozs.
Item 1 cowpe [bowl] for the sacrament with 1 pece and 1 spoon all gilded weighing 45 ozs.
Item 1 oil fat of silver weighing 8 ¾ ozs.
Item 3 ampuls [flasks] of silver weighing [blank].
Item 1 box of ivory bound with silver, *p'c* – [blank].
Item 2 censers of silver weighing 58 ozs.
Item 2 candlesticks of silver weighing 75 ozs.
Item 1 ship of silver with 1 spoon weighing 21 ozs.
Item 1 paxbread of silver weighing 15 ozs.
[Scored: Item 2 cruets of silver weighing 6 ozs.]
[Different hand and scored: Item 2 cruets of silver weighing 7 ½ ozs of the gift of John Leynell and Katherine his wife.]
[Different hand] Item 2 cruets of silver weighing 14 ozs and 4 pennyweights [different hand: that was made with 2 pairs of cruets afore crossed, made in the year of John Jenkyns and Richard ?Sutton.]
[Different hand(?the infirm hand)] Item a cross of silver and gilt with Mary and John of the gift of Alice Chestre weighing [blank].
[Different hand] Item 2 copper and gilt cross staves, one for the best cross and another for the second cross which was the gift of Sir John Thomas, vicar of the said parish.

(346)
Richard Haddon and John Schoppe
Inventory of chalices
In primis 1 chalice with a paten all gilt weighing 24 ozs.
Item 1 chalice with paten weighing 12 ¼ ozs.
Item 1 chalice and 1 paten all gilt weighing 14 ⅜ ozs.
Item 1 chalice and 1 paten all gilt weighing 15 ½ ozs.
All gilt and broken[:Margin] Item 1 chalice and 1 paten weighing 15 ½ ozs.
Parcel gilt[:Margin] Item 1 chalice and 1 paten weighing 13 ¾ ozs.
[Different hand] Item a chalice with paten of the gift of John Leynell and Katheryn his wife all gilt weighing 24 ½ ozs and all gilt.

[Different hand] Halleways chantry viz Chalice
In primis a chalice all gilt weighing 19 ¾ ozs.
Item a white chalice party gilt 13 ozs.

(347)
Richard Haddon and John Schoppe
Inventory of corporas
In primis 1 case of blue baudkin with 1 corporas of diaper.
Item 1 black corporas with 1 crown of gold.
Item 1 case of black with ?beasts of needlework with 1 corporas.
Iten 1 case of green needlework with 1 corporas.
Item 1 case of green with flowers of gold with 1 corporas.
Item 1 old case with 1 ?lappeover with 1 corporas.
Item 1 yellow case with 1 corporas.
Item 2 purses of needlework.
[Different hand] Item a corporas case of blue velvet embroidered with
gold, of the gift of Katherine Leynell.

(348)
Richard Haddon John Schoppe
Inventory of pillows
[Blank]

(349)
Richard Haddon John Schoppe
Inventory of paxbreads and cruets
[Blank]

(350)
Richard Haddon John Schoppe
Inventory of linen cloths for the best vestments
[Blank]

(353)
This is an inventory made for all manner evidence that has been found
in the said church
In primis for the Green Lattice 9 evidences.
Item for the house next to the steeple 2 evidences.
Item of Thomas Fyler's house next to the Great [recte: Green] Lattice
on the south side.

Rent assizes that are paid.
In primis in Skadpull Street now called Marsh Street 7 pieces.
Item in Saint Peter's Street 2 pieces.
Item of the house next to the conduit in Corn Street 1 piece.
Item of the house in Lewinsmead 2 evidences with 1 copy of part of testament.
Item of 1 house in Baldwin Street of 12s with 12 pieces.
Item for the baste door in the churchyard 1 evidence.

Item for 1 gutter going out of the churchyard as for 1 state made to the chantry priests of Redcliffe and Saint Nicholas for the term of 49 winters the which term is passed – 1 evidence.

(354)
This is an inventory of rent assizes which have not been paid for many years
In primis of the house next to Thomas Abingdon in Venny Lane now called the Almshouse 2 pieces.
Item 1 house in Wine Street 1 piece.
Item in Redland 1 piece.
Item at the Barres under the common seal 1 piece.
Item of Robert Pykard in Baldwin Street of 2s, 1 evidence.

(355)
This is an inventory of other divers evidence that we find
In primis 1 patent under [blank]
Item 1 patent under king [blank]
Item 1 evidence under the dean's seal as for a strife made in the church that the church should not stand suspended.
Item 1 deed of feoffment for the livelode of the church.

(356)
This is an inventory of other deeds in the church
In primis 1 evidence of Roger Gurdeler to curse all those that alienate the bowl, cup or spoon.
Item 1 testament of Sir William Selke.
Item 4 letters of indulgence.
Item 3 evidences for the house of the Kalendars.
Item 2 evidences under the bishop of Worcester's seals for the anniversary of Sir Thomas Marshall.

(357)
This is an inventory of all manner of copies that we find in the church
In primis 1 copy of 1 deed of the house next to the steeple.
Item 1 copy of 1 testament of Richard Brompton as for the house in Baldwin Street.
Item 1 copy of 1 testament of Joan Brompton for the said house.
Item 1 copy of the plea for the house next to the steeple.

(358)
This is an inventory of evidence of bonding of livelode of the church
In primis 1 rental of the reign of King Richard the second's 7th year [1383–84].
Item 1 rental of bonding of all the livelode of the said church in the 14th year of the reign of King Richard the second [1390–91]. John Ashton, carpenter, and John Turner, mason, proctors of the said church.
Item 1 rental made by Robert Cor and William Colyns, proctors of the said church, bonding all the livelode in the 28th year of Henry VI [1449–50].

*   *   *

(375)
These are the names of the churchwardens of All Hallows' in Bristol of which we find Rentals and Accounts.

In primis John Derby and William Backe in their days let make the presbytery, the pulpit and the fashion of 2 silver censers – £3 5s 4d, and clear of all costs and quit they brought to the church – 11s 11 ½d. God have mercy on their souls.
Item the black vestment with stars of gold and the seats for the children in the choir.

Lawrens Brocke and William Baten their days let make 2 chairs for the choir and 4 cushions of stained work with eagles for the presbytery and for the said chairs, and brought clear in to the church – £4 11s 7d. God have mercy on their souls.

John Baker and John William brought clear in to the church – £3 5s 2½d. God have mercy on their souls. Item they let made the cross in the churchyard and brought in the new legendary of the *sanctorum*.

William Spycer and John Talbot brought clearly in to the church – £5 16s 7 ½d. God have mercy on their souls. Item they let paint the high altar with 2 angels.

Thomas Halleway and William Spycer in their days the rent of assize next to Roger Abyndon's house, now called the Almshouse, was withheld and withdrawn – 12d; and they clearly brought to the church – £9 1s 8 ½d. God have mercy on their souls.

(376)
The names of the Church Wardens
John Monke and William Raynes brought clearly in to the church – £5 16s 6d. God have mercy on their souls.

Richard Brewer and John Coke, osteler, owe to the said church – £5 17s 4 ½d.

William Lenche and Stephen Knyght let write 1 inventory of all the goods pertaining to the said church. God have mercy on their souls.

John Aschton, carpenter, and John Torner, mason, in their days let write as for 1 memorial to be had forever the names of the benefactors who had given livelode to the said church and the bonding of the said livelode where it lies. God have mercy on their souls.

Thomas Halleway and William Tempyll in their days let make the hanging for the paschal and the tressel and brought clearly to the church

– £4 13s 4d. God have mercy on their souls. Item they received for 1 gutter going through the churchyard under the beer house – 5s. [Margin: Look the gutter under the beer house.]

William Raynes and Thomas Chestyr let make in their days the sepulchre and brought clearly to the church – 7d. God have mercy on their souls.

Thomas Fyler and William Haytfeld in their days let bound books and brought clearly to the church – 13s 8 ½d. God have mercy on their souls.

(377)
Pers Chaplen and Richard Abyndon brought clearly to the church – £3 12s 8 ½d. God have mercy on their souls.

William Raynes and David Sokett in their days brought and sued an ?Isyprys for 1 yearly rent of assize that Thomas Erle withdrew from the church in Lewinsmead of the house that Roger Lywe dwelt in, and so by the law was reckoned yearly 12d. And brought clearly to the church – £3 11s 11d. God have mercy on their souls.

William Ward and William Baten in their days let make the enterclose, the rood loft and let paint it and brought in the great pair of latten candlesticks and the latten bowls in the rood loft. God have mercy on their souls.

Thomas Fyler and Robert Walsche, cook, brought clearly in to the church – 56s 1d. God have mercy on their souls.

William Chestyr and John Leynell in their days let made the enterclosing about the nether altars and closed the tower with windows, and brought clearly to the church – 25s 3d. God have mercy on their souls. Item they let make the place by the holy-water stock for dealing holy bread.

John Whytsyde and Roger Abyndon in their days defended the plea against John Suthfolke undertaken between the church and him for the house in Wynche [ie Wine] Street that John Pers gave to the church. Item they paved the churchyard and made great reparations on John Whytsyde's house and brought clearly in to the church – 14s. God have mercy on their souls.

(378)
Names of the Church Wardens
Thomas Halleway and John Gosselynge in their days changed the bells from 3 to 4, and took 1 view for the ground of the churchyard that Roger Abyndon had built over. And in their days they began the writing of the new ordinal, and all things clear the church owed them – 5s ½d.

And in their days took assize against Roger Acton knight for the house that Thomas Fyler dwelt in in Corn Street before the mayor's counter. God have mercy on their souls.

William Raynes, barber, and John Taylor, osteler, in their days kept the plea against Roger Acton for the house aforesaid. And paid for the noting of the new ordinal. And defended the plea against John Suthfolke, weaver, for the house in Wine Street that John Pers gave unto the church. And in their days made new orfreys to the blue suit, *p'c* – £6 3s 4d. God have mercy on their souls.

Richard Androwe and Roger Abyndon 3 year proctors, in their days kept plea against Roger Acton, knight, for the said house and made great reparations upon Martin Layfyll and William Ward's house and on the steeple. And brought clearly into the church for the said 3 years – £10 6s 8d. And ?reckoned in the law against the said knight. God have mercy on their souls.

William Warde, mercer, and David Sokett, tailor, brought clearly in to the church – £4 3s 5d. God have mercy on their souls.

(379)
William Raynes and Richard Warde in their days made great repairs and ?costs on all the books, *p'c* – £3 3s ½d. And brought clearly to the church – 32s 6 ½d. God have mercy on their souls.

Roger Abyndon and Richard Andrew in their days repaired the walls of the churchyard. And under the mayor's seal recorded the plea between the church and Roger Acton knight. And brought clearly to the church – 51s 2 ½d. God have mercy on their souls.

John Leynell and Thomas Aden in their days bought the great latten basin before Our Lady's altar and brought clearly to the church [blank].

Roger Abyndon and Robert Core in their days defended the plea against John Suthfolke for John Pers's house, and made great repairs both in the church and in the tenements. And brought clearly to the church – 17s 8½d. God have mercy on their souls.

Richard Knyght, cook, and Richard Androwe, corvesor, brought clearly in to the church – 36s 11 ½d. God have mercy on their souls.

(380)
John Leynell and Hugh Sadler brought clearly to the church in their days – 27s 3 ½d. God have mercy on their souls.

William Peyntour and Robert Walsche, cook, in their days was brought in on All Hallows' eve the best suit, *p'c* – £100[sic]. And on Saint

Katherine's eve following 1 pair of organs *p'c* – £6 6s 8d. And brought clearly in to the church – 36s 5d. God have mercy on their souls.

William Isgar and Thomas Fyler in their days paid for 1 part of the payment for the organs – 54s 8d. And brought clear to the church – 28s 11 ½d. God have mercy on their souls.

Richard Knyght and Richard Baker in their days let stain 2 pieces of cloth for the high altar. And brought clearly to the church – 22d. God have mercy on their souls. Item they received of Thomas Fysche at ?Corner for hire of the beer house to put in timber – 2s.

William Boxe and John Schoppe in their days paid to John Leynell in part payment of £20 for the best suit – £7 1s 2d. and brought clearly to the church – £12 12s 2 ½d. God have mercy on their souls.

(381)
Hugh Sadler and John Schoppe brought clearly to the church in their days – £4 4s. God have mercy on their souls.

John Schoppe and Hugh Sadler A.D. 1462 and 2 Edward IV brought clearly to the church – 43s 2 ½d. God have mercy on their souls. And in the said year John Shipward, merchant, withdrew from 1 house in Skadspyll Street now called Marsh Street, in the which house dwelt Nicholl Stocke, mariner, and 2s has been paid out of mind. God amend him.

Thomas John, tailor, and Thomas Gold, barber, renewed and refreshed the oilfat and brought clearly unto the church – 34s 9d. God have mercy on their souls.

Clement Wilteshire and Howell apRees brought clearly in to the church – 11s 11d. God have mercy on their souls. And in their year 2 houses next the steeple were burned by 1 drunken pointmaker.

William Boxe and John Schoppe in their days repaired a part of the said burnt houses, and brought clear to the church – 20d. God have mercy on their souls.

(382)
William Jenkyns and Thomas Phylyps in their days made repairs on Thomas Aden's house and Margery Monymony's house and brought clearly to the church – £3 6s 5d. God have mercy on their souls.

William Rowley and John Compton in their days took 1 action and 1 suit both in spiritual and temporal law against Thomas Fyler citizen of London for the withdrawing of 1 tenement that Agnes Fyler his mother bequeathed and gave unto the said church, and so they brought in the evidence under record of the dean's seal and the mayor's seal, and brought clear to the church – 50s 6d. God have mercy on their souls.

Martin Symond's son and John Branfeld in their days let made 3 seats in Our Lady's aisle, *p'c* – 56s cost without a profit, and brought clear to the church – £3 13s 8d.

Richard Haddon and John Schoppe in their days had great repairs made on vestments and let made a frontal of black velvet embroidered for the high altar, and let made 3 ampuls of silver for the oilfat. And for 1 evidence to be had for ever let ordained this book, for every man's account to be written in as for 1 evidence of old time of rents that have been gathered and paid time out of mind, and also in the said year they let made an inventory of all the goods of the church where none before might be found.

*   *   *

(437)
[Undated]
The account of John Derby and William Backe proctors of the said church, before Sir Thomas Marshall then vicar.

Receipts
In primis on Good Friday and Easter day – 20s 7 ½d.
Item for the crown and the cross at divers times – 12s 1d.
Item for 2 seats – 2s.
Sum – 34s 8 ½d

Item received of Roger Gurdeler and John Forge, cook, for the new gable window – £6.

Receipts of rent
In primis of Harry Tyler in the High Street – £3.
Item of Philip Somersett for 2 houses between the Steeple and the Corner house – 40s.
Item so of James Cockes for rent of assize – 4s.
Item of John Forge, cook – 2s 6d.
Item of William Yonge in Skadspyll Street now Marsh Street – 2s.
Item of John Droyse in Lewins Mead – 12d.
Item of Thomas Yonge – 6d.
Sum – £5 10s.

Sum total of receipts £13 4s 8 ½d.

(438)
Payments
In primis to the mother church of Worcester – 2s.
Item for lime stones and washing the church – 6s 4d.

[Margin: Children's seats]Item for children's seats in the choir – 16d.
Item for 2 torches and wax – 29s 2 ½d.
Item for mending of 1 cope – 2s 6d.
[Margin: The Presbytery]Item for making of the presbytery – 12s 5 ½d.
[Margin: The Pulpit]Item for making of the pulpit – 7s 11 ½d.
Item for 1 ?tabyllonyr over Our Lady's altar and painting it – 6s 5d.
Item for mending 1 clapper of 1 bell – 7d.
Item for making 1 great key – 6d.
Item for plastering the rood loft – 22d.
Item for 3 girdles – 2d.
Item for bearing the cross and censers on Corpus Christi day – 6d.
Item for making 2 surplices – 4s 5d.
Item for making the enterclose – 30s 10d.
Item for washing by the year – 12d.
[Margin: The 2 censers]Item paid for the over-weight of the 2 censers –
£3 5s 4d.
Item for 1 new window in Our Lady's aisle – £3 2s 1d.
Item for rushes – 5d.
Item to the raker – 8d.
Item for 1 truss of ?stree at 2 times for the church – 6d.
Item for besoms – 1d.
Item for 1 paring iron – 5d.
Item for stopping of divers holes – 4d.
[Margin: The black vestment with stars of gold]Item for 1 black
vestment with stars of gold – 29s 3d.
Item for a new pipe of lead in the churchyard – 5d.
Item for the churchyard doors – 3s 10d.
Item for making 1 clapper to 1 little bell – 2s 8d.
(439)
Item for paving before the rood altar – 2d.
Item for 2 gymmose[hinges] for Our Lady altar – 3d.
Item for writing 1 inventory and the parchment – 16d.
Sum – £13 16s 8 ½d.

And there remains clear to the church – 11s 11 ½d.

(440)
[1408–09].
The accounts of Laurence Brocke, cook, and William Baten, vintner,
proctors of All Saints, Bristol, before Sir Thomas Marshall then vicar,
10 Henry IV

Receipts
In primis on Good Friday and Easter Day – 17s 10 ½d.
Item for the cross and the crown – 3s.
Item for 3 burials – 20s 8d.
Sum – 41s 6 ½d.

Receipts of rent
In primis of William Knoking in the High Street – £3.
Item of Nicholas Somersett, tailor, and 1 man of little stature – 40s.
Item of James Cockys – 4s.
Item of Thomas Yonge – 6d.
Item of Roger Lybbe in Lewins Mead – 12d.
Item of Thomas Fysche in Skadspyll Street now Marsh Street – 2s.
Item of Everard Frensche's chantry – 2s 6d.
Sum – £5 10s.

Sum total – £7 11s 6 ½d.

(441)
Payments
In primis for mending 2 cruets – 3d.
Item for washing – 22 ½d.
Item for 4 cushions and all stuff – 4s 4 ½d.
Item for besoms – 1d.
Item for rushes and straw – 13 ½d.
Item for making 1 judas – 8 ½d.
Item for wax by the year – 24s 5 ½d.
Item to the church of Worcester – 16d.
Item for bearing the cross and the banners – 10d.
Item for scouring – 2s 8d.
Item for mending 1 glass window – 2s 4d.
Item for 1 plank and 1 board – 8d.
Item to 1 carpenter – 10d.
Item for mending 1 pax – 2d.
Item for lamp oil – 21 ½d.
Item for the General Mind – 4s 10 ½d.
Sum – 48s 4 ½d.

And there remains clear to the church – £4 11s 7d.

(442)
[1409–10]
The account of John Baker and John William proctors of the aforesaid church, before Sir Thomas Marshall, then vicar, 11 Henry IV.

Receipts
In primis on Good Friday and Easter day – 19s.
Item for the cross and the crown – 9s 10d.
Item for 2 seats – 18d.
Item of 1 goldsmith for 1 harness girdle – 10s 9 ½d.
Item for 1 book – 14s.
Sum – 54s 11 ½d.

Receipts of rents
In primis of Harry Tyler – £3.
Item of Nicholas Somersett – 40s.

Item of James Cockys – 4s.
Item of William Yonge in Skadspyll Street now Marsh Street – 2s.
Item of John Droyse in Lewins Mead – 12d.
Item of Thomas Yonge – 6d.
Item of Everard Frensche's chantry – 2s 6d.
Sum – £5 10s

Sum total – £8 4s 11 ½d.

(443)
Payments
In primis for wax for all the year – 29s 3 ½d.
Item to the church of Worcester – 2s.
Item for washing by the year – 18d.
Item for carrying of rubble – 2s 5d.
Item for rushes and straw – 11 ½d.
Item for bearing of the cross and the banners – 14d.
Item for the writing of this account – 6d.
Item for sand – 2s 6d.
Item to 1 mason – 2s 4d.
Item for lime and sand – 13d.
Item for making the cross in the churchyard – 21s 6d.
Item for binding and ?lymnyng the new Legendary – 31s 2d.
Item for the General Mind – 2s 5d.
Sum – £4 19s 9d.

And there remains clear to the church – £3 5s 2 ½d.

(444)
[1410–11]
The account of William Spicer and John Talbot proctors of the aforesaid church, before Sir Thomas Marshall then vicar, 12 Henry IV.

Receipts
In primis on Good Friday and Easter day – 17s 2d.
Item for the cross and the crown – 19s 7d.
Item for 2 burials – 13s.
Item for 1 bequest – 17s 10d.
Sum – £3 8s 9d.

Receipts of the rents
In primis of Harry Tyler – £3 10s.
Item of Nicholas Somersett – 40s.
Item of James Cockys – 4s.
Item of William Yonge in Skadspyll Street now Marsh Street – 2s.
Item of John Droyse in Lewins Mead – 12d.
Item of Thomas Yonge – 6d.
Item of Everard Frensche's chantry – 2s 6d.
Sum – £6.
Sum total – £9 8s 9d.

(445)
Payments
In primis for hanging 1 bell – 16d.
Item for rushes and straw – 17 ½d.
Item for washing – 12d.
Item to the raker – 12d.
Item for wax – 32s 7d.
Item for bearing banners and the cross – 17d.
Item to the church of Worcester – 2s.
Item for 1 baldric to 1 bell – 13d.
Item for 1 stock, 1 staple and 1 ring – 4d.
Item for besoms and scouring – 5d.
Item for 1 ladder – 8d.
Item for 1 surplice to the clerk – 4s.
Item for making the church clean – 6d.
Item for keeping the sepulchre – 5d.
Item for clamps and bolts to the great bell – 7s 8d.
Item for mending 1 glass window – 6d.
Item for lamp oil – 2s 4d.
Item for painting 2 angels at the high altar – 10s.
Item for the General Mind – 4s.
Sum – £3 12s 8 ½d

And remaining clear to the church – £5 16s 7 ½d.

(446)
[1411–12]
The account of Thomas Halleway and William Spycer proctors of the aforesaid church, before Sir Thomas Marshall then vicar, 13 Henry IV.

Receipts
In primis on Good Friday and Easter day – 18s 5 ½d.
Item for the cross and the crown – 18s 8d.
Item from Emott Chylcombe 1 chalice of 13 3/4 ozs, *p'c* – 40s.
Item for 2 burials – 13s 4d.
Sum – £4 10s 7 ½d.

Item for seats – 7s 4d.
Item for vestments – 10s 4d.

Receipts of rents
In primis of Harry Tyler – £3
Item of Nicholas Somersett – 40s.
Item of James Cockes – 4s.
Item of Everard Frensche's chantry – 2s 6d.
Item of William Yonge in Skadspyll Street now Marsh Street – 2s.
Item of John Droyse in Lewins Mead – 12d.

Item of Thomas Yonge – 6d.
Sum – £5 10s.
Sum total – £10 18s 3 ½d.

(447)
Payments
In primis for wax – 11s 3 ½d.
Item for 1 cord to the paschal – 6d.
Item for the raker – 2d.
Item for rushes and straw – 9 ½d.
Item to the church of Worcester – 2s.
Item for bearing banners and the cross – 14d.
Item for mending of the candlestick – 3d.
Item for 1 staff to the cross – 3s 4d.
Item for the General Mind – 3s 10d.
Item for 1 ¼ hundredweights and 7 lbs of iron – 12s 3d.
Item for lamp oil – 12d.
Sum – 36s 7d.

And there remains to the church – £9 1s 8 ½d.

[Margin: Look well the Almshouse] Memorandum that in the time of Thomas Halleway and William Spycer, proctors of the said church, the house that stands next to Roger Abyndon's, yielding a rent assize of 12d, was withdrawn, the which house was called the Almshouse.

(448)
[1412–13]
The account of John Monke and William Raynes proctors of the aforesaid church, before Sir Thomas Marshall then vicar, 14 Henry IV.

Receipts
In primis on Good Friday and Easter Day – 17s 1d.
Item for the cross and the crown – 7s 8d.
Item for 2 burials – 13s 4d.
Item for seats – 6s 6d.
Sum – 43s 7d.

Receipts for rents
[As previous, but differently ordered, and save for new tenant, John Castell, in High Street]
Sum – £5 10s.
Sum total – £7 14s 7d.

(449)
Payments
In primis to the raker – 6d.
Item for straw and rushes – 14d.
Item for washing – 15d.

Item to the church of Worcester – 2s.
Item for keeping the sepulchre – 2d.
Item for wax by the year – 18s 7d.
Item bearing banners and the cross – 12d.
Item for painting the judas – 12d.
Item for tallow candles – 10d.
Item for altar pins – 4d.
Item for scouring – 7d.
Item for 3 ells of canvas – 18d.
Item for the General Mind – 9s 2d.
Sum – 38s 1d.

And there remains to the church – £5 16s 6d.

(450)
[1414–15]
The account of Richard Brewer and John Coke, osteler, proctors of the aforesaid church, before Sir Thomas Marshall then vicar of the church, 2 Henry V.

Receipts
In primis on Good Friday and Easter Day – 16s.
Item for the cross and the crown – 11s.
Item of William Newberry for 1 bequest – 20s.
Sum – 53s 8d.

Receipt of rents
[As previous]
Sum – £5 10s.

(451)
Payments
In primis for washing – 6 ½d.
Item for straw and rushes – 16d.
Item for the banners and the cross – 8 ½d.
Item to the church of Worcester – 2s 4d.
Item to the raker – 4d.
Item for mending of the judas bells – 2d.
Item to the waxmaker for the year – 27s 10d.
Item for changing of lead – 2 ½d.
Item for 1 wire to the Lent cloth – 2 ½d.
Item for cloth to 1 surplice – 5s 4d.
Item for lamp oil – 12d.
Item for keeping of the sepulchre – 8d.
Item for the General Mind – 4s 4 ½d.
Item for writing this account – 16d.
Sum – 46s 3 ½d.

Item the said proctors owe to the said church – £5 17s 4 ½d.

(452)

[1421–22]

The account of Thomas Halleway and William Tempyll proctors of the aforesaid church, before Sir Thomas Marshall then vicar, [roman numeral vii is scored; nono inserted] 9 Henry V.

Receipts

In primis on Good Friday and Easter Day – 16s 6 ½d.

Item for 2 graves – 13s 4d.

Item for the crown and the cross – 4s 8d.

[Margin: The gutter under the beerhouse] Item for 1 gutter going through the churchyard – 5s.

Item for seats – 4s 6d.

Sum – 44s ½d.

Receipts of rents

[As previous]

Sum – £5 10s.

(453)

Payments

In primis for rushes and straw – 17d.

Item for mending of the best cross – 4d.

Item for 1 dozen linen girdles – 8d.

Item for timber and boards to 1 wheel for the paschal and to the carpenter – 5s 6d.

Item for iron work – 3d.

Item to 1 mason – 11d.

Item for 1 load of tile stone – 3s.

Item for lime, sand, laths, boards, nails, crests and tile pins – 15d.

Item to 1 tiler – 3s 9d.

Item to 1 plumber – 22d.

Item for washing – 4d.

Item to the raker – 2d.

Item for besoms – 1d.

Item for bearing of banners – 5d.

Item for bearing of the cross – 5d.

Item for scouring – 4d.

Item for mending 1 clapper to the little bell – 2d.

Item for mending a pavement – 2d.

Item to the church of Worcester – 2s.

Item for lamp oil – 2s.

Item for the General Mind – 3s 7d.

(454)

Item to the waxmaker for wax and waxmaking for the year – 32s 3 ½d.

Sum – £3 9d.

And remaining to the church – £4 13 4d.

(455)
[1422–23]
The account of William Raynes, barber, and Thomas Chestyr, cook, proctors of the said church, before Sir Thomas Marshall then vicar, 1 Henry VI.

Receipts of rents
[As previous]
Sum – £5 10s.

Receipts
In primis on Good Friday and Easter day – 20s.
Item for the cross and the crown – 20s.
Item for 2 burials – 13s 4d.
Item for seats – 7s 11d.
Sum – £3 1s 3d.

(456)
Payments for making the sepulchre
In primis for 3 ?Estyrlygge boards – 18d.
Item to 1 carver – 10s 9d.
Item to 1 mason – 9d.
Item to Richard, painter – 23s 4d.
Item to the proctors of St Nicholas – 3d.
Item for iron gear – 8d.
Item for 1 frontal and 1 fringe – 9s.
Item for lime, nails and ?rekholys – 2 ½d.
Item in bread and ale – 8 ½d.
Sum – 47s 2d.

(457)
Payments for other costs
In primis to Byford for the hire of his crane – 2d.
Item for thread to mend the albs – 3d.
Item for 2 ¼ ells of linen cloth – 20d.
Item to Agnes Fyler for 1 quart of wine – 2d.
Item for 1 cord to 1 lamp – 3d.
Item for rushes and straw – 13d.
Item to the church of Worcester – 2s.
Item to the raker – 4d.
Item for staining 1 altar cloth – 12d.
Item for bearing banners – 5d.
Item for mending 1 gutter – 5d.
Item for making wax – 24s 1d.
Item for bearing the cross – 4d.
Item for scouring – 4d.
Item for mending 1 torch – 4d.
Item for washing – 8d.

Item for besoms – 1d.
Item for 2 torches of wax – 33s 1d.
Item to Huckford, mason, for ale – 1d.
Item to William Hukford and William Tempyll in ale – 3d.
Item to William Hukford for his earnest – 2d.
Item to Colle, mason, for ale – 2d.
Item to Colle, mason, for his earnest – 1d.
Item in drink – 2d.

(458)
Item to William Hukford mason – 40s.
Item for writing of 2 endentures – 8d.
Item for the General Mind – 5s 3d.
Sum – £5 13s 7d.

And there remains to the church – 7d.

(459)
[1427–8]
The account of Thomas Fyler and William Haytfeld proctors of the
aforesaid church before Sir Thomas Marshall, on the last day of March
1427, 2 Henry VI [recte 6 Henry VI].

Receipts
In primis on Good Friday and Easter day – 20s 5 ½d.
Item for seats – 5s 9d.
Item for 1 censer – 5s.
Item for 3 burials – 20s.
Item for torches – 8d.
Sum – 31s 1d.

Receipts of rents
In primis of William Warde in the High Street – £3.
Item of John Whytsyd – 26s 8d.
Item of Nicholas Hoper in Baldwin Street – 12s.
Item of Thomas Fysche in Corn Street – 4s.
Item of Everard Frensche's chantry – 2s 6d.
Item of Nicholas Stocke in Skadspyll Street now called Marsh Street – 2s.
Item of Thomas Baker in Lewins Mead – 12d.
Item of Joan Yonge – 6d.
Sum – £5 8s 8d.

Sum total receipts – £8 4 ½d.

(460)
Payments for divers costs
In primis for William Newbery's mind – 6s 1d.
Item for wax for Easter – 18s.

Item for making of old wax – 19 ½d.
Item for oil – 5s 5d.
Item for torches – 10s 11 ½d.
Item for timber – 15d.
Item for nails – 2d.
Item for boards – 4d.
Item for timber – 9s 5d.
Item for carriage of the timber – 3 ½d.
Item for the carpenter – 8s 1d.
Item to masons – 53s 3d.
Item for taking down of glass – 2s.
Item to 2 ?veyerys – 2s.
Item for rushes at Easter – 6d.
Item for straw at Christmas – 9d.
Item for washing of cloths – 6d.
Item for besoms – ½d.
Item for 1 chain and 1 lock – 6d.
(461)
Item for bearing of banners – 3d.
Item for 1 new amice – 8d.
Item for bearing the cross – 4d.
Item to the church of Worcester – 2s.
Item for burnishing of 2 censers – 2s 6d.
Item for girdles to vestments – 3d.
Item for paper – 1d.
Item for carriage of 15 ?dos rubbish – 4s 1d.
Item for the General Mind – 2s 6d.

Costs done upon mending of books
In primis for 3 calves skins – 21d.
Item for 3 red skins – 15d.
Item for 4 clasps – 12d.
Item for 3 white skins – 9d.
Item for 4 skins of parchment – 8d.
Item for silk to bind the books – 5d.
Item for binding 3 books – 3s.
Item for mending 1 mass book – 8d.

Sum total – £7 3s 5d.

And there remains to the church – 13s 8 ½d.

(462)
[1428–9]
The account of Peter Chaplen and Richard Abyndon proctors of the aforesaid church, before Sir Thomas Marshall, then vicar, on the last day of March A.D. 1428.

Receipts
In primis of Good Friday and Easter day – 14s 4d.
Item for the cross and the crown – 4s 8d.
Item for half a dozen spoons – 15s.
Sum – 34s.

Receipts of rents
[As previous, save Roger Lybbe in Lewins Mead].
Sum – £5 8s 8d.
Sum total of the receipts – £7 2s 8d.

(463)
Payments for divers costs
In primis for 1 baldric to the great bell – 11d.
Item for mending of the clapper – 5d.
Item for 1 stock to the great bell – 2s.
Item for 1 baldric to the second bell – 5d.
Item for iron gear – 2s.
Item for 1 clapper of the great bell – 3s 4d.
Item for bolts, staples and 1 clapper to the second bell – 19s 4d.
Item for ale to the labourers – 2d.
Item for boards and nails – 5d.
Item for mending of the beer house – 2d.
Item for besoms and cleaning the church – 3d.
Item for scouring – 4d.
Item for bearing banners – 6d.
Item for bearing the cross – 4d.
Item to the church of Worcester – 2s.
Item for cleaning the glass windows – 8d.
Item for rushes at Easter and Whitsuntide – 10d.
Item for washing of cloths – 10d.
Item for straw at Christmas – 7 ½d.

(464)
Item for the ?velle of William Ward's house – 4s.
Item for writing 1 deed of the same place – 20d.
Item for mending 1 censer – 2d.
Item for weighing half a dozen spoons – 2d.
Item for 1 rope to the little bell – 2d.
Item for 40 lbs of wax at 4 ¼d the pound – 14s 2d.
Item for making the said wax – 18d.
Item for renewing the wax at All Hallows' tide – 13s 4d.
Item for the General Mind – 3s 6d.

Sum total – £3 14s 2 ½d

And there remains clear to the church – £3 12s 8 ½d.

(465)

[1429–30]

The account of William Raynes and David Sokett proctors of All Saints, Bristol, A.D. 1429 6 Henry VI [recte 8 Henry VI], before Sir Thomas Marshall then vicar; John Newton mayor, John Sharp sheriff, and Andrew Parle and John Eyr bailiffs.

Receipts

In primis on Good Friday and Easter day – 16s 1d.
Item of Roger Abyndon – 3s 4d.
Item of Thomas Halleway – 5d.
Item for 2 candlesticks – 20d.
Item for the crown – 6d.
Item for 2 ½ feet of glass – 10d.
Sum – 22s 10d.

Receipts for seats

Richard Androwe – 18d.
Item of John Baker, barber – 12d.
Item of William Johnson – 12d.
Item of Lewys Brewer – 8d.
Item of John Goslyng, bellmaker – 20d.
Sum – 4s 2d.

Receipts for rents

In primis of William Warde – £3.
Item of Everard Frensche's chantry – 2s 6d.
Item of John Whytsyde – 26s 8d.
Item of Perse Hoper in Baldwin Street – 12s.
Item of William Chestre – 4s.
Item of Nicholas Stoke in Skadspyll Street now called Marsch Street – 2s.

(466)

Item of Joan Goldsmith for 1 house next John Whytsyde for 1 quarter – 4s.
Item of Joan Yonge – 6d.
Sum – £5 11s 2d.

Sum total of receipts – £6 18s 2d.

Payments for divers costs

In primis for washing 1 ?pynon in the churchyard – 6d.
Item for mending 1 lock to the great coffer – 2d.
[Margin: Look Thomas Erle for 12d in Lewins Mead] Item for 1 dinner to the quest between Thomas Erle and the church for rent of assize of 12d a year to the said church that lies in Lewins Mead that Roger Lybbe dwells in – 4s 9d.
Item for mending the vicar's surplice – 1d.
Item to the mother church at Worcester – 20d.

Item to the raker – 3d.
Item for the annivesary of William Newbery – 6s 1d.
Item for washing of altar cloths – 4d.
Item for bearing banners – 3d.
Item for the cover to a ?ber – 2s 3d.
Item for 6 linen girdles – 9d.
Item for bearing the cross on Corpus Christi day – 4d.
Item for mending the churchyard wall – 21d.
Item for lime and sand – 8d.
Item for doors, locks and iron gear – 5s 8 ½d.
Item for casting 33 lbs of lead – 4d.
Item for ?skobur nails – 1 ½d.
Item for wax at Easter and Whitsuntide – 7s 4d.
Item for washing altar cloths and surplices – 6d.
Item for staining 1 pane and 1 altar cloth – 16d.
Item for scouring candlesticks – 4d.
(467)
Item for 4 lbs of tallow candles for the rood loft – 6d.
Item for John Perse's ?gve [?grave] – 6s 8d.
Item for the General Mind on Ash Wednesday – 2s 6d.
Item for wax at All Hallows' tide – 18s.
Item for soldering the gutter – 4d.
Item for oil for Our Lady's lamp – 2s 8d.
Sum – £3 6s 3d

And there remains clear to the church – £3 11s 11d.

(468)
[1430–31]
The account of William Warde and William Baten proctors of the church of All Saints', Bristol, A.D. 1430, 7 Henry VI [recte 9 Henry VI], before Sir Thomas Marshall vicar, Roger Lyvedon mayor, Henry Gildeney sheriff, John Talbott and John Troyte bailiffs.

Receipts
In primis on Good Friday and Easter Monday – 20s 1 ½d.
Item for dishes of pewter – 3s 6d.
Item for 1 latten censer – 3s 4d.
Item money given to Our Lady's light – 6s 3d.
Item for 1 coffer – 12d.
Item for old glass – 8s.
Sum – 42s 2 ½d.

Receipts of rents
[As previous. At the end of the receipts is an entry in diferent coloured ink noting that Roger Lybbe, tenant of the disputed Lewins Mead property, pays 12d rent to the church].
Sum – £5 8s 8d.

Receipts of money given by divers people of the parish for the great candlesticks, sum – £5 8s 6d.

Sum total of receipts – £13 18s 4 ½d.

(469)
Payments for divers costs
In primis for the great candlesticks – 51s 8d.
Item for washing 1 surplice – 2d.
Item for rushes and besoms – 8 ½d.
[Margin: Costs of the Enteclose] Item for nails to the enterclose – 5 ½d.
Item to the carpenter for his handiwork – 11s.
Item for iron gear – 22d.
Item for ?noneschynes to the carpenter – 2d.
Item to Hucksowe, mason – 6d.
Item to John plasterer – 4d.
Item to Richard Peynter – 16s.
[Margin: Latten bowls in the rood loft] Item for 12 dishes of latten for the rood – 32s.
Item for carrying them from London – 10d.
Item for rushes at Whitsuntide – 2d.
Item for carrying 1 piece of timber – 2d.
[Margin: Costs of the rood loft] Item to William Tempyll for timber boards and his handiwork to the rood loft – 15s 8d.
Item to William Tempyll – 9s 9d.
Item to William Tempyll – 4s 5 ½d.
Item to William Tempyll – 5s 8d.
Item to William Tempyll – 5s 6d.
Item to William Tempyll – 7s 7d.
Item to William Tempyll – 8d.
Item for carrying 2 pieces of timber – 2d.
Item for ?noneseynes – 7d.
Item for nails – 6d.
Item to William Tempyll – 10s 2d.
[Margin: The painting of the rood loft]. Item Edward Peynter – 16s 4d.
Item to the plasterer – 5d.
Item to the glasier – 4d.
Item for 1 wire to stay the light – 2 ½d.
Sum – £9 14s.

(470)
Item for painting the judas – 4s 6d.
Item for painting the base of the best cross – 16d.
Item for making the base and 2 images – 4s.
Item for making the long desk in Our Lady chapel – 9s.
Item for making 9 judas in Our Lady chapel – 2s.
Item for making the judas – 2s 8d.
Item for cutting 1 table of St Thomas' altar – 1d.

Item to William Tempyll for sklattstone – 2s 11d.
Item for sand and ?hair lime – 3d.
Item for tile pins – 1d.
Item to the tiler for his handiwork – 4s 4d.
Item for straw at All Hallows' tide – 8d.
Item for pack thread – ½d.
Item for ale for hanging the church – 1d.
Item for 2 girdles – 1d.
Item to the raker – 3d.
Item for ?noneseyngs to the carpenter, tiler and mason – 19d.
Item for 2 dozen pins for the altars – 1d.
Item for 2 ½ lbs of wax – 16d.
Item to the waxmaker – 10s.
Item to Thomas Halleway for wax – 13s.
Item for 1 frontal to Our Lady altar – 6d.
Item for 1 lock to the churchyard stile – 7d.
Item for washing the altar cloths – 5d.
Item for ?noneseggs – 2 ½d.
Item for mending 1 censer – 2d.
Item to the mother church at Worcester – 2s.
Item for bearing banners – 6d.
Item for bearing the cross on Corpus Christi day – 4d.
Item for bearing 4 torches – 4d.
Item for washing surplices – 4d.
Sum – £3 1s 8d.
(471)
Item in wine for the priests on Corpus Christi day – 2d.
Item for making 1 rochet – 5d.
Item for the General Mind on Ash Wednesday – 3s 10d.
Item for painting 1 table to St Thomas' altar – 2s.
Item for 1 lock and 1 ring to the desk in Our Lady's chapel – 8d.
Item for washing 3 rochets – 2d.
Item for washing an altar cloth – 4d.
Item for oil to Our Lady's lamp – 20d.
Sum – 9s 3d.

Sum total – £13 4s 11d.

(472)
[1434–35]
The account of Thomas Fyler and Robert Walsche proctors of the church of All Saints' in 1434, before Sir Thomas Parkhouse then vicar.

Receipts
In primis on Good Friday and Easter day – 17s 9d.
Item of the prior of the Kalendars – 16d.

Item of the women on Easter day for ?ball silver – 4d.
Item for 1 old chasuble – 4s.
Item of pilgrims going to Saint James' – 18d.
Item of John at the wood – 2d.
Item of the waxmaker's wife – 2d.
Item of the vicar of Portbery – 5d.
Item of John Hosyer for 2 seats – 2s.
Sum – 27s 8d.

Receipt of rents
In primis William Warde – £3
Item of John Whytsyde – 26s 8d.
Item of Pers Hoper in Baldwin Street – 12s.
Item of John Fredryk, goldsmith – 16s.
Item of the said Fredryk – 8s.
Item of Thomas Ashe, baker – 2s.
Item of Everard Frensche's chantry – 2s 6d.
Item of Joan Yonge – 6d.
Item of Nicholas Stocke in Skadspyll Street now Marsh Street – 2s.
(473)
Item of Thomas Fysche – 4s.
Item of John Fredrycke – 4s.
Item of Roger Lywe – 12d.
Sum – £6 18s 8d.

Sum total – £8 5s 10d.

Payments for divers costs
In primis for washing of 2 surplices – 4d.
Item for timber to the roof of the church – 7s 10d.
Item to the carpenter – 7s 10d.
Item for 4 poles to underset the church – 20d.
Item to the mother church of Worcester – 16d.
Item for bearing the cross of Saint George's day – 2d.
Item for hauling of 4 ?sumarys – 4d.
Item to the raker – 1d.
Item for taking down timber from 2 pillars – 3d.
Item for carrying of rubble – 3s 11d.
Item to a labourer – 4 ½d.
Item for bearing of banners – 3d.
Item for washing of albs and amices – 2d.
Item for William Newbery's mind – 6s 1d.
Item for bearing the cross on Corpus Christi day – 4d.
Item for washing Our Lady altar's curtains and mending 1 iron rod – 4d.
(474)
Item for the resting of John Frederick's goods – 2d.
Item to Longford – 20d.
Item for writing the names of the good doers – 1d.

Item for washing of the vicar's surplice – 4d.
Item for besoms – 2d.
Item to 1 carpenter for mending 1 stair in John Whytsyde's house – 2d.
Item for washing of 3 amices – 1d.
Item to John Whytsyde for writing a record under the Official's seal for the house that John Perse gave to the church – 3s.
Item for 2 candlesticks of latten – 4s.
Item for scouring the basin of the lamp in the chancel – 4d.
Item for scouring of candlesticks – 2d.
Item to Longford – 3s.
Item for washing of 2 surplices – 4d.
Item to 1 tiler for mending Whytsyde's house – 16d.
Item for 1 branch of wax burning before the rood – 6d.
Item for 3 lbs candles at Christmas – 4d.
Item for the General Mind on Ash Wednesday – 2s.
Item for hauling 6 poles – 2d.
Item for writing and paper – 1d.
Item to William Tempyll for 2 poles and hiring 4 men – 3s 5 ½d.
Item for wax at Easter and Christmas – 9s 3d.
Item for 3 poles – 16d.
Item to the mason – 10s.
Item to William Tempyll for his ?honde and for 1 pole of iron – 9d.
(475)
Item for boards, nails and tile stones – 18d.
Item for soldering and mending the gutter in Fredryck's house – 18d.
Item to the mason – 23s 4d.
Item to the tiler for nails, pins, lime and for ?dubbing 1 new arch – 17d.
Item to the tiler for his hire – 2s 10d.
Item for the ceiling – 16d.
Sum – £5 9s 9d.

And there remains clear to the church – 56s 1d.

(476)
[1437–38]
The account of William Chestyr and John Leynell proctors of the church of All Saints', Bristol, before Sir William Rodberd then vicar, the 14th day of March A.D. 1437.

In primis on Good Friday and Easter day – 17s 7d.
Item for candlesticks – 16d.
Item for the crown – 11d.
Item for the candlesticks – 4d.
Item for the black cloth – 2s.
Item for the black cloth and the candlesticks – 8d.
Item for keeping 1 coffer of the barber's – 22d.
Item for 1 free stone – 21d.
Item for 10 feet of old glass – 2s 6d.

Item of Sir David – 4d.
Item of Ewyn Bucklond – 6d.
Item of John Whytsyd for 1 coffer – 5d.
Sum – 35s 8d.

Receipt of seats
In primis John Olde – 12d.
Item of Roger Osteler – 10d.
Item of ?Gyeas Goldsmith – 8d.
Item of Richard Hosyer – 8d.
Item of James Chambyrleyn – 2s 4d.
Item of the Cordener's wife – 8d.
Sum – 6s 2d.

(477)
Receipt of rents
In primis of William Warde – £3.
Item of Everard Frensch's chantry – 2s 6d.
Item of Thomas Fysche – 4s.
Item of Thomas Baker in Lewins Mead – 12d.
Item of John Wytheford in Skadspyll Street now Marsh Street – 2s.
Item of Janet Kanynges – 6d.
Item of Perse Hoper in Baldwin Street – 12s.
Sum – £4 2s.

Item of Sir Richard Parkhouse – 40 lbs of wax
which we put towards making 2 torches – 19 lbs.
Item to making 10 tapers – 20 lbs
and so there remains of the said wax – 5 lbs.
the which lies in a coffer before Our Lady's altar in 1 ?keche y multe at
4d the pound.
Sum – 13s 4d.

Item received of Sir Thomas Parkhouse, 2 torches to serve at the high
altar, *p'c* – 8s.
Item received of the said Thomas a pair of green vestments of cloth of
gold for the soul of Sir Richard Parkhouse, *p'c* – £3.
Sum – [blank].

Sum total of receipts – £6 17s 2d.

(478)
Payments for divers costs
In primis for a load of freestone to the entreclose of the altars – 3s 11d.
Item for carrying this stone from St Thomas' street – 4d.
Item for washing of 2 surplices – 4d.
Item for keeping the sepulchre – 5d.
Item to Thomas Halleway for iron – 8d.
Item for 1 lamp before Our Lady – 1d.

Item to the raker at Easter – 3d.

Item for boards to the rood loft and for almery [?aumbry] doors – 12d.

Item for nails, boards and ?leggys for the ?beerys [?beirs] – 6d.

Item to the carpenter for his hand in the same work – 22d.

Item for 2 stones for battlements for the altars – 8d.

Item to the mason for his handiwork for 18 ½ days – 10s.

Item to the plasterer – 1d.

Item to the mother church of Worcester – 2s.

Item for washing of 5 albs, 10 altar cloths and 4 amices – 8d.

Item for washing of 5 albs and 5 amices – 5d.

Item for setting on of the said albs – 6d.

Item for making 1 seat – 14 ½d.

Item for William Newbery's mind – 6s 1d.

Item for bearing of banners – 5d.

Item on Corpus Christi for bearing the cross – 4 ½d.

Item for bearing censers on the said day – 2d.

[Margin: Look the seige of Calais]Item for bearing the cross on the Sunday before Saint Laurence's day for [the] breaking of the seige of Calais – 2d.

Item for 1 lock and staple to the rood loft door – 12d.

Item for 1 lock and key to an almery [?aumbry] at Our Lady's altar – 3d.

Item for besoms – ½d.

Item for making clay ?ballys for the candles at Christmas – 1d.

(479)

Item for paper and ink for this account – 1d.

Item for hinges for the rood loft and almery [?aumbry] – 1 ½d.

Item for washing of 1 amice and 3 altar cloths – 2d.

Item for wax at Easter – 6s 4d.

Item for wine to Thomas Halleway, Pavy and John Whytsyde for seeing the evidence of the church – 6d.

Item paid for 1 box for the deeds of John Perse's house – 1d.

Item for mending the cloths that hang in the choir – 4d.

Item to Richard Carge of Bedminster for [blank]

Item for 7 yards of black buckram – 5s 3d.

Item for blacking of 1 old cloth – 8d.

Item paid for 1 quarter of linen cloth – 2d.

Item for staining of the same cloth – 15d.

Item for making of the same cloth – 12d.

Item for scouring of the candlesticks and bowls – 5d.

Item for washing of surplices and altar cloths – 5 ½d.

Item for making 1 bar of iron and 2 rings to stay Our Lady's tapers – 3 ½d.

Item for 2 loads of paving stone – 5s 4d.

Item for 1 dozen candles at Christmas in the rood loft – 15d.

Item for 11 rings for hanging the riddel before Saint Saviour – 3d.

Item for John Perse's mind – 6s 8d.

Item for making the seat to deal the holy bread – 13s 8d.

Item to William Norton carpenter for boards and nails for windows in the steeple – 8s 6 ½d.

Item to the said Norton for boards and nails and his handiwork – 18d.
Item to the same Norton for mending windows – 12d.
Item for laths and nails to close the boards of the steeple – 4d.
Item for 1 lock to the window of the steeple – 3d.
(480)
Item for 1 ?laborell [?labourer] to make clean the steeple – 2d.
Item for the General Mind on Ash Wednesday – 9d.
Item for mending the school house door – 3s 3d.
Item for mending 1 lock to the said door – 3d.
Item for 1 double window in the steeple to the gutter – 19d.
Item for glasing 1 window over the rood altar – 10d.
Item for 2 bolts of iron, staples and locks – 7d.
Item for hallowing 1 pair of vestments – 12d.
Item to 1 labourer for ?berer [?bearing] of ?half a hundredweight of
wainscot – 1 ½d.
Item to 1 mason for setting of staples and locks – 6 ½d.
Item for setting 1 bar in the vestry door – 1d.
Item for wax at All Hallows' tide – 3s 8d.
Item for making the said wax – 19d.
Item to the waxmaker for flourishing the taper – 2s 1d.
Item for making 2 torches and 7 lbs of ?weak yarn and 2 lbs of wax and
8 lbs of rosen [?rosin] – 3s 5d.
Item to Thomas Yowley, smith, for 3 twists, 3 bolts and 4 pins mending
of 1 clapper of 1 bell – 2s 5d.
Sum – £5 11s 11d.

And there remains clear to the church – 25s 3d.

(481)
[1437–38]
[Different ink] The account of John Whytsyde and Roger Abyndon
before Sir William Rodberd then vicar, A.D. 1438, 16 Henry VI.

Receipt of rents
In primis of William Warde – £3.
Item of Robert Walshe, cook – 2s 6d.
Item of John Whytsyde for 2 years' rent – 53s 4d.
Item of Pers Hoper in Baldwin Street for 2 years' – 24s.
Item of William Chestyr by the hand of Thomas Fysche – 4s.
Item of Nicholas Stocke in Skadspyll Street now called Marsh Street –
2s.
Item of Janet Canynges – 6d.
Item of Thomas Baker in Lewins Mead – 12d.
Sum – £7 7s 4d.

Other receipts
In primis on Good Friday and Easter day – 18s 4d.
Item for 24 small pieces of glass – 6d.

Item for an elm board – 2d.
Item for William Baten's grave – 6s 8d.
Item for the crown with angels – 2s 8d.
Item for the black cloth – 8d
Item for a seat – 2s.
Item of John Hussey for a seat – 2s.
Item of John Nele for wall stone – 16d.
Item for Richard Abyndon's pit – 6s 8d.
Item of Sir Denys for the loan of 2 tenaclys [tunicles] and a cope – 4d.
Sum – 61s 4d.
Sum total receipts – £9 8s 8d.

(482)
These are the parcels paid at divers times by the said proctors.
In primis for scouring of candlesticks and ?tynnyn bowls – 3d.
Item to the raker – 3d.
Item to the suffragan for keeping the sepulchre – 2d.
Item for washing of surplices and altar cloths – 12d.
Item to the mother church at Worcester – 2s.
Item for washing of albs and towel – 3d.
Item for bearing of banners – 6d.
Item for bearing the cross on Corpus Christi day – 4d.
Item for making iron gear before the Salvator – 20d.
Item for an iron ladle to fetch fire – 4d.
Item for washing of 4 albs and 4 amices and the setting out of them – 8d.
Item for half a bushel of limestone and the workmanship thereof – 4d.
Item for mending a glass window – 4d.
Item for hooks to the new pillars – 2d.
Item for Newbery's mind – 6s 1d.
Item for John Perse's mind – 6s 8d.
Item for the General Mind on Ash Wednesday – 2s 1d.
Item for candles at Christmas – 14d.
Item for nails and iron to hang a bell – 20d.
Item for a carpenter and his man – 4s 6d.
Item to 2 tilers – 2s 2d.
Item for 2 quarters of lime – 5d.
Item for 1 seme stones – 3d.
Item for besoms – 1d.
Item to the waxmaker for wax and its making – 19s.
Sum – 52s 4d.

(483)
Expenses touching the plea of John Sowthfolk's shop and the goldsmith's house in Wine Street.
In primis to Pavy and to Vyell – 3s 4d.
Item in wine and in ale to the said Pavy – 2d.
Item to Vyell to inquire for certain names – 1d.
Item in wine to the said men – 2d.

Item to the ?Bayley Croud – 2s.
Item to Bolton – 2s.
Item for 1 copy of the deed – 4d.
Item to Pavy, Vyell and Chocke at the day of assize – 10s.
Item to Chocke on St Lucy's day for another assize – 3s 4d.
Item to Pavy and the Vyell on the same day of assize – 3s 4d.
Item for the copy of a writ – 2d.
Item to a sergeant and the entering of a plaint – 4d.
Item to Selwod the man of law – 20d.
Item for writing of 2 obligations – 4d.
Sum – 27s 3d.

Expenses for paving the churchyard.
In primis for 12 quarters of lime – 2s 11d.
Item for 2 dozen of sand – 18d.
Item to the mason – 8s.
Item for making a gutter in the churchyard – 20d.
Item for 4 quarters of lime – 10d.
Item for 1 load of paving stones – 3s 4d.
Item to a labourer – 3d.
Item for carrying away rubble – 2d.
Sum – 18s 8d.

Expenses for making the chimney in John Whytsyde's house and for making a gutter in the same house.
In primis for 1 butt of stones – 3s 6d.
Item for carriage of the said stones – 11d.
Item for 2 jambs – 14d.
Item for 1 panier – 3d.
Item for carrying of the said jambs – 3d.
Item for 1 clavey to the chimney in the hall – 2s 6d.
Item in bread and ale – 1 ½d.
Item for 1 dozen ?sand – 10d.
Item to the mason – 6s 8d.
Item for candles to the mason – 1d.
Item for 2 quarters of lime – 5d.
Item to the said mason – 6s 8d.
Item for a tiler 3 ½ days – 22 ½d.
Item for 3 waterboards for the gutter – 9d.
Item for 1 ½ ?hundredweight of Asyn stone – 9d.
Item for lime – 4s 2d.
Item to a carpenter and a haulier – 10d.
Item to the mason – 6s 8d.
Item for 1 new gutter of 15 feet – 22 ½d.
Item for new lead – 4s.
Item for carrying away of rubble – 9d.
Item for 2 stones – 5d.
Item to 1 carpenter – 8d.

Item for nails – 2d.
Item to 1 plasterer – 5d.
Sum – 46s 4 ½d.
(485)
Item for 1 clavey to a chimney – 6d.
Item to the mason – 3s 4d.
Item for his ?nonesygges – 3d.
Item to 1 labourer – 2s 3d.
Item for lime – 20d.
Item for carrying away rubble – 3s 6d.
Sum – 11s 6d.
Item to Hugh Mason – 2s 5d.
Item to 1 labourer – 19d.
Item to another labourer – 6 ½d.
Item for 2 stones to cover a chimney – 4d.
Item to 2 masons – 2s 6d.
Item for their ?nonsegges – 2d.
Item to 1 labourer – 8d.
Item for 1 ?lentell and 1 ?rabetz – 16d.
Item for 5 quarters of lime – 12 ½d.
Item for making of 1 door – 8d.
Item for nails – 2d.
Item for 2 boards – 6d.
Item for lock and key – 6d.
Item for 1 pair of hinges – 4d.
Item for carrying of rubble – 1d.
Item to 1 carpenter and for timber – 3s.
Item for 4 ?hundredweight of Asyn stone – 2s.
Item for 50 laths – 4d.
Item for 200 lath nails – 4d.
Item for hache nails – 4d.
Item for 9 waterboards – 9d.
Item for 4 boards – 3d.
Item for 1 ?lover and wind bargys – 4d.
Item for 1 seme of tile stone – 3d.
Item to 2 tilers – 2s 8d.
Sum – 24s 3 ½d.

And there remains clear – 14s, which was laid down.

Item Agnes Fyler owes for her husband's pit – 6s 8d, for the which Thomas Fyler ?has borrowed.

(486)
[1438–39]
The account of Thomas Halleway and John Gosselyng proctors of the church of All Saints' before Sir William Rodberd then vicar, 17 Henry VI.

Receipts
In primis on Good Friday and Easter day – 17s 4d.
Item for old glass – 2s.
Item for a pole – 3d.
Item of William Bryd – 8d.
Item for the black ?psalter – 8d.
Item for the black cloth – 8d.
Item for the cross – 16d.
Item of a gentlewoman – 12d.
Item for the cross and the crown – 2s.
Item for 6 seats – 6s 4d.
Sum – 33s 7d. 32s 3d. [sic]

Receipts of the rent
In primis of William Warde – £3.
Item of John Whytsyde – 26s 8d.
Item of Thomas Fysche – 4s.
Item of Nicholas Stocke in Skadspyll Street now Marsh Street – 2s.
Item of Robert Walshe, cook – 2s 6d.
Item of Thomas Asche, baker, in Lewins Mead – 12d.
Item of Janet Yonge – 6d.
Item of Pers Hoper in Baldwin Street – 12s.
Sum – £5 8s 8d.
Sum total – £7 11d.

(487)
These are the payments
In primis for carrying of rubble – 1d.
Item for washing of 2 surplices and altar cloths – 4d.
Item for scouring and keeping of the sepulchre – 5d.
Item to the mother church of Worcester – 2s.
Item for bearing the cross on Saint George's day – 2d.
Item for bearing of the banners – 2d.
Item for bearing the cross on Corpus Christi day – 4d.
Item for William Newbery's mind – 6s 1d.
Item to the waxmaker – 12s.
Item to William Warde for 17 ells of linen cloth – 12s.
Item for making 2 rochets and an alb and an amice – 4s 5d.
Item for besoms – 1d.
Item for 4 torches – 18s 4d.
Item for scouring of the candlesticks and latten bowls – 13d.
Item for wax – 3s 4 ½d.
Item for making 64 lbs – 2s 8d.
Item for 1 pair of trestles to set the treasure coffer on – 6 ½d.
Item for washing and mending of surplices – 9d.
Item for making of iron gear – 8d.
Item for 2 quarters of lime to Jenkin Whytsyde's house – 5d.
Item for 2 seme sand – 2d.

Item for 3 boards – 3d.
Item for nails – 12d.
Item to 2 tilers – 3s 3d.
Item for laying a stone and covering a pit – 7d.
Item for 1 crest – 1d.
Item for Asyn stone – 6d.
Item for 3 bell ropes – 2s 6d.
Item for the General Mind – 4s.
Item for 1 ¼ gallons of lamp oil – 17 ½d.
Sum – £3 19s 5d.

(488)
Costs in plea and to men of law against Roger Acton knight.
In primis to Thornton – 3s 3d.
Item to the said Thornton to be our attorney in London – 6s 8d.
Item to Richard Chocke for Roger Acton knight – 20d.
Item at the day of assize between the said Roger and us to Pavy and Vyell – 3s 4d.
Item at Christmas to Chocke, Pavy and Vyell – 5s.
[Margin: Look the view] Item for a view taken between Roger Abyndon and us for 1 house by the churchyard – 10d.
[Margin: Look for the Kalendaries] Item paid to Hychekocke the Summoner to cite Master William Twyte, Sir Harry Colas and Sir Thomas Halleway for negligence of divine service – 4d.
Sum – 24s 5d.

Item to Edmund clerk of Saint Stephen's for writing 13 quires of the ordinal – 13s 4d.
Item for 1 baldric to a bell – 12d.
Item for writing 2 pairs of indentures – 12d.
Item for the mayor's seal – 6d.
Item to Pavy the man of law – 3s 4d.
Item for 2 loads of paving stone – 6s.
Item for 6 quarts of lamp [oil] – 21d.
Sum – 26s 11d.

Item for nails – 9d.
Item for timber to the kitchen – 10d.
Item to a tiler – 3d.
Item to a carpenter – 2s 8 ½d.
Item to a mason – 16d.
(489)
Item for lime and sand – 5d.
Item for 2 crests – 2d.
Item for nonsyges – 2d.
Item for 1 seat to a privy – 4d.
Item for twists and hooks – 1d.
Item for 6 loads of Asyn stone to a privy – 18d.

Item for lime and sand – 11d.
Item to a mason – 22d.
Item to 1 labourer – 13d.
Item for candles – 1d.
Item for stones and boards – 3s 3d.
Sum – 16s 6 ½d.

Sum total – £7 7s 3 ½d.
And so the church owes the proctors – 5s ½d.

(490)
[1439–40]
The account of William Raynes and John Tailour, hosteler, proctors of All Saints' before Sir William Rodberd, then vicar, 1st day of March A.D. 1439 and 18 Henry VI.

Receipts
In primis for the loan of the cross and the crown – 3s 4d.
Item on Good Friday and Easter day – 16s 2 ½d.
Item of Richard Chocke – 4d.
Item of William Harrys for 1 pit – 6s 8d.
Item for loan of candlesticks – 6d.
Item of Robert Stayner for 2 seats – 2s.
Sum – [blank]

Receipts for rents
In primis of John Whytsyd – 26s 8d.
Item of Janet Yonge – 6d.
Item of William Warde – £3.
Item of Thomas Baker in Lewins Mead – 12d.
Item of Nicholas Stocke in Skadspyll Street now called Marsh Street – 2s.
Item of Robert Walshe, cook – 2s 6d.
Item of Thomas Fysche – 4s.
Item of Pers Hoper in Baldwin Street – 12s.
Sum – [blank].

(491)
These are the payments
In primis for 2 torches of 28 lbs – 7s.
Item to the raker – 2d.
Item for making of 2 albs and 2 amices – 8d.
Item for washing of surplices and altar cloths – 10d.
Item for setting on of the apparel – 2d.
Item for noting of the ordinal and for writing the kalendar and for velum and binding – 14s 5d.
Sum – 23s 3d.

Costs for the assize between Roger Acton knight and us.
In primis Chocke, Pavy and Vyell – 6s 8d.
Item to Bolton – 3s.
Item to the Bayley Croud – 2s.
Item at Michaelmas to Bolton for writing a bill and the quest – 2s 4d.
Item for a copy of the plea – 4d.
Item to the attorney – 4d.
Item to Jocke, Pavy and Vyell – 8s 4d.
Item to T. Bolton – 12d.
Item to the Bayley Croud for assize at Christmas – 2s.
Item to Chocke and Vyell – 4s.
Item for the Statute merchaunt to Thornton – 6s 8d.
Item to Bolton for a certificate of the same – 2s 6d.
Sum – [blank]

(492)
Costs of the plea between John Suthfolke in Wine Street and us for John Pers's house
In primis to Thornton our attorney – 6s 9d.
Item to Thornton for a ?Syrefacyes against Suthfolke – 2s 6d.
Item to Thornton for John Perse – 6s.
Sum – [blank]

Costs paid for the church
In primis to the mother church at Worcester – 12d.
Item for mending vestments – 12 ½d.
Item for William Newbery's mind – 6s 1d.
Item for wax at Easter – 5s 5d.
Item for bearing of banners – 1 ½d.
Item for bearing the cross on Corpus Christi day – 4d.
Item for washing of cloths – 10d.
Item for mending of locks and keys – 4d.
Item for pins to the altars – ½d.
Item for making of a stock and ring for the cross that stands in the High Street – 2d.
Item for mending of 2 baldrics – 2d.
Item for mending and painting of battlements – 16d.
Item for wax at All Hallows' tide – 9s 9d.
Item for washing at All Hallows' tide – 8d.
Item for John Pers's mind – 6s.
Item for the General Mind – 2s 6d.
Item for William Warde for his costs to London – 3s 4d.
Item for mending John Whytsyde's chimney – 9s 11d.
Item for lamp oil – 2s 4d.
Item for new orfreys to the blue suit – £6 3s 4d.

Sum – [blank].

[The account ends abruptly.]

[493]
[1443–44]
The account of Richard Andrew and Roger Abyndon proctors of the church aforesaid before Sir William Rodberd, 25th day of March A.D. 1443, 22 Henry VI.

Receipts of rents
In primis of Robert Walsche – 2s 6d.
Item of John Whytsyde – 26s 8d.
Item of William Chestyr – 4s.
Item of Nicholas Stocke in Skadspyll Street now Marsh Street – 2s.
Item of William Canynges – 6d.
Item of Thomas Baker in Lewins Mead – 12d.
Item of Martin Lafyle – 16s 8d.
Item of John Leynell – 20d.
Sum – £3 17s ½d.

Receipts
In primis for the black cloth – 4d.
Item of Pers Ledbury – 8d.
Item for the black suit – 12d.
Item for the cross and the candlesticks – 3s 2d.
Item for William Tempyll's grave – 6s 8d.
Item for Pers Chapmon's grave – 6s 8d.
Item for 4 torches – 20d.
Item of Sir Harry – 2s 6d.
Item for 2 seats – 12d.
Item for the black cloth – 6d.
Item for 2 seats – 2s.
Item for the black cloth – 12d.
Item of a hardware man – 2s 2d.
Item for 2 seats – 14d.
Item of Walschote's wife for her grave and another grave – 13s 4d.
Item of the church goods – £5 6s 8d.
Sum – £11 14s 2 ½d.

(494)
These are payments
In primis for wax against Easter – 12s 8d.
Item for wax at All Hallows' tide – 6s 6d.
Item for washing of surplices and altar cloths – 8d.
Item for scouring – 8d.
Item for 2 baldrics – 14d.
Item to the mother church at Worcester – 16d.
Item for bearing the cross on Saint George's day and on Corpus Christi day – 6d.
Item for Newbery's mind – 6s 1d.
Item for bearing of banners – 4d.

Item for bearing of 2 censers – 2d.
Item for paving the treasure house – 3s 9d.
Item for carrying of rubble – 8d.
Item for 3 quarters of lime – 7 ½d.
Item for mending of 2 cushions – 8d.
Item for lamp.oil – 3s.
Item for scouring – 12d.
Item for washing of surplices and altar cloths – 7d.
Item for the General Mind – 2s 6d.
Item to John Jose for a plea to London for the house that William Warde holds – 6s 8d.
Item for 1 wire to the choir – 3d.
Item for besoms – 1d.
Item in expenses for the church – 12d.
Item for candles at All Hallows' tide and Christmas – 12d.
Item for setting in of 2 ?Irys about Our Lady in the pillar – 4d.
Sum – 49s 2 ½d.

(495)
Costs for Martin Lafyll's house
In primis for 12 quarters lime – 2s 6d.
Item to 3 carpenters – 19 ½d.
Item to 1 labourer – 13 ½d.
Item for carrying of stones – 8d.
Item for 8 ton of stones – 16d.
Item to 2 masons – 2s 6d.
Item for candles – 2d.
Item for 1 load of stone – 2s.
Item top 2 carpenters – 4s 10 ½d.
Item for nails – 4d.
Item to 1 carpenter – 2s 5d.
Item for nails – 6d.
Item for tack nails – 6d.
Item for 17 bushels of plaster – 7s 1d.
Item for 100 water boards – 7s 6d.
Item 2 dozen studs – 2s 7d.
Item for 2 groundsels – 12d.
Item for carrying 100 boards – 2d.
Item to 2 carpenters – 6s 6d.
Item to Parkhouse the Man of Law – 6s 8d.
Item for 2 blades of a stair and 2 poles – 20d.
Item for nails – 8d.
Item for 16 bushels of plaster – 6s 8d.
Item for boards – 2s 6d.
Item for 2 elm planks – 10d.
Item to 2 carpenters – 4s 4d.
Item for board nail – 6d.
Item for 500 hache nail – 15d.

(496)
Item for 50 tack nail – 13d.
Item for 8 bushels of plaster – 3s 4d.
Item to 2 carpenters – 6s 6d.
Item for 1 piece of timber – 22d.
Item for 2 seme stone – 5d.
Item for 36 bushels of plaster – 15s.
Item to 1 carpenter – 19 ½d.
Item for 1 load of paving stone – 2s 11d.
Item to 1 mason – 19 ½d.
Item to 1 labourer – 13 ½d.
Item for 12 bushels of plaster – 5s.
Item for 1 quarter of 1 ?hundredweight of new lead – 23d.
Item to 1 carpenter – 2s 8 ½d.
Item to 1 sawyer – 8d.
Item for 100 water boards – 7s 8d.
Item to 1 carpenter – 4s 3 ½d.
Item for nails – 6d.
Item for 1 ?bolke – 16d.
Item for hooks and twists – 11d.
Item for laths – 8d.
Item for carrying rubble – 12d.
Item for ?stappys – 3s 3d.
Item for 1 load of stone – 3s.
Item for 6 quarters of lime – 15d.
Sum – £7 5s 3d.

Sum total – £9 14s 5 ½d.
And there remains clear in the church – 39s 9d.

(497)
[1444–45]
The account of Richard Androwe and Roger Abyndon proctors of the aforesaid church before Sir William Rodberd then vicar, the 25th day of March A.D. 1444, 23 Henry VI.

Receipts
In primis on Good Friday and Easter Day – 20s 4d.
Item for the black cloth – 12d.
Item for old glass – 4d.
Item for the black cloth – 12d.
Item for the cross and the black cloth – 4s.
Item for the crown and the black cloth – 20d.
Sum – 28s 4d.

Receipts of rent
In primis of Robert Walsche, cook – 2s 6d.
Item of John Whytsyde – 26s 8d.

Item of William Chestyr – 4s.
Item of Nicholas Stocke in Skadspyll Street now Marsh Street – 2s.
Item of William Canynges – 6d.
Item of Thomas Baker – 12d.
Item of Martin Layfyll – 25s.
Item of John Leynell – 3s 4d.
Item of 1 hardwareman – 5s.
Item of William Warde – £8 6s 8d.
Sum – £11 16s 8d.

(498)
Payments for the church
In primis for washing of surplices and altar cloths – 14d.
Item for scouring – 8d.
Item to the raker – 4d.
Item for 4 pensells to the paschal – 8d.
Item for keeping the sepulchre – 6d.
Item for wax at Easter and All Hallows' tide – 18s 6d.
Item for Newbery's mind – 6s 1d.
Item for mending of vestments – 6d.
Item to John Jose, the man of law, for William Ward's house – 13s 4d.
Item for 1 quire of parchment to write a copy of the deeds belonging to the church – 5s 8d.
Item for bearing of banners – 4d.
Item for bearing of the cross and censers – 8d.
Item to John Jose at midsummer term – 3s 4d.
Item for 8 tons of stone to make 1 gutter out of Ward's house into the High Street – 2s 10d.
Item for hauling of the stones – 12 ½d.
Item to 1 mason – 3s 3d.
Item to 1 labourer – 13 ½d.
Item for 1 wey of lime – 15d.
Item to ?Wynebusche – 3s 4d.
Item in costs for Ward's house to the quest – 4s.
Item for writing 6 deeds – 12d.
Item for 1 altar cloth that was stolen – 3 ½d.
Item for besoms – 1d.
(499)
Item to John Jose at Michaelmas term – 11s 8d.
Item for 1 box to put the deeds in – 1d.
Item for scouring – 8d.
Item for washing of surplices and altar cloths – 12d.
Item to 1 tiler – 8d.
Item for 4 crests – 4d.
Item for lime and sand – 3d.
Item for candles at All Hallows' tide and Christmas – 14d.
Item to John Joce at Christmas term – 13s 4d.

Item for writing the deeds between Sir John Gyllard and Richard Haddon, the executors of Christine Haddon, and the parish of All Hallows' – 3s 4d.
Item for the General Mind – 2s 10d.
Item 10 ells of linen cloth for the vicar's surplice – 8s 4d.
Item in expenses done for the church – 16d.
Item for lamp oil – 2s 4d.
Sum – £6 4s 4 ½d.

Costs done on William Ward's house in the High Street
In primis for ½ a ?hundredweight of cornish stone – 3d.
Item for 1 board – 3d.
Item for making of 2 small pentes [?lean-tos] – 2s 8d.
Item for hasps and staples – 10d.
Item for latches, catches, bolts, twists and hooks – 19d.
Item for 1 latch with 1 ring – 4d.
Item for 3 elm boards – 12d.
Item for 9 locks and keys – 3s 1d.
(500)
Item for 9 rings with roses – 2s.
Item for 4 staples – 2d.
Item for 12 boards – 14d.
Item to 1 carpenter – 5s 5d.
Item for 5 ½ bushels of plaster – 2s 3d.
Item for laths and nails – 22s 1d.
Item for the ?ceiling – 10s 4d.
Item for 14 quarters of lime – 2s 1d.
Item for 106 new bars – 11s ½d.
Item for timber – 6d.
Item to 1 carpenter – 15d.
Item for 1 load of paving stone – 3s 4d.
Item for paving – 18d.
Item for making of 1 lattice in the parlour – 10 ½d.
Item to 1 plasterer – 10 ½d.
Sum – £3 15s 8 ½d.

And there remains clear to the church – £5 12d.

(501)
[1445–46]
The account of Richard Androwe and Roger Abyndon proctors of the aforesaid church, before Sir William Rodberd then vicar, the 15th day of March A.D. 1445, 24 Henry VI.

Receipts
In primis on Good Friday and Easter day – 22s.
Item for the black cloth and candlesticks – 8d.

Item of Garlond for 2 seats – 20d.
Item of 1 hardware man – 5s.
Item for the black suit – 12d.
Sum – 30s 4d.

Receipts of rents
In primis of William Ward – 13s 4d.
Item of Robert Core – 33s 4d.
Item of Thomas Fyler – 26s 8d.
Item of John Leynell – 3s 4d.
Item of Robert Hoper for 3 quarters' rents – 9s.
Item of Robert Cook – 2s 6d.
Item of William Chestyr – 4s.
Item of Nicholas Stocke in Skadspyll Street now Marsh Street – 2s.
Item of William Canynges – 6d.
Item of Thomas Baker – 12d.
Sum – £4 15s 8d.

(502)
Costs paid for the church
In primis for washing of surplices and altar cloths – 14d.
Item for 1 link to 1 censer – 3d.
Item for making 1 holy water stick of iron – 4d.
Item to the raker – 4d.
Item for mending of the green suit and for silk – 8d.
Item for scouring – 8d.
Item for keeping the sepulchre – 6d.
Item to Jose the Man of Law – 10s.
Item for Newbery's mind – 6s 1d.
Item to the mother church of Worcester – 2s.
Item for making 1 pair of sleeves to an alb and mending surplices – 18d.
Item for bearing the cross and censer on Corpus Christi day – 8d.
Item for mending of 1 leaden pipe – 14d.
Item for 4 torches – 18s 1d.
Item for wax at All Hallows' tide and Easter – 27s 11d.
Item for making 1 wheel for the paschal – 10d.
Item for 1 judas and 1 iron bar before the rood – 7d.
Item for assize that the chantry priests of Saint John's served against us to Pavy, Gylmyn and Jose – 10s.
Item in expenses at divers times on the quest – 3s 4d.
Item for 1 suit taken in the market court against the said chantry priests – 8s 8d.
Item for 1 baldric to 1 bell – 8d.
Item for 1 key to the coffer for torches – 3d.
Item for bearing of banners – 4d.
Item for washing of altar cloths and surplices – 10d.
Item for besoms – 1d.

Item for 1 load of tile stone – 3s.
[Margin: Costs for the steeple] Item for 4 quarters of lime for the steeple – 10d.
(503)
Item to tilers – 8s 9 ½d.
Item for boards and nails – 8d.
Item for 1 gutter of 22 feet – 2s 11d.
Item for boards – 5d.
Item for nails – 6d.
Item for lime – 5d.
Item to 1 tiler – 6s 1 ½d.
Item to William Wanstre for making of the cross – 3s 8d.
Item for casting of 3 ?hundredweight of lead – 4s.
Item for ½ a ?hundredweight of new lead – 3s 6d.
Item for 20 ½ lbs of solder for the hond [?handiwork] – 4s 3d.
Item to the plumber for lead to the cross and for his hond [?handiwork] – 3s 10d.
Item to 1 tiler – 2s 4d.
Item for lime – 10d.
Item for 1 gutter of 5 feet – 7 ½d.
Item for nails – 2d.
Item for 1000 pins – 2 ½d.
Item for making of iron gear – 3s.
Item for making the gutter between John Leynell and Thomas Fyler – 14d.
Item for candles at All Hallows' tide and Christmas – 18d.
Item for 2 keys to 1 coffer that Richard gave into the treasure house – 12d.
Item for 4 lbs of solder to the little vestry – 10d.
Item for 4 ?skarrys – 8d.
Item for the General Mind – 2s 6d.
Item for carrying of rubble – 4d.
Item for 3 lbs mede wax – 15d.
Item for allowance for gathering rent – 12d.
Item for lamp oil – 2s 4d.
Item for scouring – 8d.
Sum – £8 1d.

And there remains clear to the church – £3 6s 11d.

(504)
[1446–47]
The account of William Warde and David Sokett proctors of the aforesaid church before Sir William Rodberd then vicar, the 25th day of February A.D. 1446, 25 Henry VI.

Receipts
In primis on Good Friday and Easter Day – 19s 8d.
Item for the crown and the cross – 3s 4d.
Item for the crown and the cross – 2s 4d.
Sum – 26s 4d.

Receipts of rents
In primis of Janet Fyler – 26s 8d.
Item of Robert Core – 33s 4d.
Item of Pers Hoper – 12s.
Item of Robert Walshe, cook – 2s 6d.
Item of Thomas Asche, baker – 12d.
Item of Nicholas Stocke in Skadspyll Street now called Marsh Street – 2s.
Item of John Leynell – 3s 4d.
Item of William Chestre – 4s.
Item for William Warde's house – £5.
Item of William Canynges – 6d.
Sum – £10 11s 8d

(505)
Payments made for the said church
In primis for washing surplices and altar cloths – 10d.
Item for carrying of rubble – 4d.
Item for scouring – 9d.
Item for bearing the cross on Saint George's day – 4d.
Item to the mother church at Worcester – 20d.
Item for wax at Easter – 9s 5 ½d.
Item for washing of cloths – 12d.
Item for keeping the sepulchre – 11d.
Item for mending 1 sacring bell – 2d.
Item to Jose the Man of Law – 6s 8d.
Item for Newbery's mind – 6s 1d.
Item for mending of 1 vestment – 2d.
Item in receiving of Janet Fyler's rent – 1 ½d.
Item for hanging of the choir – 2d.
Item for wax – 2s 7d.
Item to Jose the Man of Law – 3s 4d.
Item for 1 piece of timber – 2s 4d.
Item for candles at Christmas – 3d.
Item for mending of 2 keys – 2d.
Item for mending of vestments – 6d.
Item for the General Mind – 2s 1 /2d.
Sum – 42s 4d.

And there remains clear – £4 3s 5d.

(506)
[1447–48]
The account of William Raynes and Richard[:scored; superscript William, also scored] Ward proctors of the aforesaid church before Sir William Rodberd then vicar, the 26th day of March A.D. 1447, 26 Henry VI.

Receipts
In primis on Good Friday and Easter Day – 15s 4 ½d.
Item for the cross – 12d.
Item of Thomas Dene – 8d.
Item for the Crown – 12d.
Item 31 lbs of pewter – 6s 2d.
Item 27 lbs of pewter – 3s 4 ½d.
Item for 1 crock of 12 lbs – 23d.
Item of Master William Twerty for 1 legacy – 13s 4d.
Item for 1 seat – 11d.
Item for 3 seats – 2s 6d.
Sum [blank]

Receipts of rent
In primis of Robert Core – 33s 8d.
Item of Thomas Fyler – 26s 8d.
Item of John Foster in the High Street – £5.
Item of Pers Hoper – 12s.
Item of William Canynges – 6d.
Item of William Chestre – 4s.
Item of Thomas Asche in Lewins Mead – 12d.
Item of Robert Walshe in the High Street – 2s 6d.
Item of John Leynell – 3s 4d.
Item of Nicholas Stocke in Skadspyll Street now called Marsh Street – 2s.
Sum – £9 5s 4d.

(507)
Payments for the church
In primis for 1 bar to the church door – 1d.
Item for besoms – 1d.
Item for 1 hook to the sepulchre – ½d.
Item for keeping the sepulchre – 10d.
Item to the raker – 9d.
Item for washing of altar cloths and surplices – 2s 9d.
Item for 1 key to the church door – 3d.
Item for bearing the cross on Saint George's day – 4d.
Item to the mother church of Worcester – 2s.
Item for bearing of banners – 3d.
Item for mending a desk in the choir – 2d.
Item for 1 plaint on John Suffolke – 15d.
Item for the cross on Corpus Christi day and censers – 6d.
Item for mending of 1 surplice – 2s 8d.
Item to the raker – 2d.
Item for making the mitre and the cross of Saint Nicholas – 22d.
Item for making the churchyard style – 23d.
Item for candles at Christmas – 4 ½d.
Item for 2 lanterns – 2d.
Item for mending the font – 9d.

Item for 1 amice – 4d.
Item for mending the churchyard – 3d.
Item for 1 lover [?louvre] to Robert Core's house – 8 ½d.
Item to the plasterer for John Leynell's house – 21d.
Item to the waxmaker for a whole year – 23s 11d.
Item for lamp oil – 21d.
Item to Richard Haddon for William Ward's place – £4 6s 8d.
Item for writing the said account – 6d.
Item for Newbery's mind – 6s 1d.
(508)
Item for John Pers's mind – 23d.
Item for the General Mind – 3s 10d.
Sum – [blank]

Expenses upon books
In primis for 1 deer's skin – 20d.
Item for 3 skins – 12d.
Item for making the same – 3s.
Item for 32 bosses of latten – 5s 4d.
Item for 1 deer's skin – 20d.
Item for 1 sheep's skin – 4d.
Item for glue – 1 ½d.
Item for latten wires and rivets – 4 ½d.
Item for 1 red skin and silk – 7d.
Item for 1 deer's skin – 21d.
Item for parchment to the ?Custos for books – 17d.
Item for silk and white thread – 9 ½d.
Item for 1 deer's skin and 2 sheeps' skins – 18d.
Item for 2 red skins – 10d.
Item for leather ?hungur – 1d.
Item for 1 deer skin and 1 sheep's skin – 18d.
Item for silk and thread – 12d.
Item for cheverell – 2d.
Item to Thomas Molle for his handiwork – 39s 6d.
Sum – £3 3s ½d.

Sum total – [blank]
And there remains to the church – 32s 6 ½d.

(509)
[1448–49]
The account of Roger Abyndon and Richard Androwe proctors of the aforesaid church before Sir William Rodberd then vicar, the 12th day of March A.D. 1448, 27 Henry VI.

Receipts
In primis on Good Friday and Easter Day – 18s 1d.
Item for 1 crock of 12 lbs – 2s 1d.
Item for 1 crock of 26 lbs – 4s 4d.

Item for Margery Abyndon's crane – 6s 8d.
Item for 1 seat – 12d.
Item for 1 basin and laver – 20d.
Sum [blank]

Receipts of rents
In primis of Janet Foster – £5.
Item of Robert Walsche – 2s 6d.
Item of Robert Core – 33s 4d.
Item of Pers Hoper in Baldwin Street – 12s.
Item of Nicholas Stocke in Skadspyll Street now called Marsh Street – 2s.
Item of William Canynges – 6d.
Item of Thomas Asche in Lewins Mead – 12d.
Item of Thomas Fyler – 26s 8d.
Item of John Leynell – 3s 4d.
Sum – [blank]

(510)
Payments for the said church
In primis for washing of surplices and altar cloths – 2s 1d.
Item for keeping the sepulchre – 8d.
Item to the raker – 4d.
Item for mending of 1 tynnell – 2d.
Item for scouring – 18d.
Item to the church of Worcester – 2s.
Item to Richard Haddon for Forster's house – £4 6s 8d.
Item for Newbery's mind – 6s 1d.
Item for bearing of banners – 3d.
Item for the cross on Holy Thursday – 4d.
Item to ringers against [ie on the occasion of] the king – 8d.
Item for setting in of 1 orfrey – 2d.
Item for lime stone and washing of the steeple – 3d.
Item for 1 coffer with 2 ledys [?lids] – 2s 2d.
Item for 2 locks to the churchyard doors – 6d.
Item to 1 mason – 2s 3d.
Item for cornish tile – 10d.
Item for 3 quarters of lime – 10d.
Item for mending of 1 chalice – 4d.
Item for 2 ?Irys for Our Lady's altar – 2d.
Item for the General Mind – 3s 5d.
Item for record of the plea between Roger Acton and the parish – 8s 6d.
Item for wax for the whole year – 23s 10d.
Item for 4 torches of 72 lbs – 20s 11 ½d.
Item for binding and helyng [ie mending] of 1 processional – 2s.
Item for soldering of 1 gutter – 10d.
Item for besoms – 1d.
Sum – £8 7s 11 ½d.

And there remains clear – 51s 2 ½d.

(511)
[1449–50]
The account of John Leynell and Thomas Dene proctors of the said
church before Sir William Rodberd then vicar, the 11th day of March
A.D. 1449, 29 Henry VI [recte 28 Henry VI?].

Receipts
In primis on Good Friday and Easter day – 18s 11d.
Item for the black cloth – 4d.
Item for Richard Isgar's grave – 6s 8d.
Item of John Isgar – 12d.
Item for seats – 7s 2d.
Item for William Wytteney's grave – 6s 8d.
Sum – 40s 9d.

Receipts of rent
In primis of John Forster in the High Street – £5.
Item of Robert Walshe, cook – 2s 6d.
Item of Robert Core – 33s 4d.
Item of Pers Hoper in Baldwin Street – 12s.
Item of William Chestyr – 4s.
Item of Nicholas Stocke in Skadspyll Street now Marsh Street – 2s.
Item of Richard Asche in Lewins Mead – 12d.
Item of Thomas Fyler – 26s 8d.
Item of John Leynell – 3s 4d.
Sum – £9 4s 10d.
Sum total – £11 5s 7d.

(512)
Payments for the church
In primis for scouring for all the year – 21d.
Item for 1 cord to the paschal – 2d.
Item to the raker – 4d.
Item for washing for all the year – 2s ½d.
Item for keeping the sepulchre – 13d.
Item to the mother church – 2s.
Item for bolts, locks and keys – 7 ½d.
Item for bearing of banners – 4d.
Item for 1 cloth of her [?hair] to the high altar – 11d.
Item for Newbery's mind – 6s 1d.
Item for bearing the cross on Corpus Christi day – 4d.
Item to the waxmaker for the whole year – 27s 10d.
Item for cleaning of 1 gutter – 2d.
Item for hanging the cloths at All Hallows' tide and at Saint James – 5d.
Item for ringing against the king – 3d.
Item for overseeing the bells – 2d.
Item for 1 cruet to the high altar – 3 ½d.

Item for 1 latten basin to Our Lady's altar – 23s 4d.
Item for 1 cord – 3d.
Item for besoms – 1d.
Item for 5 girdles to vestments – 2d.
Item for candles at Christmas – 6d.
Item for mending of 1 coffer – 2d.
Item for the General Mind – 3s 9d.
Item for lamp oil – 2s.
Item to Richard Haddon for the Green Lattice – £4 6s 8d.
Sum – £8 21 ½d.

And there remains clear to the church – [blank].

(513)
[1450–51]
The account of Roger Abyndon and Robert Core, proctors of the aforesaid church before Sir William Rodberd then vicar, A.D. 1450, 30 Henry VI [recte 29 Henry VI?]

Receipts
In primis on Good Friday and Easter day – 23s 3d.
Item for 1 brass pot – 6s 8d.
Item for 1 pan – 3s 4d.
Item for 7 graves – 46s 8d.
Item for the crown and the cross – 12d.
Item for 4 torches – 16d.
Item for 4 seats – 8s 8d.
Item of the false vestment-maker – 7s 10 ½d.
Item for 1 stresse [?distress] taken of Pers Hoper in Baldwin Street – 14s 11 ½d.
Item for 1 stresse [?distress] of John Goldsmith – 3s 3d.
Sum – £5 14s 11 ½d.

Receipts of rent
In primis of Joan Ward – £5.
Item of Robert Walsche – 2s 6d.
Item of Robert Core – 33s 4d.
Item of Thomas Fyler – 26s 8d.
Item of John Leynell – 3s 4d.
Item of the Master of the Tailors – 12s.
Item of Nicholas Stocke in Skadspyll Street now Marshe Street – 2s.
Item of William Canynges – 6d.
Item of Thomas Asche in Lewins Mead – 12d.
Item of William Chestyr – 4s.
Sum total – £15 2s 3 ½d.

(514)
Payments
In primis for 1 hinge and nails – 2d.
Item for 1 paring iron – 5d.

Item for besoms – 1d.
Item to the vicar for the bede-roll – 8d.
Item to the raker – 4d.
Item for washing by the year – 22d.
Item for 1 bar of iron to the south door – 5d.
Item for 1 ladle of iron – 3d.
Item for scouring at 2 times – 22d.
Item for keeping the sepulchre – 6d.
Item to the mother church – 2s.
Item for bearing the cross on Saint George's day and on Corpus Christi day – 8d.
Item for banners – 3d.
Item for mending vestments – 4s 1d.
Item for prysing [?appraising] Pers Hoper's and John Goldsmith's goods – 2s 4d.
Item for mending 2 robes of Our Lady in the pillar – 8d.
Item for entering a plaint on the false vestment-maker – 4d.
Item for 2 clasps to the best mass book – 13d.
Item for candles – 2 ½d.
Item for lamp oil – 2s 7d.
Item to Richard Haddon for the Green Lattice – £4 6s 8d.
Item to Sir John Gyllard for the candlesticks of silver – £3 6s 8d.
(515)
Item for 4 new torches – 23s 8d.
Item for wax – 6s 11d.
Sum – £10 4s 7 ½d.

Costs for the repairs on Robert Cor and Thomas Fyler's houses.
In primis to 1 mason – 14s 8d.
Item to 1 labourer – 5s 5d.
Item for lime – 7s 3 ½d.
Item for nails – 2d.
Item to tilers – 18 ½d.
Item for jambs and 1 ?clavey and the carriage – 3s 2d.
Item for solder – 2d.
Item for paving stone – 6d.
Item for sand – 4d.
Item for 26 lead [sic] – 18d
Item for carriage of rubble – 20d.
Sum – 36s 11d.

Costs on seats and on the window in the steeple
In primis for boards – 2s 8d.
Item for nails – 5 ½d.
Item for hinges – 15d.
Item to 1 carpenter – 4s 4d.
Item for casting 5/8th of a ?hundredweight of lead – 10d.
Sum – 9s 6 ½d.

(516)
Costs of the obits
In primis for Newbery – 6s 1d.
Item for John Pers – 2s 8d.
Item for the General Mind – 2s 4d.
Item for costs on the false vestment-maker – 12d.
Sum – 12s 1d.

Costs of the plea for John Suffolke
In primis to men of law – 13s 6d.
Item for entering the plaint – 4d.
Item to the sergeant – 2s 4d.
Item to our attorney – 2d.
Item for entering the plea and the ?pces – 4s 5d.
Item for 2 ?contynewas – 8d.
Sum – 21s 5d.

Sum of all payments – £14 4s 7d.
And there remains clear to the church – 17s 8 ½d.

(517)
[No date given, but after 1450–51 and pre-dating June 1453 when Rodberd is said to have died.]

The account of Richard Knight and Richard Androwe proctors of the aforesaid church before Sir William Rodberd then vicar.

Receipts
In primis on Good Friday and Easter Day – 15s 6 ½d.
Item for Alison Knight's mother's pit – 6s 8d.
Item for the cross and the crown – 3s 8d.
Item for 1 seat – 16d.
Sum – 27s 2 ½d.

Receipts of rent
In primis of John Leynell – 23s 4d.
Item of Pers Grenfeld – 15s.
Item of Robert Coke – 2s 6d.
Item of Thomas Baker – 12d.
Item of William Canynges – 6d.
Item of William Chestyr – 4s.
Item of Nicholas Stocke in Skadspyll Street now Marsh Street – 2s.
Item of Thomas Phelyppe, Master of Tailors – 12s.

Sum total – £4 7s 6 ½d.

(518)
Payments
In primis for painting the cross – 8s 4d.

Item for Newbery's mind – 6s 1d.
Item for washing by the year – 2s 2d.
Item for setting in of orfreys – 7d.
Item for scouring – 8d.
Item for keeping the sepulchre – 8d
Item to the raker – 4d.
Item to the church of Worcester – 16d.
Item for costs on Corpus Christi day – 12d.
Item for wax – 14s 1d.
Item for the General Mind – 5s 4d.
Item for candles at Christmas – 6d.
Item for making the silver pax – 5s.
Item for 6 staves for the Dance of Pauls – 20d.
Item for planks and boards – 4s 2d.
Item for mending of locks and keys – 18d.
Item for spikes to the enterclose – 10d.
Item for mending of 2 spryngell [?sprinklers] – 2d.
Item to Richard Haddon – 13s 4d.
Sum total – 51s 4d.

And there remains clear to the church – 36s 9 ½d.

(519)
[No date given, but clearly subsequent to Rodberd's death in 1453.]

The account of John Leynell and Hugh Sadler proctors of the aforesaid
church before Sir William Wer then vicar.

Receipts
In primis on Good Friday and Easter Day – 21s 1/d.
Item for seats – 10s 2d.
Item for the crown and the cross – 16d.
Item for Wat Burges's grave – 6s 8d.
Item of Sir William Rodberd 1 pair of cruets of silver of 6 ozs & 2d.
Item of the said Sir William, 1 processional.
Item of the said Sir William, 1 coverlet to lie before the high altar.
Item of the said Sir William, 6 torches.
Item of John Schoppe – 9d.

Receipt of rents
In primis of Thomas Aden, Master of the Tailors – 12s.
Item of Pers Grenfeld – 20s.
Item of John Leynell – 23s 4d.
Item of Nicholas Stocke in Skadspyll Street now Marsh Street – 2s.
Item of William Canynges – 6d.
Item of Thomas Asche in Lewins Mead 12d.
Item of William Chestyr – 4s.

Item of Richard Haddon – 13s 4d.
Item of Robert Walshe, cook – 2s 6d.
Sum – £3 18s 8d.

(520)
Payments for the church
In primis for washing by the year – 3s ½d.
Item for paving before the church door – 5s 2d.
Item for lime – 22 ½d.
Item to the raker – 4d.
Item for keeping the sepulchre – 11d.
Item for scouring – 20d.
Item for 1 cord to the paschal – 3 ½d.
Item to the church of Worcester – 2s.
Item for Newbery's mind – 6s 1d.
Item for bearing of banners – 5d.
Item for mending of 1 house – 4d.
Item for soldering of 1 gutter – 3d.
Item on Corpus Christi day – 4d.
Item for paving stone – 6d.
Item for sand – 2d.
Item for 1 stone – 4d.
Item to 1 mason – 16 ½d.
Item to 1 plumber for lead and solder – 9s 9 ½d.
Item for making of 4 hooks – 5d.
Item for cornish tile – 1 ½d.
Item for nails – 2d.
Item for boards – 1d.
Item for ?mese – 2d.
Item to 1 tiler – 19 ½d.
Item for 1 baldric to 1 bell – 10d.
For hanging of 1 pipe of lead – 7d.
Item for hanging the cloths on Saint James' day – 2 ½d.
Item for wax by the year – 24s ½d.
Item for 2 lb candles at Christmas – 3d.
(521)
Item for making a window in John Leynell's kitchen – 15d.
Item to 1 tiler – 7 ½d.
Item for the General Mind – 4s 8d.
Item for carrying of rubble – 2d.
Item to Richard Haddon for the Green Lattice – 13s 4d.
Item for lamp oil – 2s 9d.
Sum – £4 6s 4d.

And there remains clear to the church – 27s 3 ½d.

(522)
[1453–54]
The account of William Isgar and Thomas Fyler proctors of the

aforesaid church before Sir Maurice Hardwick then vicar, the 20th day of March A.D. 1455 [recte 1453?], 32 Henry VI.

Receipts
In primis on Good Friday and Easter day – 20s 1 ½d.
Item for seats – 11s 2d.
Item of William Peynter, y wote ner wher for [I don't know what for] – 2s 6d.
Item for 1 ?lery hog's head – 6d.
Sum – 34s 3 ½d.

Receipts of rents
In primis for the Green Lattice – £5.
Item of Pers Grenfeld – 20s.
Item of John Leynell – 23s 4d.
Item of William Chestyr – 4s.
Item of Thomas Ashe in Lewins Mead – 12d.
Item of William Canynges – 6d.
Item of Nicholas Stocke in Skadspyll Street now called Marsh Street – 2s.
Item of John Albyrton – 12s.
Item of Robert Walshe – 2s 6d.
Sum – £9 4d.

[Sic:] Organs – £6 6s 8d.
[Scored: Item for wine and woad for the new vestments – 54s 8d.]
[Scored: Sum total – £13 9s 3 ½d.]

[Margin: For the organs, price – £6 6s 8d.]
Item for 1 pair of organs received in wine and woad from William Chestyr and Nicholas Longe – 54s 8d.

Sum total – £13 9s 3 ½d.

(523)
Payments
In primis for washing by the whole year – 15d.
Item to the raker – 15d.
Item for keeping the sepulchre – 8d.
Item for scouring – 8d.
Item to the mother church – 2s.
Item for William Newbery's mind – 6s 1d.
Item to Richard Haddon for the Green Lattice – £4 6s 8d.
Item for bearing of the banners and the cross – 9d.
Item to the waxmaker – 28s 3d.
Item for 3 gurdyls [?girdles] – 2d.
Item to ?jokys for the organs – 39s 10d.
Item for candles at Christmas – 10d.

Item for hanging up the cloths twice – 10d.
Item for besoms – 1d.
Item for lamp oil – 2s 6d.
Item in ?halfepens – 8d.
Item to John Leynell [scored: for the vestments – 23s 4d.]
Item to John Leynell for the organs – 40s.
Item for the General Mind – 4s 6d.
Sum – £12 4d.

And remaining to the church aforesaid – 28s 11 ½d.

(524)
[1454–55]
The account of William Jenkins, painter, and Robert Walsche, cook, proctors of the church aforesaid before Sir Maurice Hardwick then vicar, the 27th day of March A.D. 1456 [recte 1454?], 33 Henry VI.

Receipts
In primis on Good Friday and Easter day – 15s 1 ½d.
Item for the cross – 8d.
Item for seats – 22d.
Item for the black cope – 3 ½d.
Item for stones – 7d.
Sum – 18s 6d.

Receipt of rent
In primis of Richard Haddon for the Green Lattice – 13s 4d.
Item of Robert Coke – 2s 6d.
Item of Pers Grenfeld – 20s.
Item of John Leynell – 23s 2d.
Item of William Chestyr – 4s.
Item of Thomas Asche – 12d.
Item of William Canynges – 6d.
Item of Nicholas Stocke in Skadspyll Street now called Marsh Steet – 2s.
Item of the Master of the Tailors – 12s.
Sum – £3 18s.
Sum total – £4 16s 6d.

(525)
Payments
In primis for nails, twists and boards for 1 seat – 8d.
Item for 1 cloth for the font – 9d.
Item for 1 new lock – 4d.
Item for wine on Palm Sunday to the priests – 4d.
Item for scouring – 12d.
Item for washing – 22d.
Item for keeping the sepulchre – 8d.

Item for bearing of the cross and banners – 10d.
Item for Newbery's mind – 6s 1d.
Item for the church of Worcester – 2s.
Item to the raker – 8d.
Item for wax – 19s.
Item for making 1 almory[?aumbry] – 2s 5d.
Item to Thomas Fyler for his costs to ride to London for the new suit – 13s 4d.
Item for making 1 clapper for the great bell – 2s.
Item for 1 shovel – 1d.
Item for soldering of 1 gutter – 7d.
Item for candles – 2d.
Item for carrying of timber to the Treanglc – 3d.
Item for the General Mind – 6s.
Item for lamp oil – 2s 6d.
Item for making 1 new rental – 3d.
Item for writing the said account – 4d.
Sum – 58s 11d.

And there remains in the church – 36s 5d.

(526)
[?1456–57]
The account of Richard Knight and Nicholas Baker proctors of the said church before Sir Maurice Hardwick then vicar, the 2nd day of April 14[?57], 35 Henry VI.

Receipts
In primis on Good Friday and Easter day – 12s 3 ½d.
Item of 1 hardwareman – 10d.
Item of Thomas Turner for the Beer house – 20d.
Item for seats – 2s 8d.
Sum – 17s 5 ½d.

Receipts of rents
In primis of Richard Haddon for the Green Lattice – £5.
Item of Robert Coke – 2s 6d.
Item of Pers Grenfeld – 26s 8d.
Item of John Leynell – 23s 4d.
Item of Thomas Asche – 12d.
Itenm of John Albyrton in Baldwin Street – 12s.
Item of William Canynes for rent of assize that John Adyrton, stainer, holds of him – 6d.
Item of Nicholas Stocke in Skadspyll Street now Marsh Street – 2s.
Item of Thomas Halleway's chantry and for William Waren's chamber – 6s 8d.
Sum – £8 18s 8d.
Sum total of all receipts – £9 16s 1 ½d.

(527)
Payments
In primis for scouring – 2s 3d.
Item for washing – 12 ½d.
Item for making 1 wheel for 1 bell – 3s 10 ½d.
Item to the raker – 13d.
Item for 1 bill made to the bishop against the prior of the Kalendars and his bretheren – 4d.
Item for keeping the sepulchre – 8d.
Item for wine to the priests on Palm Sunday – 4d.
Item to the church of Worcester – 20d.
Item for Newbery's mind – 6s 1d.
Item for a dinner for the priests on Corpus Christi day – 2s 4d.
Item for bearing of the cross – 4d.
Item for 1 lock and key to the vestry door – 2s 2d.
Item for mending of 1 lock – 4d.
Item for bearing of banners – 6d.
Item for 1 bar of iron – 1 ½d.
Item for 2 ells of linen cloth for the high altar – 18d.
Item for the waxmaker – 42s 10d.
Item for lamp oil – 3s 7d.
Item to William Peynter for staining the said cloth – 6s 8d.
Item to Richard Haddon – £4 6s 8d.
Item to the suffragan – 3s 4d.
Item for mending of 1 gutter – 9 ½d.
Item for the General Mind – 11s ½d.
Item for 1 lock – 1 ½d.
Item for 1 load of stone – 2s 6d.
Sum total – £9 14s 3d.

And there remains clear to the church – 23d.

(528)
[1457–58]
The account of William Boxe and John Schoppe proctors of the church aforesaid before Sir Maurice Hardwick then vicar, the 27th day of the month of March 36 Henry VI.

Receipts
In primis for seats – 6s 4d.
Item on Good Friday and Easter day – 19s 6 ½d.
Item for 1 legacy from Sir William Welschott – 6s 8d.
Item for 1 plank and 1 pole – 5s.
Item for 1 legacy – 8s.
Item for 1 legacy – 6s 8d.
Item for 2 graves – 13s 4d.
Item for 1 legacy from Richard Hatter – £3 6s 8d.
Item of Agnes Fyler to the new suit – 6s 8d.
Item for Sir Thomas Serle's grave – 3s 4d.

Item of 1 hardwareman – 16d.
Item for selling ale for the best suit – £11 19s 4d.
Sum – £19 2s 10 ½d.

Receipts of rents
In primis of John Compton for the Green Lattice – £5.
Item of Pers Grenfeld – 26s 8d.
Item of John Leynell – 23s 4d.
Item of William Chestyr – 4s.
Item of Thomas Asche in Lewins Mead – 12d.
Item of John Albyrton in Baldwin Street – 12s.
Item of William Canynges – 6d.
Item of Nicholas Stocke in Skadspyll Street now Marsh Street – 2s.
Item of Thomas Halleway's chantry for Sir William Waren's chamber – 6s 8d.
Sum – £8 18s 8d.

(529)
Payments
In primis for besoms – 1d.
Item for nails – 6d.
Item for 1 deed of feoffment – 6d.
Item for 1 carpenter – 16d.
Item for twists – 2d.
Item for 1 elm board – 9d.
Item for washing of the church – 6s 6d.
Item for washing by the year – 22d.
Item to the raker – 4d.
Item for keeping the sepulchre – 9 ½d.
Item to the church at Worcester – 2s.
Item to 1 plumber – 2s 2 ½d.
Item for Newbery's mind – 6s 1d.
Item for mending the great bell – 3s 4d.
Item for scouring – 16d.
Item for taking down of the cloths – 8d.
Item for bearing of banners – 10d.
Item for entering a plaint against William Raynes – 4d.
Item for mending the glass windows – 2s 4d.
Item to the waxmaker – 24s 10d.
Item for 1 fire pan – 6d.
Item for a dinner to the priests of Corpus Christi day – 2s.
Item for 1 cord to the trestle – 4d.
Item to 1 upholsterer – 9d.
Item for mending the great clapper – 20d.
Item to John Leynell to the best suit – £4 13s 4d.
Item to 1 tiler – 7d.
Item for candles at Christmas – 2d.
Item for a letter of testimonial under the dean's seal – 14s 6d.

(530)
Item to Richard Haddon for the Green Lattice – £4 6s 8d.
Item to John Leynell for the new suit – 57s 10d.
Item for making of 1 ladder – 10d.
Item for lamp oil – 2s 9d.
Item for painting of the trestle – 8d.
Sum – £15 9s 4d.
Sum total paid to John Leynell by the said proctors for the best suit – £7 14d.

Sum total receipts – £28 18 ½d.
And there remains clear to the church – £12 12s 2 ½d.

(531)
[1460–61]
The account of Hugh Sadler and John Schoppe proctors of the aforesaid church before Sir Maurice Hardwick then vicar, 39 Henry VI and 1 Edward IV, A.D. 1459 [recte 1461], 27th day of March.

Receipts
In primis on Good Friday and Easter day – 12s 8d.
Item of 1 hardwareman – 5s.
Item for the crown and the candlesticks – 10d.
Item for 1 free stone – 10d.
Item for William Raynes' pit – [blank]
Sum [blank]

Receipt of rents
In primis of David Lynell, writer – [blank].
Item of John Leynell – 23s 4d.
Item of William Canynges – 6d.
Item of Robert Walshe, cook – 2s 6d.
Item of John Albyrton in Baldwin Street – 12s.
Item of John Compton – £5.
Item of Thomas Asche in Lewins Mead – 12d.
Item of Nicholas Stock in Skadspyll Street now Marsh Street – 2s.
Item of William Chestyr – 4s.
Item of Thomas Halleway's chantry for Sir William Waren's chamber – 6s 8d.
Sum – [blank]
Sum total – £9 6s 4d.

(532)
Payments
In primis for washing by the year – 6d.
Item for scouring – 16d.
Item for keeping the sepulchre – 8d.
Item to the church of Worcester – 20d.
Item to the raker – 5d.

Item for Newbery's mind – 6s 1d.
Item to the priests on Corpus Christi day – 2s 6 ½d.
Item for cleaning of 1 gutter – 18 ½d.
Item for hanging up the Dance of Pauls – 8d.
Item for the waxmaker – 23s 5 ½d.
Item for locks and keys – 17d.
Item for 1 rope to the little bell – 2d.
Item for besoms and 1 panier – 2d.
Item for candles at Christmas – 2d.
Item to Richard Haddon for the Green Lattice – £4 6s 8d.
Item for lamp oil – 2s 3d.
Item for the General Mind – 9s ½d.
Item for 1 load of stone – 2s 6d.
Sum – £6 2s 4d.

And there remains clear to the church – £3 4s.

(533)
[1461–62]
The account of Hugh Sadler and John Schoppe proctors of the aforesaid church before Maurice Hardwick then vicar, the 15th day of April A.D. 1462, 2 Edward IV.

Receipts
In primis on Good Friday and Easter day – 13s 4 ½d.
Item for seats – 18d.
Sum – 14s 10 ½d.

Receipt of rent
In primis of David Lynell – 20s.
Item of John Leynell – 23s.
Item of John Albyrton in Baldwin Street – 12s.
Item of Thomas Asche in Lewins Mead – 12d.
Item of Robert Walshe, cook – 2s 6d.
Item of John Compton – £5.
Item of William Canynges – 6d.
Item of Thomas Halleway's chantry for Sir William's chamber – 6s 8d.
Sum – £8 6s.

Sum total – £9 10 ½d.

Memorandum that John Shipward withheld and withdrew first the rent of assize of the house in Skadspyll Street, now Marsh Street, in which dwelt Nichol Stocke, mariner, and [time] out of mind was paid – 2s. God amend him.

(534)
Payments

In primis for washing – 18d.
Item to the singers on Palm Sunday – 3d.

Item for washing – 7 ½d.
Item to the raker – 15d.
Item to 1 plumber – 14d.
Item to the church of Worcester – 20d.
Item for bearing of banners – 6d.
Item for Newbery's mind – 6s 1d.
Item for 1 load of tile stone – 2s 6d.
Item for the priests on Corpus Christi day – 2s 7d.
Item for hanging the Dance of Pauls – 8d.
Item for mending glass windows – 8d.
Item to 1 mason – 9d.
Item for making of 1 window – 12d.
Item for 1 surplice to the vicar – 9s.
Item for candles at Christmas – 3d.
Item for besoms – 1d.
Item for bearing of the cross – 4d.
Item for scouring – 16d.
Item for keeping the sepulchre – 10d.
Item to Richard Haddon – £4 6s 8d.
Item for lamp oil – 3s 3d.
Item to 1 tiler – 3s 8d.
Item for the General Mind – 7s 4d.
Item in allowance for Nicholl Stocke in Skadspyll Street – 2s.
Item [blank] – 9d.
Sum – £6 17s 8 ½d.

And there remains clear to the church – 43s 2 ½d.

(535)
[1462–63]
The account of Thomas John and Thomas Gold proctors of the church aforesaid before Sir Maurice Hardwick then vicar, on the last day of March 1463, 3 Edward IV.

Receipts
In primis on Good Friday and Easter day – 12s 4d.
Item for seats – 4s 1d.
Item from Harry Chestyr for the candlesticks – 4d.
Item for 1 iron brooch – 3s.
Item for 3 burials – 20s.
Sum – 39s 9d.

Receipts of rent
In primis of John Compton – £5.
Item of Joan Walshe, cook – 2s 6d.
Item of Thomas Pointmaker for 1 quarter – 4s.
Item of John Leynell – 23s 4d.
Item of Thomas Asche in Lewins Mead – 12d.

Item of John Albyrton in Baldwin Street – 12s.
Item of William Canynges – 6d.
Item of Thomas Halleway's chantry – 6s 8d.
Sum – £7 10s.
Sum total – £9 9s 9d.

(536)
Payments
In primis for washing – 16d.
Item for keeping the sepulchre – 9d.
Item to the raker – 8d.
Item to the mother church – 12d.
Item for Newbery's mind – 6s 1d.
Item for bearing of banners and the cross – 8d.
Item to the priests on Corpus Christi day – 2s 6d.
Item for scouring – 16d.
Item for hanging the Dance of Pauls – 8d.
Item for mending and gilding the oilfat – 4s 4d.
Item for mending the organs – 12s.
Item for 2 lbs of candles – 3d.
Item for a cord for the Lent cloth – ½d.
Item for besoms – 1d.
Item for lamp oil – 2s 1 ½d.
Item to Richard Haddon – £4 6s 8d.
Item to the suffragan – 17d.
Item to the waxmaker – 12s 4 ½d.
Item for the General Mind – 8s 8d.
Item to 1 plumber – 3s.
Item to 1 tiler – 2s 8d.
Item 1 labourer – 10d.
Item for lime – 15 ½d.
Item for making a key to the church door – 12d.
Item for mending the glass windows – 2s 4d.
Item for writing the said account – 12d.

Sum – £7 14s 11d.
And there remains clear to the church – 34s 9d.

(537)
[1463–64]
The account of Clement Wilteshire and Howell apRes proctors of the aforesaid church before Sir Maurice Hardwick then vicar, on the last day of March A.D. 1464, 4 Edward IV.

Receipts
In primis on Good Friday and Easter day – 12s 7 ½d.
Item for the crown and the cross – 12d.
Item for old timber – 6s 8d.
Item of treasury coffer – 29s 9d.

Item for ale selling – £4 5s 4d.
Item of Halleway's chantry for money that was borrowed from the church – 20s.
Item in our allowance for received rent – 11d.
Item for seats – 3s 4d.
Item for 4 burials – 26s 8d.
Item of Nicholas Baker – 20d.
Item for 2 burials – 10s.
Sum – £9 17s 11 ½d.

Receipts of rent
In primis of John Compton – £5.
Item of Joan Walsche, cook – 2s 6d.
Item of Thomas Pointmaker for half the year – 8s.
Item of John Leynell – 5s 10d [for] 1 quarter.
Item of Thomas Phylyps, barber, for 2 ½ years – 10s.
Item of John Sybylle, baker, in Lewins Mead – 12d.
Item of John Alberton in Baldwin Street – 12s.
Item of William Canynges – 6d.
Item of Halleway's chantry – 6s 8d.
Sum – £7 6s 6d.

(538)
Payments
In primis for washing – 12d.
Item for scouring – 16d.
Item for keeping the sepulchre – 10d.
Item to the raker – 8d.
Item to the church of Worcester – 12d.
Item to the priests on Palm Sunday for wine – 3d.
Item for bearing of [the] cross and the banners – 8d.
Item for Newbery's mind – 6s 1d.
Item for the Dance of Pauls – 8d.
Item for a dinner on Corpus Christi day for the priests – 3s 6d.
Item for candles at Christmas – 3d.
Item to the suffragan for his hire – 2s 2d.
Item for 1 rope to the salve bell – 5d.
Item to Richard Haddon for the Green Lattice – £4 6s 8d.
Item for lamp oil – 3s.
Item for mending of 1 lock and 1 key – 8 ½d.
Item for besoms – 1d.
Item for hanging of 1 bell – 3d.
Item to 1 carpenter – 5s 3d.
Item in allowance for rent – 11d.
Item for writing this said account – 21d.
Item to the waxmaker – 22s 5d.
Item for the General Mind – 10s 8 ½d.
Sum [blank]

(539)

Costs for 2 tenements that were burned next to the steeple in Corn Street.

In primis to [scored: 2] labourers to sese [?cease] the fire – 2s 2d.

Item to 4 labourers and the raker – 3s 8d.

Item to Thomas Carpenter and other carpenters – £7 5 ½d.

Item to 1 haulier – 18d.

Item to 1 tiler – 21s 4 ½d.

Item for lath nails and other nails – 9s.

Item to Balle, carpenter – 6d.

Item to 1 mason – 5s 11d.

Item to 1 labourer – 3d.

Item for boards – 6d.

Item for iron gear – 6d.

Item to 1 plumber – 10s 10 ½d.

Item for tile stones – 30s.

Item for sand – 6d.

Item for 3 dozen and 2 crests – 19d.

Item for lime – 22 ½d.

Item for ?muse – 12d.

Sum – [blank]

Sum total of all the payments – [blank]

And there remains clear to the church – 11s 11d.

(540)

[1464–65]

The account of William Boxe and John Schoppe proctors of the aforesaid church before Sir Maurice Harwick then vicar, the last day of March A.D. 1465, 5 Edward IV.

Receipts

In primis on Good Friday and Easter day – 14s 2d.

Item of John ?Lonkodon – 3s 4d.

Item for Janet Raynes' grave – 6s 8d.

Item for seats – 4s 4d.

Item of Halleway's chantry – [scored: 6s 8d] £4 4s 5 ½d.

Item received of the church money – 11s 11d.

Sum – £6 4s 10 ½d.

Receipts of rent

In primis of John Compton – £5.

Item of John Branfeld, cook – 2s 6d.

Item of Thomas Adene for 3 quarters – 13s 4d.

Item of Thomas Phelpys, barber – 4s.

Item of John Albyrton in Baldwin Street – 12s.

Item of William Canynges – 6d.

Item of Syble, baker, in Lewins Mead – 12d.
Item for Halleway's chantry – 6s 8d.
Sum – £7.
Sum total – £13 4s 10 ½d.

(541)
Payments
In primis for washing – 14 ½d.
Item for scouring – 16d.
Item for keeping the sepulchre – 10d.
Item to the church of Worcester – 12d.
Item to the raker – 8d.
Item for bearing banners and the cross – 8d.
Item for the dinner on Corpus Christi day – 3s 6d.
Item for Newbery's mind – 6s 1d.
Item for the Dance of Pauls – 8d.
Item for candles – 2d.
Item for besoms and 1 panier – 2d.
Item for lamp oil before the cross altar – 2s 3d.
Item to Richard Haddon for the Green Lattice – £4 6s 8d.
Item to the suffragan for his hire – 2s 8d.
Item to the waxmaker – 20s.
Item for the General Mind – 9s 3 ½d.
Item in allowance for rent – 11d.
Item for making this account – 21d.
Sum – £6 18s 9d.

(542)
Costs for repairs done on the house next to the steeple
In primis for carpenters – £3 4s 4d.
Item for nails – 3s 7 ½d.
Item to the haulier – 2s 7d.
Item to the plasterer – 21s 5d.
Item to labourers – 4s 1 ½d.
Item for lime – 5 ½d.
Item for boards – 6s 9 ½d.
Item to masons – 4s 5d.
Item for salt to 1 chimney – 2d.
Item for sand – 14d.
Item for free stone – 9d.
Item for 1 load of paving stone – 22d.
Item for iron gear – 2s 11d.
Item to 1 lattice – 6d.
Item for 1 rope to the stair – 2d.
Sum – £5 11s 4 ½d.

Sum total – £13 3s 2 ½d.
And there remains clear in the church – 20d.

(543)
[1465–66]
The account of William Jenkins, painter, and Thomas Philypps, barber, proctors of the church aforesaid before Sir Maurice Hardwick then vicar, the last day of March A.D. 1466, 6 Edward IV.

Receipts
In primis on Good Friday and Easter day – 12s 3 ½d.
Item of Kateryn Hardwareman – 20d.
Item for seats – 15d.
Item for the cross – 4d.
Item of Harry Chestyr for candlesticks – 4d.
Item for 2 burials – 13s 4d.
Item for 1 basin – 4s.
Sum – 33s 2 ½d.

Receipts of rent
In primis of John Compton – £5 6s 8d.
Item of John Branfeld, cook – 2s 6d.
Item of Thomas Adene – 20s.
Item of Margery Manymoney for half a year – 6s 4d.
Item of Thomas Phylyps, barber – 4s.
Item of John Albyrton in Baldwin Street – 12s.
Item of William Canynges – 6d.
Item of Syble, baker, in Broad Mead – 12d.
Item of Halleway's chantry – 6s 8d.
Sum – [blank]

(544)
Payments
In primis for washing – [blank].
Item for keeping the sepulchre – 10d.
Item for scouring – 16d.
Item to the church of Worcester – 12d.
Item to the raker – 8d.
Item for bearing of banners and the cross – 8d.
Item for the dinner on Corpus Christi day – 2s 2 ½d.
Item for Newbery's mind – 6s 1d.
Item for 2 lbs candles – 2d.
Item for besoms – 1d.
Item to the suffragan for his hire – 3s.
Item for mending 1 pair of vestments – 8d.
Item for mending the best cross – 11d.
Item for 1 new lock and key – 4s.
Item for 1 ring to the church door – 16d.
Item for mending glass windows – 7s 1d.
Item for mending of 1 fire pan and 1 paring iron – 5d.
Item for 1 hanging lock to the treasure coffer – 7d.

Item on Palm Sunday to the priests – 6d.
Item for parchment for the rental – 1d.
Item for cleaning of gutters – 2d.
Item for a freestone – 12d.
Item for lamp oil to the rood altar – 15d.
Item to the suffragan – 18d.
Item for allowance of the rent – 19d.
Item to the waxmaker – 28s 9d.
Item for the General Mind – 9s 3d.

(545)
Costs for repairs done on Thomas Adeane's house
In primis for boards and ledges – 22d.
Item for hooks and twists – 16d.
Item to 1 carpenter – 18d.
Item for timber and boards – 7s 6d.
Item to 1 plasterer – 4d.
Item for 1 new lattice – 17d.
Item to 1 plumber – 5s.
Item for 2 planks – 22d.
Item for 1 lattice – 8d.
Item to 1 carpenter – 12d.
Item for locks and keys – 21d.
Item for cornish tiles – 4s 4d.
Item for lime and sand – 3 ½d.
Item for tile pins – 1 ½d.
Item for 1 lattice – 21d.
Item for paving stone – 2s 2d.
Item to 1 mason – 13d.
Item for lime and sand – 11 ½d.
Item for making 2 doors into the churchyard, and lead and iron spikes –
10s 2 ½d.
For writing this said account – 14d.

Sum – £6 6s 5 ½d.
And there remains clear in the church – £3 6s 5d.

(546)
[1466–67]
The account of John Compton and William Rowley proctors of the
aforesaid church before Sir Maurice Hardwick then vicar on the last day
of March A.D. 1467, 7 Edward IV.

Receipts
In primis on Good Friday and Easter day – 15s 10d.
Item for seats – 6s.
Item for Joan Phylypps' grave – 6s 8d.
Item for 1 ?forser that John Leynell gave to the church – 8s.
Sum [blank]

Receipt of rents
In primis of John Compton – £5 6s 8d.
Item of Kateryn Hardwareman – 3s 4d.
Item of Margery Manymoney – 13s 4d.
Item of Thomas Adene for 3 quarters – 15s.
Item of John Albyrton in Baldwin Street – 12s.
Item of Thomas Halleway's chantry – 6s 8d.
Item of John Branfeld, cook – 2s 6d.
Item of Thomas Phylypps, barber – 4s.
Item of William Canynges – 6d.
Item of John Syble in Lewins Mead – 12d.
Sum [blank]

(547)
Payments
In primis for wine to the priests on Palm Sunday – 2 ½d.
Item for keeping of the sepulchre – 8d.
Item for scouring – 12d.
Item to the church of Worcester – 12d.
Item for washing – [blank].
Item to the suffragan – 20d.
Item for besoms and 1 panier – 2 ½d.
Item to the raker – 8d.
Item for Newbery's mind – 6s 1d.
Item for bearing of banners and the cross – 8d.
Item to the waxmaker – 19s 7d.
Item for making a partition in Margery Manymoney's house – 2s 1 ½d.
Item for making 1 window in John Compton's ?pamente – 14d.
Item for 2 little bells and the hanging of them – 4s.
Item for the Dance of Pauls – 8d.
Item for writing and sealing Agnes Fyler's testament – 11s 8d.
Item for entering a plaint against Thomas Fyler – 8d.
Item for 1 court of ?pypondyrs – 4s 2d.
Item for the declaration of the process – 12d.
Item in wine to men of law – 22d.
Item to Harry Weston and Mawnsell – 11s 8d.
Item for the continuance and the withdrawing of the court – 6d.
Item to the mayor and the town clerk for writing and sealing – 9s.
Item for besoms – 1d.
Item for mending of a lock – 2d.
(548)
Item for soldering of a gutter – 5 ½d.
Item for making a chimney and 1 ?foren in John Compton's house – 28s 3d.
Item for 9 ells of holland cloth for 1 surplice – 8s 4d.
Item for breaking of a gutter – 7d.
Item for mending of 1 glass window – 6d.
Item for 5 ells of linen cloth for 1 alb and amice – 4s 4d.

Item for writing an indenture between the church and Thomas Fyler – 8s 4d.
Item for allowance of rent – 9d.
Item for 1 quart of lamp oil – 3d.
Item for the General Mind – 13s 8d.
Item for paper and writing this account – 12d.
Sum – £7 11s 10d.

And there remains clear in the church – 50s 6d.
These are the debts owing to the said church that we have not received
In primis of Thomas Adene for a quarter's rent of this our year as it appears by our receipts – 5s.

(549)
[1467–68]
The account of Martin Symonson and John Branfeld, cook, proctors of the aforesaid church before Sir Maurice Hardwick then vicar, the 28th day of March A.D. 1468, 8 Edward IV.

Receipts
In primis on Good Friday and Easter day – 8s 10d.
Item for seats – 4s.
Item of 1 hardwareman – 4d.
Item for the burial of Thomas Chestre and Margaret Abyndon – 13s 4d.
Sum – 26s 6d.

Receipts of rent
In primis of John Compton – £5 6s 8d.
Item of John Branfeld – 2s 6d.
Item of Thomas Aden for 3 quarters – 15s.
Item of Margery Manymoney – 13s 4d.
Item of Katherine Hardwareman for 1 wardroppe – 3s 4d.
Item of Thomas Phylyps, barber – 4s.
Item of John Syble, baker, in Lewins Mead – 12d.
Item of John Albyrton in Baldwin Street – 12s.
Item of William Canynges – 6d.
Item of Thomas Halleway's chantry – 6s 8d.
Sum – £8 10s.

(550)
Payments
In primis for washing – [blank].
Item for keeping the sepulchre – 12d.
Item for scouring – 16d.
Item for wine for the priests on Palm Sunday – 2 ½d.
Item to the church of Worcester – 12d.
Item for Newbery's mind – 6s 1d.

Item for bearing of banners – 4d.
Item for bearing of the cross – 4d.
Item for a dinner to the priests on Corpus Christi day – 3s 1d.
Item for hallowing a pair of vestments – 2d.
Item for the suffragan's hire – 2s 4d.
Item for the Dance of Pauls – 8d.
Item for 2 lbs of candles at Christmas – 2 ½d.
Item for besoms – 1d.
Item to the raker – 8d.
Item for mending 1 lock to the treasure house – 5d.
Item for mending of the ber [?bier] – 6d.
Item for 1 post to hang the churchyard door – 14d.
Item to Roger Kemys for overseeing the evidence between John Shipward, merchant, and the church – 3s 1d.
Item to the waxmaker – 16s 8 ½d.
Item for the General Mind – 11s 2d.
Sum [blank]

(551)
Costs for repairs
In primis on the house that Thomas Adene dwells in – 3s 9d.
Item for 1 gutter made in John Compton's house – 3s 2d.
Item on Margery Manymoney's house – 2s 11 ½d.
Item for 3 seats in Our Lady's aisle – 56s.
Cost without avail [blank]

Sum total of receipts – £9 18s 6d.

Sum total of payments – £6 4s 10d.

And there remains clear to the church – £3 13 8d.

Memorandum that Thomas Adene owes for 1 quarter's rent – 5s.

(553) [Different hand and presentation]
[1472–73]
The account of Clement Wilteshire and John Chestre proctors of the church of All Hallows' from the feast of the Annunciation of Our Lady in the 12th year of the reign of King Edward IV unto the said feast in the year next ensuing, so containing a whole year

Receipt of rents
In primis Morgan Lewis per annum – £5 6s 8d.
Item the chantry of Edward Frenche for John Baynfold's baste door and for his water gutter – 2s 6d.
Item Thomas Denne per annum – 20s.
Item Margery Money silk woman per annum – 13s 4d.
Item Katherine Hardware per annum – 3s 4d.

Item Thomas Philypp, barber, rent assize for his place – 4s.
Item John Syble, baker, in Lewins Mead, rent assize for his house per annum – 12d.
Item the Master of the Tailor's rent assize for the place that John Alberton dwells in in Baldwin Street, per annum – 12s.
Item John [sic] Canynges' rent assize for the place in Saint Peter's parish which John Steynour dwelt in, per annum – 6d.
Item John Shipward the elder's rent assize for the place in Marsh Street that Nicholas Stocke sometime held – 2s.
Item the chantry of Thomas Halleway for the house in the churchyard per annum – 6s 8d.
Sum total of rents – £8 12s.
Item received of John Paynter for the Beer House – 2s.
Sum total of this side – £8 14s.

(554)
Receipts at Easter and other casualties
In primis on Sheer Thursday, on Easter eve and Easter day on the box – 17s 10d.
Item of James Hardwareman for a seat – 8d.
Item of the widow of Gloucester for a seat – 16d.
Item of ?Agnes Palmer for a seat – 8d.
Item of William Bowde for a seat – 12d.
Item of John Martylment for a seat – 16d.
Sum – 22s 10d.

Item ye shall understand that we received for your old organs – 53s 4d.
Item of the parishioners and other divers strangers, the sum of – £9 17s 7d.
Sum – £12 10s 11d.

Allowance
In primis for the place in Marsh Street which Nicholas Stocke sometime held, the which John Shipward witholds now from us wrongfully – 2s.
Item of the rent assize for the place in St. Peter's parish the which Sir William Canynges wrongfully withholds from us – 6d.
Sum – 2s 6d.

Payments for the church
In primis on Palm Sunday for a pottle of osey for the priests and clerks that sang the passion in the rood loft – 6d.
Item against Easter and All Hallows' tide for washing surplices and other cloths – 11d.
(555)
Item for keeping the sepulchre and the light for 2 nights watching – 8d.
Item for bread and ale and coals for the said keepers – 2d.
Item for scouring of your bowls and candlesticks against Easter – 16d.
Item for making clean of the churchyard lane – 1d.
Item for carrying away the church dust – 8d.

Item to the suffragan that he was behind in his wages – 23d.

Item for the hallowing of 3 altar cloths – 4d.

Item to Isabell Wyn for making 2 of the best altar cloths and the best houseling towel with silk that Mistress Chestre gave – 4d.

Item for scouring the basin in the choir before the high altar – 8d.

Item for a rope to hang the said basin on – 4d.

Item for a lamp for the same basin – 1d.

Item for hanging up the Dance of Pauls twice a year and for rolling it up again – 8d.

Item for mending the best suit of vestments – 12d.

Item to the mother church of Worcester – 12d.

Item for 2 lbs of tallow candles for the rood loft on Christmas day in the morning – 2 ½d.

Item for a new key to the little vestry door at the rood altar end – 2d.

Item for bearing the banners in Rogation week – 4d.

Item for bearing the best cross on Corpus Christi day – 4d.

Item for the dinner for the priest and the clerks on the day aforesaid after the procession – 3s.

Item for William Newbery's mind – 6s.

Item for a new rope for the salve bell – 5d.

Item for besoms to streke [sweep] the church with – 1d.

Item for making the rent roll – 1d.

Sum – 31s 5 ½d. [lightly scored, and added: Verum sum solue – 21s 1 ½d.]

(556)
Costs of lights to the church

In primis to John Mayowe, waxmaker, for making of 53lbs of your own wax that was of your square lights and round lights – 2s 2 ½d.

Item to the said waxmaker for 22 lbs of new wax to part-form your square lights and round lights and your font taper, price 10d the pound – 18s 4d.

Item to John Waxmaker for making the paschal taper of his own wax and for waste – 2s 6d.

Item for making your round lights for All Hallows' tide and for new wax to part-form the said light – 2s 8 ½d.

Item for 2 new torches for the high altar weighing 42 lbs, at 3d the pound – 10s 6d.

Sum of the foresaid costs – 36s 3d.

Costs of your General Mind

In primis for loaf bread, cakes and spices that went thereto – 3s 2d.

Item for a deson [?dozen] ale – 12d.

Item for baking of your said cakes – 2d.

Item for red wine and sweet wine – 4s 4d.

Item to 6 priests and to the clerk – 22d.

Item for ringing of the bell – 16d.

Sum of the costs of the General Mind – 11s 10d.

Costs done on the steeple and the bells
In primis for a stock which has been fitted upon the great bell – 2s 6d.
Item for hauling the said stock – 1d.
Item for 2 new spindles of iron for the great bell – 16d.
Item for iron work to hang the great bell with the second bell – 16d.
Item for mending 2 baldrics of the 2 bells – 6d.
(557)
Item for the ?hadocks of the 2 bells – 4d.
Item for 6 bundles of laths for the steeple windows – 2s.
Item for 500 tack nails for the said windows – 2s.
Item for 4 penny boards for the said windows – 4d.
Item to John Dawe, carpenter, and to his man for hanging the said 2 bells and closing the said windows of the steeple – 8s 6d.
Sum – 18s 2d.

Costs [of work] done on the church gates
In primis for a piece of timber to make posts for the said gate – 2s.
Item for hauling the said piece of timber – 1d.
Item for 7 oak boards for the said doors – 2s 2d.
Item for 2 quarters of lime and a load of sand – 5d.
Item for a mason for setting the 4 posts of the gates – 8d.
Item for 2 pair hinges of iron and 2 bolts – 22d.
Item to Richard Red, smith, for the iron work of the said gates – 16d.
Item for 100 door nails and 50 hach nails – 8 ½d.
Item to Richard Carpenter for the making of the 2 gates – 2s 2d.
Item to John Whithypoll for half a hundredweight and 4 lbs of lead – 3s 4d.
Sum – 14s 8 ½d.

Reward to the tenants and cost for making this account
In primis to the tenants – 13d.
Item for making the account – 20d.
Sum – 2s 9d.

Costs of the rood loft and the entreclose beneath.
In primis to John Hyll, carpenter, for making of the rood loft that the organs stand upon and for the enterclose underneath, taking for his timber and his handiwork task work – 53s 4d.
Item for 4 pairs of hinges that the choir doors hang with – 14d.
Item for board nails and lath nails for flooring the rood loft and for sealing underneath – 6d.
Item for iron work for the desk in the rood loft – 8d.
Sum – 55s 8d.

(558)
Cost of the new organs in the rood loft
In primis to Thomas Wotton, organmaker, for the said organs in the rood loft – £13 6s 8d.
Item for the hire of the house that the said organs were made in – 5s.

Item to Watkyn Plommer for 26 lbs of lead the which is the peyce of the organs – 10s.
Sum costs of the said organs – £14 20d.

Sum total of the payments and costs – £22 15s.

There rests clear to the proctors – 7s 3d.

(559)
[1473–74]
The account of John Chestre and Clement Wilteshire proctors of the aforesaid church before Sir William Howe then vicar, 13 Edward IV.

Receipts of rents
[As previous, save John Shipward's rent assize is absent]
Sum – £8 12s.

Receipts on Easter day and Seats
In primis on Sheer Thursday, on Easter day, on Easter eve – 16s 8d.
Item of Mathew Cotyngton for his seat – 8d.
Item of Robert Cachemay for his seat – 4d.
Sum – 17s 8d.
Sum total of receipts – £9 11s 8d.

Allowance
In primis for the place which sometime Nicholas Stocke held, which John Shipward withheld from us wrongfully in Marsh Street – 2s.
(560)
Item of a rent assize for the place in St Peter's parish, which Sir William Canynges wrongfully withholds from us – 6d.
Sum – 2s 6d.

Payments
In primis on Palm Sunday for a pottle of osey for the priests and clerks that sung the passion – 5d.
Item to Alison Monke for washing the church surplices and altar cloths – 8d.
Item for keeping the sepulchre and the lights as for 2 nights – 8d.
Item for bread, ale and coals for the said keeping – 2d.
Item for making clean the churchyard – 1d.
Item for scouring your candlesticks and bowls against Easter – 16d.
Item for carrying away the church dust – 8d.
Item for hanging up the Dance of Pauls twice a year and the hanging up [sic] again – 8d.
Item to the mother church at Worcester – 12d.
Item for 2 lbs of tallow candles for the rood loft on Christmas day in the morning – 3d.
Item for bearing of your banners in Rogation week – 4d.
Item for bearing the best cross on Corpus Christi day – 4d.

Item for the dinner to the priests and clerks on Corpus Christi day after the procession – 3s.
Item for William Newbery's mind – 6s.
Item for a new rope to the salve bell – 4d.
Item for besoms to streke the church with – 1d.
Item for making the rent roll – 1d.
Item for paper to write the account in of both the books – 1d.
Item for writing these accounts – 12d.
Item for washing of surplices and altar cloths against All Hallows' tide – 6d.
(561)
Item to John Plommer for mending of the church gutters – 12d.
Item for mending of the glass windows – 3s 4d.
Item for a board which ?closes corbells on the choir – 16d.
Item for 1 deed for the hardwareman's house – 8d.
Item to John Taverner for 1 quarter's rent for the house that Matthew Cotyngton dwells in – 11s 3d.
Item for mending the organs – 4d.
Sum total – 37s 8d.

Costs of lights in front of the rood and beneath
In primis to John Mayowe, waxmaker, for the making of ?58 lbs of old wax of your square lights and rounds – 2s 5d.
Item to the said waxmaker for 17 ½ lbs of new wax to part-form the said lights and your font taper – 10s 2 ½d.
Item to John Waxmaker for making the paschal taper of his own wax and for wasted wax – 2s 7d.
Item for making the round light for All Hallows' tide and making 26 lbs of your own wax – 13d.
Sum – 16s 3 ½d.

Costs of the General Mind
In primis for loaf bread and cakes and the spices that went thereto, and to the baker for baking – 3s 3 ½d.
Item for ale – 16d.
Item for wine – 2s.
Item to 5 priests and to the clerk – 18d.
Item for ringing the bells – 16d.
Item to the suffragan – 1d.
Sum – 9s 6 ½d.

Item rewarded to the tenantry at paying rent.
In primis at divers times – 12d.
Sum – 12d.

(562)
Costs of the plea between Richard Haddon and the church.
In primis to John Bagote for the search of the mortifications above[?] at London – 10s.

Item for a gallon of wine for Master William Nante and Roger Kemes –
8d.
Item for a man to ride out with John Chestre to speak with Sutton who
was Abbot of St Austins – 6s 8d.
Item for hiring horses – 2s.
Item for the proctors' costs for riding to the vicar of ?Chewe to be of
councel – 4d.
Item to Roger Kemes to be of councel with us – 10s.
Item for the vicar of Chewe's dinner and for Roger Kemes' dinner –
16d.
Item to the vicar of Chewe for his labour – 6s 8d.
Item on Saint Margaret's day for his dinner – 2s.
Item for costs of the days men the which ?Dewryd [juried?] 3 days – 4s
4d.
Item for the vicar of Chew's costs [over] 3 days – 20d.
Sum – 45s 8d.

Sum total costs and payments – £5 12s 8d.
There rests clear to the church – £3 19s.

(563)
[1474–75]
The account of Hugh Foster and Thomas Baker *alias* Spicer proctors of
the said church before Sir William Howe then vicar, 14 Edward IV.

Receipts of rents
Item Morgan Lewis – £5 6s 8d.
Item chantry of Everard Frensche – 2s 6d.
Item Thomas Deene per annum – 20s.
Item Margery Money silk woman per annum – 13s 4d.
Item Katherine Hardware – 3s 4d.
Item Thomas Philippys – 4s.
Item Syble, baker, per annum – 12d.
Item Master of Tailors' rent – 12s.
Item Canynges' rent – 6d.
Item John Shipward – 2s.
Item Thomas Halleway for Sir William Waren's chamber – 6s 8d.
Sum – £8 12s. [To which is added: Sum vera – £8 11s 8d.]

Receipts of the church
In primis on Good Friday, on Easter eve and Easter day – 10s 2d.
Item for John Leynell's pit – 6s 8d.
Item of Maud Atkyns for her seat – 6d.
Item of Hugo Foster for his seat – 6d.
Item of William Wodyngton for the foot of the cross – 2d.
Item of John Jenkins for his seat – 8d.
Item of Isabelle Skey for the best ? – 4d.
Item of Nicholas Baker for a seat – 6d.

Item of Richard Mede for the foot of the cross – 4d.
Item of William Jenkyns for the beer house in the churchyard – 2s.
Item of John Baten for his seat – 6d.
Sum – 22s 4d.
Sum total of the receipts – £9 14s [4d scored].

(564)
Allowance of rent.
In primis of rent assize for the place in Saint Peter's parish – 6d.
Item of rent assize in Marsh Street which John Shipward the elder
withholds from us – 2s.
Sum – 2s 6d.

Payments
In primis for washing of the church – 19d.
Item for mending of an alb – 2d.
Item for mending the bocys [box?] of the best mass book – 2d.
Item for carrying away the church dust – 8d.
Item for a new lock and 2 new staples – 2s 2d.
Item to the mother church of Worcester – 12d.
Item for William Newbery's mind – 6s.
Item for bearing of the banners in Rogation week – 4d.
Item for a dinner to the priests on Corpus Christi day – 5s 8d.
Item for bearing the best cross on the same day – 4d.
Item for a surplice without sleeves – 2s 4d.
Item for 2 little hand towels – 4d.
Item for scouring of the basin before Our Lady – 20d.
Item for making of the paring iron – 4d.
Item for tallow candles against Christmas – 1 ½d.
Item for a key new – 2d.
Item for tucking girdles – 2d.
Item for a new rope – 5d.
Item for mending of seats in the church – 2d.
Item for mending of hoop before Our Lady of Pity – 4d.
Item for a panier to bear away the church dust in – 2d.
Item for mending the wall over the little westery [vestry?] – 8d.
Item for soldering of 3 skares over the little westry – 6d.
Item for wood to heat his irons – 1d.
Item for seeing evidence – 4d.
Item for paper – ½d.
Item for besoms – 1d.
Item for mending the glass windows – 3s 4d.
(565)
Item to the recorder and to Roger Kemes to defend us against Canynges
for John Pynner's place – 4s 8d.
Item for making the rent roll – 1d.
Item for hanging the Dance of Pauls – 8d.
Item for scouring of candlesticks and bowls – 16d.

Item for rewards to the tenants – 12d.
Item for making and writing this account – 20d.
Item to Thomas Clerk, suffragan, for his wages – 3s 4d.
Item for mending the bere [?bier] – 4d.
Item for the general mind – 13s 11d.
Sum – 56s 6d.

Costs of the lights
In primis to John Mayow, waxmaker, for square lights against Easter –
16s 11d.
Item for round light – 4s 10d.
Item for torches weighing 50 lbs, at 3d the pound – 12s 6d.
Sum – 34s 4d.

Repairs done on the steeple
In primis for solder in the gutters – 10d.
Item for coals – 1d.
Item for cleaning the little pavement – 3d.
Item for 2 tilers for a day's work – 11d.
Item for 100 cornish tiles – 5d
Item for a cloth of lead weighing 72 ½ lbs – 5s 1 ½d.
Item to a mason for a day and a half – 8d.
Item for a quarter of lime – 2d.
Item for hauling away rubble – 1 ½d.
Sum – 8s 7d.

Sum total costs and payments – £5 22d.
There rests clear to the church – £4 12s 6d.

(566)
[1475–76]
The account of Thomas Abyndon and Thomas Phillypps proctors of the
aforesaid church before Sir William Howe then vicar, 15 Edward IV.

Receipts of rents
In primis of Morgan Lewis – £5 6s 8d.
Item of Everard Frensche – 2s 6d.
Item of Margery Money – 6s 8d.
Item of Amy Howell – 8s.
Item of Katherine Hardware – 3s 4d.
Item of Thomas Philipps – 4s.
Item of John Syble rent assize – 12d.
Item of John Alberton in Baldwin Street – 12s.
Item of the place in St Peter's parish rent assize – 2s.
Item of Thomas Halleway's chantry – 6s 8d.
Sum – £8 13s 4d.

Receipts of the church

In primis on Sheer Thursday and Easter eve and day – 8s.
Item of Richard Welsh, cook, of his bequest – 20d.
Item for burying Richard Baker – 6s 8d.
Item for burying Margery Money – 6s 8d.
Item for burying Alison Chestre's cook – 6s 8d.
Item of John Jenkins for his seat – 2s.
Item of Thomas Cogan for his seat – 2s.
Item of Richard Arundel for seats – 16d.
Item of William Chestre for his seat – 6d. ·
Item of Thomas Parnell for a seat – 8d.
Item of John Byrley for a seat – 12d.
Item of Robert Catchmay for his wife his seat [sic] – 8d.
Item of Thomas Dyer for a seat – 8d.
Item of William Paynter for the hire of the beer house – 2s.
Sum – 39s 10d.

(567)
Payments
In primis on Palm Sunday for wine – 3d.
Item for washing against Easter – 12d.
Item for watching the sepulchre – 8d.
Item for bread, ale and coals – 2d.
Item for carrying away of the church dust – 8d.
Item for scouring of candlesticks and bowls – 16d.
Item to the suffragan – 3s 4d.
Item for William Newbery's mind – 6s.
Item for bearing of the banners – 4d.
Item for burnishing the church jewels – 5s 4d.
Item to Our Lady of Worcester – 16d.
Item on Corpus Christi day for the dinner – 4s 4d.
Item for bearing the best cross – 4d.
Item for binding the pistyll [?epistle] book – 20d.
Item for the sequent of Sir Thomas Farbor's mass book – 4s.
Item for writing 2 new parchment leaves in the said old mass book – 6d.
Item for the covering of the said book and clasps – 4d.
Item for making a new vestment of green – 3s 4d.
Item for canvas to the said vestment – 6d.
Item for buckram to the said vestment – 4d.
Item for ribbon to the same vestment – 7d.
Item for washing of 2 surplices and a rochet – 5d.
Item for hanging up the Dance of Pauls – 8d.
Item for a new battlement in the choir – 8d.
Item for nails and hooks to the said battlement – 2d.
Item for besoms – 1d.
Item for bearing out of the church dust – 1d.
Item for 2 lbs of tallow candles – 2d.
Item for pins – ½d.
Item for washing 2 surplices and a rochet – 5d.

Item for washing a new vestment – 7d.
Item for washing 5 albs and 3 towels – 9d.
Item for the deed of Margery Mony's place – 6s 8d.
Item for wine – 8d.
Item for a gallon of wine to the recorder – 8d.
Item for making the rent roll – 1 ½d.
(568)
Item rewards unto your tenants at paying of the rent – 6d.
Item for making and writing this account – 20d.
Item for a lock and chain to make the ladders fast – 8d.
Item to the waxmaker for his light – 24s 6 ½d.
Item for the General Mind – 13s.
Item for paving the churchyard pavement – 58s 4 ½d.
Item to Robert Bonnoke for the organs – 13s 4d.
Sum – £7 8s 7 ½d

Repairs done at the Green Lattice
In primis for a load of paving stone – 2s 8d.
Item for 100 feet of oak board – 2s 10d.
Item for 4 boards of oak – 4d.
Item for hauling the foresaid boards – 1d.
Item for 6 loads of clay – 12d.
Item for 4 loads of sand – 4d.
Item for a piece of timber – 3d.
Item for a carpenter 2 days – 11d.
Item for nails – 8d.
Item to a mason for 5 days – 2s 3 ½d.
Item to a mason for 3 days – 16 ½d.
Item to a labourer for 8 days – 2s 4d.
Item for 5 quarters of lime – 10d.
Item for 3 ½ lbs of candles – 3 ½d.
Item for hauling away of the rubble – 5d.
Item for 2 labourers for the making clean of the gutter – 7d.
Item for a board – 2d.
Item for mending of a lock and a new key – 3d.
Item for 2 locks and 3 keys to the same tenement – 11d.
Item for mending of a wall – 3d.
Item paid to the langabyll [?land gavel] – 4d.
Sum – 19s 1 ½d.

(569)
Repairs done upon the pentes [the lean-to] in Cornstreet
In primis for boards of oak – 16d.
Item for a piece of timber for rafters – 2d.
Item for 3 hinges of iron – 8d.
Item for nails for the said pentes – 3d.
Item to a carpenter for a day's work – 6 ½d.
Sum – 2s 11 ½d.

Receipts
In primis received of the coffer money in the treasury house – 53s 4d.
Item for the old organs – 53s 4d.
Sum – £5 6s 8d.

Sum total receipts with the money in the coffer – £15 19s 10d.

Sum total payments costs and repairs – £9 4s
There rests clear to the parish – 53s 4d.

(570)
[1476–77]
The account of Thomas Cogan and Mathew Cottyngton proctors of the aforesaid church before Sir William Howe then vicar, 16 Edward IV.

Receipt of rents
In primis of Thomas Cogan per annum – £4 13s 4d.
Item of Everard Frensche per annum – 2s 6d.
Item of Thomas Went, tailor – 20s.
Item of Amy Howell per annum – 16s.
Item of Katherine Hardware – 3s 4d.
Item of Thomas Philippes – 4s.
Item of John Syble – 12d.
Item of the Master of the Tailors – 12s.
Item of the place in St Peter's parish – 6d.
Item of John Sheparde [Shipward] – 2s.
Item of Thomas Halleway – 6s 8d.
Sum – £8 16d.

Receipts of the church
In primis on Sheer Thursday, on Easter eve, on Easter day received on the pax – 12s 2d.
Item of John Jay for a seat – 6d.
Item of Robert Hyend for his bequest – 3s 4d.
Item of William Paynter for the beer house – 12d.
Sum – 17s.

Rents withheld
In primis a place in Marsh Street which Sheparde withholds from us – 2s.
Item a rent assize of the place in St Peter's parish – 6d.
Sum – 2s 6d.

(571)
Payments
In primis on Palm Sunday for wine and bread – 4 ½d.
Item for washing – 2s 10d.
Item for watching the sepulchre – 8d.

Item for bread and ale and coals – 2 ½d.
Item for carrying away of the church dust – 8d.
Item for scouring of your candlesticks – 16d.
Item to the suffragan for his wage – 3s 11d.
Item for holding William Newbery's mind – 6s.
Item for carrying of the banners – 4d.
Item to Our Lady of Worcester – 8d.
Item for a dinner on Corpus Christi day – 5s 4d.
Item for mending the censers – 2d.
Item for mending a baldric – 2d.
Item for mending the clappers – 3s 9d.
Item for 2 lbs of tallow for the rood loft – 2d.
Item for a new cover for the great bere [?bier] – 21 ½d.
Item for shaping a chasuble – 8d.
Item for paper – 2d.
Item for mending a seat in the church – 3d.
Item for scouring of the brode [?broad] basin – 1d.
Item for a round iron to the salve bell – 6d.
Item for a board set above the head of the Trinity at the Jesus altar, and for nails to nail the said board – 4 ½d.
Item for making a scaffold before the said altar – 7d.
Item for boards and nails for the said scaffold – 1d.
Item for 11 lbs of iron work to make fast the tabernacle to the wall – 13d.
Item to a smith for re-making the yard of iron that the stained cloth hangs upon – 12 ½d.
Item for making a battlement over the lady altar – 20d.
Item for 3 new ?cranes – 2s 10d.
Item for an altar cloth – 13d.
Item for 4 ½ ozs of new latten rings for the new stained cloth for Our Lady's altar – 4d.
Item for a piece of lead to mend the church gutters with – 6d.
(572)
Item for the soldering of a gutter between the Kalendars and the church – 14d.
Item for hanging up the Dance of Pauls twice a year – 8d.
Item for besoms to the church – 1d.
Item for the rent roll – 1d.
Item for a new coffer that the church book lies in – 5s.
Item for mending of the best suit of vestments – 3d.
Item for silk – 1d.
Item for a breakfast to the priests and clerks that kept Our Lady Mass this Lent – 17d.
Item to the waxmaker for wax and its making – 32s 4d.
Item for the General Mind – 12s ½d.
Item to your tenants at the gathering of your rent – 8d.
Item for the writing of this account – 20d.
Sum [blank]

Repairs
In primis on Friday the 26th day of September to Thomas Spicer for 6 crests – 3 ½d.
Item for nails – 1 ½d.
Item for a board of oak for the pentes [lean-to] in the fore pavement – 3 ½d.
Item to a tiler for 2 days – 12d.
Item for a board of oak – 1d.
Item for a sack of lime – 1d.
Item to a plumber for soldering – 4d.
Item for ?wood – ½d.
Item for casting new gutters – 2s 11d.
(573)
Item for a board of elm – 3d.
Item for making 2 locks – 12d.
Item for cleaning a gutter – 15d.
Item for mending a chimney – 4d.
Item for hauling – 1d.
Item for a new lattice – 21d.
Item for a new key to Went's house – 3d.
Item for a tiler – 6 ½d.
Item for a sack of lime – 1d.
Item for a lock and a key – 6d.
Sum – [blank].

Sum total of receipts – £8 18s 4d.

Sum total vacations, payments and repairs – £5 8s 6 ½d.
There rests clear to the church, which is paid and quit – £3 9s 9 ½d.

(574)
[1477–78]
The account of Davy Vaghn and Pers Grenfeld proctors of the church of All Hallows' before Sir William Howe that time vicar, the 17th year of the reign of king Edward IV.

Receipts of rents
[As previous]
Sum total rental – £8 16d.

Receipts at Easter and casualties
In primis on Good Friday, Easter eve and Easter day on the pax – 11s 11d.
Item of Thomas Box for a seat – 10d.
Item of Harry Dale for his wife's burial – 6s 8d.
Item of Richard Andrew for his wife's burial – 5s.
Item of Katherine Leynell for the burial stone – 5s.
Item of Crystiane Myllans for a seat – 4d.
Item of John Syble for a lattice – 8s.
Item for the beer house – 2s.
Sum – 39s 9d.

(575)
Allowance of void tenements withheld
[As previous]
Sum – 2s 6d.

Payments
In primis for wine on Palm Sunday – 3 ¼d.
Item for washing the church cloths – 8d.
Item for keeping the sepulchre – 8d.
Item for bread, ale and coals – 3d.
Item for scouring of the candlesticks – 16d.
Item for carrying away of the church dust – 8d.
Item for making clean the churchyard – 1d.
Item to Our Lady of Worcester – 8d.
Item for a new rent roll – 1d.
Item for William Newbery's mind – 6s.
Item for bearing of the banners – 3d.
Item for mending of your best cross – 12d.
Item for a dinner on Corpus Christi day – 6s 5d.
Item for bearing the best cross on the same day – 4d.
Item to the suffragan – 3s 1d.
Item for 9 ells of cloth for a surplice – 6s.
Item for making the said surplice – 2s.
Item for washing of the church cloths – 9d.
Item for rake hooks, nails and pins – 3d.
Item for besoms to streke the church – 1d.
Item for making clean of the churchyard at divers times – 3d.
Item for a stone in the churchyard pavement – 10d.
Item for 2 cramps of iron – 2d.
Item for a workman to make fast the said stone – 2d.
(576)
Item for hanging up the Dance of Pauls twice in the year – 8d.
Item for mending the seats – 8d.
Item for mending of the pissing gutter – 4d.
Item for against Christmas [sic] – 5d.
Item for 2 lbs of tallow candles – 2d.
Item for the ?suosce of the candlesticks – 1d.
Item for bringing Mathew Cotyngton before the mayor – 2d.
Item for 2 new twists and a key and a little coffer – 6d.
Item for a new key for the little westry [?vestry] door – 2d.
Item for a key for the door of the little myster – 2d.
Item for the key and mending the lock for the little myster door at Our
Lady's altar end – 3d.
Item for a breakfast to the priests – 2s 1d.
Item to the waxmaker at divers times for making lights – 28s 2 ½d.
Item for the General Mind – 11s 8 ½d.
Item for a scaffold which was set in the rood aisle and for the ceiling of
the same aisle – £3 1 ½d.

Item for frontals that Thomas Cogan let make for the altar and for the stuff that went to them – 12s 9d.
Item for writing and making the accounts – 20d.
Item in money which is rewarded unto tenants at the paying of their rents – 16d.
Item to the old suffragan who was bedeman, by the commandment of the parish – 20d.
Sum of the payments – £6 3s 1 ½d.

Repairs done in Corn Street.
In primis of timber and boards – 2s 8d.
Item for paving stones – 19d.
Item for stones – 10d.
(577)
Item for 3 loads of clay – 6d.
Item for 3 quarters of lime – 6d.
Item for board nails – 1 ½d.
Item for a board – 1d.
Item for 2 masons, 3 days work – 3s 4d.
Item for a labourer 3 days – 13d.
Item for candle – ½d.
Item for a key – 2d.
Item for mending of a gutter – 6 ½d.
Item for a lock and a key – 5d.
Item for a piece of timber to make a post of – 6d.
Item for 2 planks – 10d.
Item for 3 pairs of hinges – 8d.
Item for nails – 2d.
Item for a rail – 2d.
Item for a groundsel – 1d.
Item for a carpenter for his handiwork – 12d.
Item for a load of tile stones – 20d.
Item for 2 tilers for 3 ½ days – 3s 2 ½d.
Sum total the repairs – 21s 7 ½d.

Sum total vacations, payments and repairs – £8 18s 6d.

There rests clear to the church – 22s 6d.
Paid and quit.

(578)
[1478–79]
The account of David Vaghn and Peter Grenfeld proctors of the church aforesaid before Sir William Howe then vicar, 18 Edward IV.

Receipt of rents
[As previous, save for Katherine Hardware – her rent of 3s 4d is now paid by John Bowde and Paul Hardwareman]
Sum – £8 16d.

Receipts on Easter day and other casualties
In primis on Good Friday, Easter eve and Easter day on the pax – 10s 6d.
Item of John ?Sueg for his daughter's burial – 5s.
Item of John Cokke for his seats – 8d.
Item of a gown and a kirtle of the bequest of Thomas Cogan's maid ?less 8d for the ?upholsterer – 8s.
Item of Poll's wife for a seat – 8d.
Item of Christianne Millan for changing a seat – 6d.
(579)
Item of Richard Wente for his seat and his wife's – 8d.
Sum – 26s.

Allowance of vacations
[As previous, with this addition]
Item of rent assize of the place in Lewins Mead – 12d.
Sum – 3s 6d.

Payments
In primis paid on Palm Sunday for wine – 2d.
Item for washing of the church cloths against Easter – 12d.
Item for keeping the sepulchre for 2 nights – 8d.
Item for bread and ale and fire for the keepers – 2d.
Item for the loan of a Rawe cloth for Palm Sunday – 1d.
Item for scouring your candlesticks and bowls of the church – 16d.
Item for scouring the basins in the church – 2s 8d.
Item to a mason for mending a wall – 8d.
Item to the suffragan – 4s 1d.
Item for a new rope for the basin before Our Lady – 4d.
Item for a rope for the basin before the rood altar – 3d.
Item for a line to pull the cloth over the rood on Palm Sunday – 3d.
Item for carrying away the church dust – 8d.
Item for bearing of the banners in Rogation week – 4d.
Item to Our Lady of Worcester – 8d.
Item for William Newbery's mind – 6s.
Item for a dinner on Corpus Christi day – 8s 6d.
(580)
Item for bearing the best cross on Corpus Christi day – 4d.
Item for a coffer with 3 floors to lay the church books in – 7s.
Item for a pair of new trestles for the hearse board – 10d.
Item for making and setting up a battlement in the church – 14d.
Item for mending the lych bell – 6d.
Item for washing of the church cloths against Whit Sunday – 4d.
Item for washing Sir Thomas Furbor's alb and amice – 3d.
Item for mending the checker board that you bear the church cake upon – 2d.
Item for besoms to streke the church with – 1 ½d.
Item for paper to write these accounts – ½d.
Item for a pot to fill the holy stock – ½d.

Item for washing of 2 surplices and a rochet – 5d.
Item for a rope to the salve bell – 6d.
Item for nails and pins – 2d.
Item for hanging up the bedys [?beads] in the church and the taking them down – 4d.
Item for 2 lbs of tallow candles against Christmas for the rood loft – 2d.
Item for washing of the church cloths against Christmas tide – 10d.
Item for mending your organs – 20d.
Item for hanging the Dance of Pauls 2 times in the year – 8d.
Item for cleaning a gutter in Thomas Cogan's house – 12d.
Item for mending the pavement at the said Thomas' door – 2 ½d.
Item in rewards to your tenants at the paying of their rents – 16d.
(581)
Item for writing and making this account – 20d.
Item for mending the baldric for the great bell – 6d.
Item to the waxmaker for wax to the church lights and making them for the whole year – 26s 3 ½d.
Item for the General Mind – 14s 4d.
Item to the suffragan in part payment of his wages – 2d.
Sum [blank]

Costs of the gutter that lies in the entry of the house next to the Green Lattice
In primis for 4 loads of paving stones – 6s 8d.
Item for 20 loads of clay, 1 ½d the load – 2s 6d.
Item 22 bushels of lime stones – 3s 8d.
Item for a wey of lime – 12d.
Item for 18 loads of sand – 15d.
Item for 12 lbs of tallow candles – 12d.
Item for 6 bushels of lime stones – 12d.
Item for 6 loads of clay – 11d.
Item for pack thread for the masons' lines – ½d.
Item to the masons for 12 days – 11s.
Item to 2 labourers for 12 days – 7s.
Sum – 35s 10 ½d.

Costs done on the rood altar
In primis to a smith for 43 lbs of iron to make what the cloths hang upon before the rood altar – 5s 4 ½d.
Item to a mason for setting the irons into the wall – 3d.
Item for 42 rings that the cloths hang with – 10d.
Item for 4 staples of iron for the riddels – 2d.
Sum – 6s 7 ½d.

(582)
Item you shall receive for a pan and a lattice that was pledged by Thomas Adenne in part of the more – 4s.

Sum total vacations, costs and payments – £6 15s.

There remains to the church – 52s 4d.
Received and quit.

[1479–80]
The account of John Snygge and Thomas Box proctors of the church of
All Hallows' made before John Thomas then vicar there, 19 Edward IV.

Receipts of rents
[As previous]
(583)
Sum total rental – £8 16d.

Receipts of Easter and other casualties
In primis on Good Friday, Easter eve and Easter day on the pax – 12s 1 ½d.
Item for the suffragan's wages – 3s 6d.
Item of Thomas Pernell for the cross for Sir William Wele's burying – 8d.
Item of William Hosteler for his wife's burial – 6s 8d.
Item of Clement Wilteshire for T. Wyell's grave – 6s 8d.
Item of Gyllam Delafawnte for a broad stone – 10d.
Item of Botte of Gyllowys Inn for a seat – 8d.
Item of Hew Corke for his seat and his wife's – 12d.
Item of William Palmer of London for his bequest – 40s.
Item of Robert Dorking of London for his bequest – 20s.

Sum total receipts and casualties – £12 13s 5 ½d.
Sum the vacations – £4 12 1 ½d
These are the rents that stood void this same year. A place in Marsh
Street that John Shipward withholds, that is to say a rent of assize of a
place in Marsh Street sometime called Scalpyll Street where in Nicholas
Stoke dwelt – 2s.
Sum – 2s.

(584)
Payments
In primis on Palm Sunday on wine into the rood loft – 4 ½d.
Item for washing of the church cloths against Easter and Whit Sunday –
17d.
Item for keeping the sepulchre – 8d.
Item for bread, ale and coals – 2 ½d.
Item for mending of the ?spower – 1d.
Item for scouring of the candlesticks and bowls of the church – 2s 4d.
Item to the suffragan for his year's wage – 6s 8d.
Item to the raker for carrying away of church dust – 8d.
Item for the bearing of banners in Rogation week – 4d.
Item for an alb and 2 amices – 2s 5d.
Item for an amice to the high altar – 5d.
Item for 2 ells of cloth to make new banners withal – 2s 1d.
Item to Our Lady of Worcester – 8d.

Item for the priests' dinner in the Lent season for Our Lady Mass – 3s.
Item for an alb and 3 amices – 8d.
Item for a dinner on Corpus Christi day – 6s 8d.
Item for holding William Newbery's mind – 6s.
Item to a smith for mending the church door key – 3d.
Item for parchment for the rent roll – 1d.
Item for making of sheets to cover the best copes – 4d.
Item for paper – 1d.
Item for hanging up the Dance of Pauls twice a year – 16d.
Item for washing 17 pairs of albs and amices, 3 altar cloths and 3 towels
– 2s 4d.
Item for washing 3 surplices and a rochet – 7d.
Item for rack hooks, nails and pins – 2 ½d.
(585)
Item for a ?Tampyn to the font and a water pot – 1d.
Item for besoms – 1d.
Item for nails to mend the choir door – 1d.
Item for a key to the evidence coffer – 3d.
Item for small nails – ½d.
Item for cleaning and hauling rubble out of the steeple – 12d.
Item for changing 2 cruets – 4d.
Item for a lamp – 1d.
Item for a plank at the high altar – 3d.
Item for an 11 foot battlement – 11d.
Item for mending 12 pins of iron and for their plates of tin – 12d.
Item for a new fire pan – 2d.
Item to a carpenter for his labour – 4d.
Item for nails – ½d.
Item to an organ player from Christmas to Candlemas – 10d.
Item for sconces for the choir – 3 ½d.
Item for washing 2 surplices – 3d.
Item for lime to the church – 1d.
Item for writing these accounts – 20d.
Item for reward to our tenants – 16d.
Item for a dinner to receive the money bequeathed by William Harding
and Robert Derkyn – 3s 4d.
Sum total – 52s 4d.

(586)
These are the costs of the church light
In primis at Easter for making of ?52 ¼ lbs of our own wax – 2s 2 ½d.
Item for 24 lbs of new wax – 12s 3d.
Item for 4 tapers to the sepulchre – 6d.
Item for making of the paschal and for the waste – 2s 9d.
Item at All Hallows' tide for making 16 lbs of our own wax for round
lights – 8d.
Item for 10 lbs more of new wax – 5s.
Sum total – 23s 4 ½d.

The costs of the General Mind
In primis for loaf bread, cakes and spices and to the baker for his labour
– 4s 5d.
Item for a dozen of ale – 18d.
Item for wine – 4s 5d.
Item to 7 priests – 22d.
Item to the clerk for ringing – 12d.
Sum – 13s 3d.

These are the costs of repairs done upon the Church and the Church
Rent
In primis to a carpenter for a day to mend the case of the salve bell – 6d.
Item for spike nails – 1d.
Item for a load of tile stone – ?10d.
Item to John Schyre, tiler, for 3 days – 18d.
Item to Robert Meggys for 21 lbs of solder and for 8 ?skarrys soldered
on the steeple and in the gutters of the church – 6s.
Item for wood to the plumber – 2d.
(587)
Item to a tiler for 1 ½ days upon Richard Went's house and Amy
Howell's house – 8 ½d.
Item for boards to the said work – 7 ½d.
Item for mending of a lock – 2d.
Item for a key – 3d.
Item for mending of a lock and a new key to the great coffer in the rood
loft – 4d.
Item for the mending of the gutter at the Green Lattice – 10d.
Item for making a gutter clean in the said house – 12d.
Item for soldering of the church gutter – 5d.
Item for a hook of iron to stay up [ie shore up] the long iron at the cross
altar that bears the cloth – 8d.
Sum total – 14s 11d.

Costs of almerys [?aumbries] in the choir and for sealing and painting
the wall before the rood altar.
In primis for boards and timber to the said work – 16s 4 ½d.
Item to the carver mason and ?Rawing – 29s 7d.
Item for locks, twists and rings 9s 4d.
Sum – 55s 3 ½d.
As necessary a thing as was this many year.
Look well here to those that come after

Sum total of allowance – £8 2s 6d.

The rests that we owe the church clearly – £4 10s 11 ½d.
Paid forthwith.
And so discharged every man pleased.

(588)
[1480–81]
The are the accounts of John Jenkyns, stainer, and of Thomas Pernaunt, proctors of the said church of All Hallows' of Bristol, made for a whole year, before Sir John Thomas, vicar of the said church, that is to say from the feast of the Annunciation of Our Lady in the 20th year of the reign of King Edward IV unto the said feast next following.

These are the receipts
In primis of Thomas Cogan for the Green Lattice – £4 13s 4d.
Item of the chantry of Everard Frensche for a baste door in the churchyard and a gutter – 2s 6d.
Item of Paul James – 3s 4d.
Item of Richard Wente – 20s.
Item of Amy Howell – 16s.
Item of Thomas Phylypps, barber, for rent assize – 4s.
Item of the chamber of Hallewey's chantry – 6s 8d.
Item of Richard Erle's house in Lewins Mead for rent assize – 12d.
Item of the Master of the Tailors for William Newbery's house in Baldwin Street that John Albyrton dwells in, rent assize – 12s.
Item of an house in Saint Peter's parish that John Steynour dwelt in, rent assize – 6d.
Item of a place of John Shipward in Marsh Street, rent assize – 2s.
Sum total – £8 16d.

(589)
Receipts of Easter and other casualties
In primis on Sheer Thursday, Good Friday, Easter eve and Easter day – 13s 3 ½d.
Item received for Margaret Rowley, a torch.
Item of Thomas Cogan [tenant of Green Lattice] for Midsummer quarter – 13s 4d.
Item Thomas a Dene for his ?jack a stress – 8s.
Item of John Cockys for three quarters of the beer house – 15d.
Item of Davy Vaghn for rent assize of Erle's house that was unpaid – 12d.
Item of Davy for his son's grave – 5s.
Item of Thomas Goold's bequest – 12d.
Item of Thomas Skinner for his and his wife's seats – 16d.
Item for a seat for Garrett Corbeser – 7d.
Item for a seat of Rafe Bisschopp – 7d.
Item of Alson Hycks for a seat – 4d.
Sum – 45s 8 ½d.

Receipts for brass being pledged or sold
Item a pan of Isabell Key's gift, weighing 20 lb at 2d the pound – 3s 4d.
Item a brass pot weighing 12 lb – 2s.
Item a pan weighing 7 lb – 14d.
Sum – 6s 6d.

Vacations for the year
In primis the Green Lattice for three quarters – £3 10s.
Item in Saint Peter's parish rent asize – 6d.
Item in Marsh Street rent assize – 2s.
Sum – £3 12s 6d.

(590)
Payments by the said proctors on the church's behalf, of old custom and of things necessary to be done, as it appears for every thing in the quire of their accounts – 30s 6 ½d.

Repairs of other things, as follows
In primis to John Hyll, carver, for sealing the wall in the north aisle before the image of Jesus – 3s 4d.
Item for boards to seal it – 3s 8d.
Item for 3 stodys [?studs] – 4d.
Item for nails – 2d.
Item for painting and repairing the glass windows of the church – 4s 8d.
Item to the carver for making a timber case for the rope to the salve bell – 20d.
Item for 2 oak boards and nails – 9d.
Item for tallow to anoint it – 1d.
Item for clamps of iron for it – 10d.
Item to the said carver for making a new housing at Saint Thomas's altar for 3 images – 43s 4d.
Item to the clerk for the Dance of Pauls – 16d.
Item for a paring iron – 5d.
Item allowance in receiving of rent – 8d.
Item for making and writing this account – 12d.
Sum – £3 2s 3d.

Reparations in divers other places – how and where everything was spent appears in their book of reckoning – that comes to the sum of – 6s 8 ½d.

(591)
Costs of the General Mind
Item for bread, cakes and other stuff – 4s ½d.
Item for wine – 4s 2d.
Item for ale – 21d.
Item to 6 priests – 18d.
Item to the clerk – 14d.
Sum – 12s 7 ½d.

Costs for the church lights
In primis for square lights and round lights for Easter – 11s 8d.
Item for the paschal and font taper – 4s 1d.
Item for 2 new standards in the choir – 2s.
Item for renewing the same for Christmas – 5d.

Item for the charge of round light at All Hallows' tide – 3s 11 ½d.
Item for a new torch – 4s.
Sum – 26s 1 ½d.

Sum total allowances – £10 10s 9d.

And there remains clear in the church of All Hallows' – 2s 9 ½d.

(592)
[1481–82]
These are the accounts of Clement Wilteshire and Thomas Pernaunt proctors of the said church of All Hallows' for a whole year from the feast of the Annunciation of Our Lady in the 21st year of King Edward IV, unto the feast next following and before John Thomas for the parishioners.

Receipts of rents
In primis of the Green Lattice – £3 13s 4d.
Item of the chantry house of Everard Frensche for a baste door in the churchyard and a gutter – 2s 6d.
Item of Paul Hardwareman – 3s 4d.
Item of Richard Wente, tailor – 20s.
Item of Amy Howell – 16s.
Item of the Corner House, rent assize, in Corn Street by the pipe – 4s.
Item of the chamber of Halleway's chantry – 6s 8d.
Item of Richard Erle's house in Lewins Mead, rent assize – 12d.
Item of the Master of the Tailors for the house in Baldwin Street, rent assize – 12s.
Item of the house in Saint Peter's parish for rent assize – 6d.
Item of the house of John Shipward in Marsh Street for rent assize – 2s.
Sum – £8 16d.

(593)
Receipts of Easter and other casulaties as follows
In primis received of the parishioners for the suffragan's wages on Palm Sunday – 2s 7d.
Item received on Sheer Thursday, Good Friday, Easter eve and Easter day – 12s 4d.
Item received of George Badram for his pew and his wife's pew – 12d.
Item received of Richard Fender and his wife for both their pews – 12d.
Item received of William Frith and his wife for both their pews – 2s.
Item received of Thomas Snygge for a pew – 12d.
Item received of John Cocks for the beer house – 20d.
Sum – 21s 7d.

Sum total receipts – £9 2s 11d.

Vacations for the year
In primis the Green Lattice for the whole year – £4 13s 4d.
Item the house in Marsh Street of John Shipward for a whole year – 2s.
Sum – £4 15s 4d.

(594 & 595 blank)

(596)
Payments for the church
In primis on Palm Sunday to the priests in wine at the Passion – 6d.
Item in costs of dinner for Our Lady Mass – 2s 8d.
Item for scouring of things to the church – 14d.
Item for oil and scouring stones – 2d.
Item to the raker for his wages – 8d.
Item for watching the sepulchre – 8d.
Item for ale and coals – 2d.
Item for changing and hanging up the sanctus bell – 2s 5d.
Item for a line – 1d.
Item for Newbery's mind – 6s.
Item for hanging up a painted cloth with 3 stories of Our Lady before the tabernacle at the Jesus altar and for the hoops of iron and rings – 23d.
Item for a lock in Amy Howell's house – 4d.
Item for bearing of banners – 4d.
Item to the clerk for his cruyst [?crust] – 1d.
Item for binding a breviary – 3s 4d.
Item for mending of the best chasuble – 2d.
Item for the Corpus Christi dinner – 5s 4d.
Item for bearing the cross – 4d.
Item paid for a copper cross – 5s.
Item for hanging and taking down the Dance of Pauls twice – 16d.
Item for mending of the second cross – 8d.
Item for three quarters' wages to the suffragan – 7s 6d.
Item for a surplice to the clerk – 6s 3d.
Item for mending a glass window at the Green Lattice – 6d.
Item for a mason for 2 days at the said house and for mending of a ?foren in the baste house – 13d.
Item to a labourer for 2 ½ days – 11d.
Item for 3 bushels of limestones – 6d.
(597)
Item for laths and nails to the said work – 4d.
Item for washing of all manner of stuff to the church – 2s.
Item for dressing a stone to the holy-water stock – 2d.
Item for mending the second suit – 20d.
Sum total – 54s 3d.

Costs of church lights
In primis for square and round light – 12s 10d.
Item for the paschal and the font taper – 3s 2d.

Item for 2 new standards of 4 lbs – 2s 4d.
Item against Christmas for changing 2 standards – 12d.
Item for changing round lights at All Hallows' tide – 5s 5d.
Sum – 24s 9d.

Costs of the General Mind draw unto 14s 6d.

Item paid to the clerk what he lacked of his wages – 16d.

Sum total of allowances – £9 10s 2d.

So it rests that the church owes to the said proctors of this account clearly – 7s 3d.

*   *   *

(997)
Anniversaries in All Hallows' Church to be held yearly

Anniversary of Sir Thomas Marshall annually observed in perpetuity by the vicar for the time being of the church of All Saints', viz exequies on the 7th day of the month of January and the Mass on the morrow.

In primis six priests are to attend exequies and mass – 2s.
Item for wax burning there at the time of the obsequies – 12d.
Item to the clerk for his ?work at the exequies and for ringing the bells – 10d.
Item to be distributed to paupers in bread – 20d.
Item to the beadle for broadcasting the anniversary – 2d.
Item to the proctors of the church for their labour in implementing and superintending, to each of them 6d – 12d.
Sum – 6s 8d.

The anniversary of Henry Chestre and Alice his wife to be annually observed by the proctors of the church of All Saints' in the same church in perpetuity, viz the exequies on the 13th day of the month of February and the Mass on the morrow, that is on the Feast of St Valentine.

In primis the vicar or his deputy and six other priests, to each of them 4d, sum – 2s 4d.
Item that one of the proctors at the Mass should donate after the offertory – 1d.
Item to the vicar for burning wax – 8d.
Item to the clerk for bell-ringing and attending the exequies – 12d.
Item to the beadle for broadcasting the anniversary – 4d.
Item in bread to the incarcerated at Newgate – 20d.

Item in bread to the indigent poor in All Saints' lane – 4d.
Item in bread to the poor lepers at Bryghtbowe – 4d.
Item in bread to the almsmen at Longrewe – 4d.
Sum – 7s 1d.

[Different script] Humfrey Hervy died on the 5th day of the month of March A.D.1510.

*   *   *

(1055)
Reckoning of Jhc
The accounts of Jhc yearly from the 7th day of June AD 1480 and so following [scored: John Snygge and John Cockys giving their accounts.]

[Scored: In primis the said day afore writ John Snygge and John Cockes brought in clearly all things paid, so that the new procurators to pay Midsummer quarter and so yearly to continue from procurators to procurators that hath delivered for their year to Hugh Forster and to Thomas Spicer.]

In primis the said 7th day Anno 20 Edward IV [1480] Hugh Forster and Thomas Baker *alias* Spicer proctors of Jhc received of John Snygge of old money that was remaining, sum – 4s 9d.
Item received of the said John his wife – 12s 8d.
Item received of Sir John Thomas vicar that the soul of Sir John Lewys late vicar of Saint Leonard's to be prayed for at Jesus Mass – 6s 6d.
Item received of John Cockys – 16d.
Item 2 little ?purses received – 1d.
Sum – 25s 4d.

Moreover the said Hugh and Thomas the day of their reckoning and of their discharge that is to say the 25th day of June Anno 21 Edward IV [1481] brought in clearly before the vicar and divers of the parish besides the foresaid sum of 25s 4d – 13s 1d.

Sum total – 38s 5d.

Memorandum the 15th day of July following in the said year John Chestre and Thomas Phyllyppes procurators chosen of Jhc received into their keeping of John Snygge and of Thomas Spicer the foresaid sum of – 38s 5d.

(1056)
Memorandum the 16th day of the month of July Anno 22 Edward IV [1482] John Chestre and Thomas Phyllypps at their account before the vicar and the parishioners have paid for all manner charges of this year passed and besides this have paid for Midsummer quarter so that the new procurators have no thing to pay until the feast of Saint Michael.

And they brought in the money that they received of John Snygge and of Thomas Spicer that is to say – 38s 5d.
Item moreover besides this they have brought in – ?4s 6d.

Sum remaining to the church for to maintain the service of Jesus – 43s.

Memorandum it is ordained by the vicar and the parishioners that from this day forward the money that is now ?sowvyrd and shall be hereafter that it be put in the treasure coffer in a purse ?bt [?bought] by it safe to the use of Jhc.

Memorandum John Jenkins and Thomas Pernaunt procurators of Jhc all things accounted for their year brought in clearly in money – 6s 8d Ricd primo [ie 1 Richard III; 1483].

Memorandum that Thomas Snygge and William Fryth procurators of Jhc all things accounted for their year brought in clearly in money Anno Richard ? – 7s 1d.

[Different hand] Memorandum the 7th day of April Anno Dm 1491 with the money that Clement Wilteshire and Thomas Snygge brought in rests clear in the purse of Jesus – £5 12s 4d.

Item the said day rested in the treasure coffer of the church with the money that ?Paul and Thomas Abyndon brought in, that is to say – £42 8 ½d.
Item an obligation with an indenture of Thomas Cooke.
Item 2 cloths with flowers of gold of Master ?Glowe's bequest containing – 48 flowers.
Item another cloth of flowers containing 27 flowers.

(1057)
Memorandum the said 7th day of April and year aforesaid year rested in the chantry coffer in gold and in silver that is to say – £33 19s 1d.

[Different hand]Memorandum that William Cornowe and William Boole procurators of Jhc brought in clearly for their year – 2s 6d.

              *   *   *

(1090)
Key of the [sic]
Richard Bromefeld has the little ?leset in the treasure coffer.
John Batyn has the key of the little ?leset in the treasure coffer next the street.
John Snygge has the key of the treasure coffer for the middle lock and the 2 proctors the 2 others.
Thomas ?Pacy has the key of the little ?lesset next the door of the chantry coffer

(1092)
These be their names of them that have the keys of the church and of the chantry's treasury and evidences in ?keeping.

In primis the vicar has 3 keys, one of the church's evidence another of the church money and another of the chantry's money.
[Scored: John Snygge has 2 keys of 1 key of the coffin of the money within the chantry coffer, and another key of the coffin within the coffer of the church evidence.]
[Scored: John Chestyr has 1 key of the coffer of the church money.]
[Scored: Clement Wilteshire has 1 key of the chantry coffer.]
[Scored: Thomas Baker has a key of the coffin of church money.]
The 2 proctors have the 2 keys of the treasury with all other keys.
Thomas Snygge has the key of the church coffer that John Chestre had.
Thomas Pernaunt has the key of the chantry coffer that Clement Wilteshire had.
John Baten has the key of the coffin of the church money that Thomas Baker had.

(1093)
Richard Stevyns has the key of the coffin within the coffer of the church evidences that John Snygge had.
Thomas Barbor has the key of the coffin of the money within the chantry coffer that John Snygge had.

(1094)
Memorandum that Sir Maurice Hardwick vicar of the church of All Hallows' received of Sir John Thomas the year of Our Lord 1470 the 8th day of May of the service of Agnes Fyler – 29s 10d.
Item the said Maurice received of Sir Thomas priest of Llandaff the 5th day of October before Sir John Thomas of the service of the said Agnes Fyler – 18s 4d.

Sum total remaining in the vicar's hands – 48s 2d.

Memorandum the 10 day of April A.D. 1494 Master John Hawley, Thomas Snygge and John Baten before the substance of the parish have received of Sir John Thomas vicar of All Hallows' for the pension of 40s concerning unto my Lord the Abbot of Saint Austin and his convent that was sequestered in their hands by my Lord Morton Bishop of Worcester in the house of the Gaunts in the time of his visitation, that is to say the 16th day of the month of July A.D. 1493, that is to say a pares [?Paris] pece parcel gilt weighing 13 ounces the which was payable at the feast of St Andrew last past, that is to say the last day of November.

*　　　　*　　　　*

Parish Account [Fox Ms 70 (B.R.O. 08153(1))]

[The document is written on one side of a large sheet in Latin; the accounts are untabulated.]

[1427–28]
The account of Thomas Filer and William Haytfeld, churchwardens of All Saints' in the town of Bristol, from the feast of Saint Matthew the Apostle [Sci Mathee apli] in the sixth year of King Henry the sixth until the same feast in the following year.

[In margin]Common collection
In primis we collected on Good Friday [*in die parassiphe*] – 7s 2d. Item on Easter day – 11s 1d. Item from a man of Wales – 4d. Item from a man of Coventry – 2d. Item from Berkle dyer – 4d. Item from Sir John of Saint Stephen – 6d. Item from Sir Thomas of Saint Mary Port – 12d. Sum – 20s 7 ½d.

[In margin]Seats
Item from Agnes Talour for a seat – 6d. Item from the son and daughter of Thomas Haunte for 2 seats – 16d. Item from the seat of John Barbour – 20d. Item for the ?bace to the brother of the wife of Thomas Norton – 3d. Item from William Barbour – 2s. Item for 1 ?censer – 5s. Sum – 10s 9d.

[In margin]Burials and lights.
Item for the burial of Nicholas Barbour – 6s 8d. Item for lights around the body of the said Nicholas – 6s. Item for the burial of Isabelle Barbour – 6s 8d. Item for lights around the body of William recently the servant of John Haddon – 12d. Sum – 20s 4d.

[In margin]Rent
Item from William for the rent of the tenement in which he lives – £3. Item from John Whitside for the tenement in which he lives – 26s 8d. Item from Nicholas Hoper in Baldwin Street for the tenement in which he lives – 9s. Item from Thomas Fish for the tenement in which William Chester lives – 4s. Item from the chaplain of Everard Frensch for the tenement in which John Forges lives – 2s 6d. Item from Nicholas Stoke for the tenement in which he lives in Marsh Street – 2s. Item from Thomas Erle for the tenement in which Thomas Baker lives in Lewins Mede – 12d. Item from Joan Younge for the tenement in which John Rede lives ?near the castle in St Peter's parish – 6d. Sum – £5 5s 8d.

Sum of all receipts for the year – £7 17s 4 ½d.

[In margin]Newbery
Therefrom we claim allowance for the diverse expenses pertaining to the said church. In primis for the anniversary of Wiliam Newbery, that is to say for two ?wax lights – 12d. Item for bread – 2s. Item for priests at the exequies – 2s. Item for bell-ringing at the exequies – 10d. Item for the bedeman – 2d. Sum – 6s.

[In margin]Ashes
Item on Ash Wednesday for bread and services – 12d. Item for the elements – 6d. Item for bell-ringing for all the benefactors – 12d. Sum – 2s 6d.

[In margin]Wax and lights
Item in new wax, 36 lbs at 6d the pound, and for its making – 18s. Item for the making of old wax on two occasions – 19 ½d. Item for lamp oil for the ?second part of the year – 5s 5d. Item for buying old torches – 10s 11d. Sum – 35s 11 ½d.

[In margin]For mending books
Item 3 calf skins – 21d. Item 3 skins of red ?*coreo* – 15d. Item for 4 clasps – 12d. Item for 3 white skins for ?fly-leaves and covers on the ?ferials – 9d. Item for 4 skins of bergammo for ?book-binding – 8d. Item for silk to make book-tags – 5d. Item for binding 3 books – 3s. Item for buying 1 missal and making another book – 8d. Sum – 9s 6d.

[In margin]Carpentry
Item for timber – 15d. Item for timber – 12d. Item for timber – 8s 5d. Item for hauling timber from the castle and from the quay – 3 ½d. Item to William Temple for his and 2 men's labour – 8s 1d. Item for a key – 2d. Item for boards – 4d. Sum – 19s 6 ½d.

[In margin]Masons
Item to pay a stonemason for his labour – 53s 4d. Item for ?*capcone vitri ad terram* – 2s. Item to 2 ?*veietoribus* for their labour – 2s. Sum – 57s 4d.

[In margin]Small expenses
Item for rushes towards the feast of Easter – 6d. Item for straw towards the feast of All Saints' – 4d. Item for straw towards the feast of Christmas – 5d. Item for mending vestments during the year – 6d. Item for a broom – ½d. Item for 1 *cathena ad scalas ligandas* [?a chain for the ladders] – 3d. Item for a lock to the same chain – 3d. Item for carrying banners on Rogation Day – 3d. Item for a new amice – 8d. Item for carrying the cross on the feast of Corpus Christi – 4d. Item to the mother church at Worcester – 2s. Item for mending 2 censers – 2s 6d. Item for 3 white girdles – 3d. Item for paper – 1d. Sum – 8s 4 ½d.

Item to William for carting 10 ½ loads of rubble – 21d. Item to John for carting 14 loads of rubble – 2s 4d. Sum – 4s 1d.

Sum total of expenses – £7 3s 3 ½d.

Thomas Filer and William Haytfeld owe 9s for Peter Houper and 12d for Thomas Erle, in rent for the aforesaid church.

INDEX

Abbot of St Augustine's, 9, 31, 116, 138
Abyndon, Joan, 22, 30
Abyndon, Margaret, 87, 109
Abyndon, Richard, 46, 59, 70
Abyndon, Roger, 45, 46, 47, 54, 61, 69, 74, 77, 79, 81, 86, 89
Abyndon, Thomas, 10, 21–2, 30, 44, 118, 137
Abyndon's Inn, 6, 25
Acton, Roger, 47, 74, 76, 87
Adene (Aden, Denne, Dene), Thomas, 6, 47, 48, 85, 88, 92, 104, 106, 107, 108, 109, 110, 116, 127, 131
Ake, Richard, 13, 27
Albyrton, John, 4, 94, 96, 98, 99, 100, 102, 103, 104, 106, 108, 109, 111, 118, 131
Alen, Richard, 10
All Saints':
    Internal features, fittings and equipment:
    Aisles: cross aisle, 14, 27, 28; the Doom in the cross aisle, 13; Jesus aisle, 26; Our Lady aisle, 49, 50, 110; rood aisle, 27, 29, 124. Altars: Cross altar, 37; High altar, 12, 24, 26, 27, 28, 29, 45, 48, 49, 53, 92, 97, 129; Jesus altar, 24, 28, 122, 134; Our Lady altar, 9, 15, 15–6, 24, 35, 36, 37, 47, 50, 64, 65, 68, 87, 89, 122, 124; rood altar, 16, 50, 69, 107, and repairs, 127, and aumbries near, 130; St Dunstan's altar, 14, 28, 37; St John's altar, 19, 35, 37; St Thomas's altar, 20, 35, 37, 63, 64, 132. Chapels: Our Lady, 9, 13, 63, 64. Enterclose, 11, 46, 50, and costs 63; Rood loft, 12, 16–7, 20, 21, 23, 24, 27, 28, 46, 48, 50, 112,
114, 127, and costs, 63.
Bells, 46, 53, 60; Bier, 68, 110, 118, 122; Crucifix, 26; Glass, 61; Hearse board, 126; Hearse cloth, 17, 28, 38; Images, 10, 15, 16–7, 20, 21, 24, 26, 28, 33, 35, 68, 70, 78, 90, 117, 126, 132; Lamp, Our Lady's, 62, 64, 67; Morrow Mass bell, 28; Pulpit, 50; Presbytery, 45, 50; Sepulchre, 46, and making the, 57; Tabernacles, 10, 12, 13, 15, 26, 27, 28, 122; Treasury or treasure house, 8, 78, 110; Treasure coffer, 73; Windows, 8, 9, 25
External features:
    Baste door, 5, 25, 43, 110, 131, 133; Beer house, 5, 46, 48, 56, 60, 111, 121, 123, 133; Church gate repairs, 113; Churchyard, 5, 43, 45, 46, 47, 50, 61, 86, and paving the, 71; Churchyard wall, 62; Conduit, 23, 24, 30; Cross in churchyard, 52; Pissing gutter, 124; School house, 69; Stile in churchyard, 64; Steeple, 47, 49, 68, 69, 83, 87, 90; Vicarage, 8, 26
Management and procedures:
    Ale selling, 97, 103; Audit, 2–3; Bell repair, 56, 69, 113; Chancel maintenance, 31; Church roof, 65; Clerk's wages, 2, 135; Coffers and key holders, 137–8; Collections, 111; Compilation of Book 10, and also inventory, 49; Churchwardens, election of and restraints on, 3; Cleaning windows, 60; Lawsuits, 10, 61, 70–1, 74, 76, 78, 80, 82, 85, 87, 91, 98, 108, 110, 115–6, 117; Muniments, 10, 68, and box for

deeds, 80, and copy of deeds, 80; Property endowments, 4–7, 8, 10, 14, 15, 24–5, 27, 43–4; Repair of steeple, 113, 118; Repair of tenements after fire, 104–5; Repair of windows, 51, 53, 70, 98, 101, 102, 106, 115, 117, 132

Liturgy and Music:
Choir, 45; Church cake, 126; Clerk, 2, 134; Organs, 10, 12, 26, 48, 94–5, 111, 120, 121; New organs in the rood loft, 113–4; Organ player, 129; Organ repair, 102, 127; organ desk, 35; Organ stool, 35; Our Lady Mass, 31; Singers, 100; Singing in rood loft, 111, 114; Suffragans, 97, 102, 106, 107, 108, 110, 112, 118, 119, 122, 124, 126, 128, and suffragan's wages, 133, 134, and Haxby the old suffragan, 125

All Saints' Lane, 6, 44

Almshouse, All Saints', 6, 19, 44, 45, 54, 136

Almshouse, Long Row, 136

Andrew, Richard, 47, 61, 77, 79, 81, 86, 91, 123

Anniversaries: Henry and Alice Chestres', 15, and itemised, 135–6; Thomas and Agnes Fylers', 7; Thomas Halleway's, 17; John and Katherine Leynells' 17; Sir Thomas Marshall's, 8, 44, and itemised, 135; William Newbery's, 24, 58, 62, 65, 68, 70, 73, 76, 77, 80, 82, 86, 87, 88, 91, 92, 93, 94, 96, 97, 98, 100, 101, 102, 103, 105, 106, 108, 109, 112, 115, 117, 119, 122, 124, 126, 129, 134, 140, and Newbery's house in Baldwin Street, 131; John Pers's, 68, 70, 76, 86; Thomas and Maud Spicer alias Bakers', 19, 22, 23; Clement Wilteshire's, 21

ApHowell, Alice, 30

ApHowell, Thomas, 24

ApRees, Howell, 48, 102

Arundel, Richard, 119

Asche, Thomas, 65, 73, 84, 85, 87, 88, 89, 92, 94, 95, 96, 98, 99, 100, 101

Ash Wednesday, 3, 4

Asshton, John, 30, 44, 45

Asshton, Sir Roger, 6

Atkyns, Maud, 116

Backe, William, 45, 49

Badram, George, 133

Bagote, John, 115

Baker, John, 45, 51, 61

Baker, Richard, 48, 119

Baker, Nicholas, 96, 103, 116

Baker, Thomas, 58, 67, 69, 75, 77, 80, 82, 91

Baldwin Street, 4, 6, 14, 24, 25, 43, 44, 58, 69, 73, 75, 87, 88, 89, 96, 98, 100, 104, 106, 111, 131, 133, 139

Balle, carpenter, 104

Barbor, Thomas, 138

Barbour, Isabelle, 139

Barbour, John, 139

Barbour, Nicholas, 139

Barbour, William, 139

Bardman, Martin, 6–7

Barres, the, 6, 25, 44

Bartlett, Agnes, 19

Baten, John, 117, 137, 138

Baten, William, 45, 46, 50, 62, 70

Baynfold, John, 110

Bisschopp, Rafe, 131

Bolton, 71, 76

Bonnoke, Robert, 120

Books: 1395 inventory, 31–2; 1469 inventory, 38–40; antiphonals, 8, 11, 13, 25, 27; book of good doers, 26; breviaries, 7, 11, 25, 26, 134; grails, 8, 25; legendaries, 45, 52; manual, 8; Mass books, 7, 8, 13, 14, 18, 20, 23, 25, 26, 28, 29; ordinals, 7, 25, 46; primers, 14; processional, 8, 9, 25, 26, 87, 92; pricksong book, 11; psalters, 8, 25, 27; ordinals, 7, 25, 46; organ book, 12; writing the ordinal and kalendar, 74, 75; book binding and repairs, 46, 47, 59, 86, 87, 119, 140; binding the epistle book, 119

Boole, William, 137

Botte, of Gillows Inn, 128

Bowde, John, 125

Bowde, William, 111

Box, Thomas, 123, 128

Boxe, William, 48, 97, 104

Boy Bishop, 85

Branfeld, John, 5, 49, 104, 106, 108, 109

Brewer, Lewys, 61

Brewer, Richard, 45, 55

Brightbow, lepers at, 136

Broad Mead, 106

Broad Street, 15

Brocke, Lawrence, 45, 50

Bromefeld, Richard, 137

Brompton, Richard, 44

Bryd, William, 73

Bucklond, Ewyn, 67
Burges, Wat, 92
Busschope, Thomas, 5
Byford, 57
Byrley, John, 119

Cachemay, Robert, 114, 119
Calais, seige of, 68
Canynges, Janet, 67, 69
Canynges, John, 111
Canynges, William, 6, 77, 80, 82, 84, 85, 87, 89, 91, 92, 94, 95, 96, 98, 99, 100, 102, 103, 104, 106, 108, 109, 116; with-holding rent assize, 111, 114; defence against, 117
Carge, Richard, of Bedminster, 68
Carpenter, John, bishop of Worcester, 9, 13, 27
Carpenter, Richard, 113
Carpenter, Thomas, 104
Castell, John, 54
Chambyrleyn, James, 67
Chantries (in All Saints', unless otherwise stated): Henry and Alice Chestres', 15, 17, 28–9; Everard Frensche's, (in St John's), 5, 51, 52, 53, 58, 61, 65, 67, 110, 116, 118, 121, 131, 133, 139; Frensche's priests' action at law, 82; Sir Thomas Furber's, 12, 27; Agnes Fylers', 15, 28; John Haddon's, 9, 13; Thomas Halleway's, 14, 28, 30, 96, 98, 99, 100, 102, 103, 105, 106, 108, 109, 111, 116, 118, 121, 131, 133; recalling loans to Halleway's, 103, 104; Halleway's chantry priest, 74; Halleway's priest's chamber, 14, 96, 98, 99, 100, 102, 103, 105, 106, 108, 109, 111, 116, 131, 133; Halleway's chantry equipment, 43; John and Katherine Leynells', 17–8, 29; Sir Thomas Marshall's, 26; Thomas Pernaunt's, 24; John Pers's, 13, 27; John Pynke's, 18, 29; Sir William Rodberd's, 9, 26; John Snygge's, 21; Thomas and Maud Spicer alias Bakers', 19, 20, 21, 22, 23; Joan Stephen's, 30; Clement Wilteshire's, 19, 21, 29
Chantry priests: Sir William Warens, 11, 26, 96, 98, 99, 100, 116
Chaplen, Peter, 46, 59
Chapmon, Pers, 77
Chestre, Alice, 15-7, 28-9, 38, 42, 112;

burial of her cook, 119
Chestre, Henry (Harry), 15, 28, 38, 101, 106
Chestre, John, 11, 17, 29, 110, 114, 116, 136, 138
Chestre, Thomas, 46, 57, 109
Chestre, William, 85
Chestre (Chestyr), William, 46, 57, 61, 66, 69, 77, 80, 82, 84, 88, 89, 91, 92, 94, 95, 98, 99, 119, 139
Chewe, vicar of, 116
Chocke, Richard, 71, 74, 75, 76
Chylcombe, Emott, 13, 27, 53
Clerk, Thomas, suffragan, 118
Cloths: 1395 inventory, 32–33; 1469 inventory, 35–6, 37–8, 43; altar cloths, 10, 16, 21, 23, 26, 29, 30 &c.; making and hallowing altar cloths, 112; corporas cloths, 18, 26, 29 &c.; corporas case, 11; frontals, 11, 20, 26; painted cloths, 134; for the tabernacle, 15; hanging at principal feasts, 26; Hardwick's gift, 10–11
Cockes, James, 49, 51, 52, 53, 131, 136, 133, 139
Cogan, Agnes, 19, 29
Cogan, David, 30
Cogan, John, 19, 29
Cogan, Thomas, 41, 119, 121, 125, 126, 127, 131
Coke, John, 45, 55
Coke (Cook), Robert, 82, 91, 95, 96
Cokke, John, 126
Colas, Harry, priest, 74
Colle, a mason, 58
Colyns, William, 44
Compostella, 14, 65
Compton, John, 10, 48, 98, 99, 100, 103, 104, 106, 107, 108, 109, 110
Cooke, Thomas, 137
Cor, Robert, 44, 90
Corbeser, Garrett, 131
Cordener, wife of, 67
Core, Robert, 47, 82, 84, 85, 86, 87, 88, 89
Corke, Hugh, 128
Corn Street, 5, 43, 47, 58; rent assize from Corner House in, 133; repairs to pentes in, 120
Cornmonger, Geoffrey, 6, 25
Cornowe, William, 137
Corpus Christi day, 28, 30, 50, 62, 64, 65, 68, 70, 73, 76, 77, 82, 85, 88, 90, 92, 93, 97, 98, 100, 101, 102, 103, 105, 106, 110, 112, 114, 115, 117, 119, 122, 124, 126, 129, 134, 140; instructions for Corpus Christi day dinner, 3
Cottyngton, Matthew, 114, 115, 121; Cottyngton, brought before the

mayor, 124
Crane, Alice Chestre's gift, 17
Crane, 87
Crane hire, 57
Cross and Crown, 49, 50, 51, 52, 53, 54, 55, 56, 57, 60, 73, 75, 79, 83; crown 61
Cross in High Street, 76

Dale, Harry, 123
Dance of Pauls, 14, 27, 88, 92, 93, 95, 98, 100, 101, 102, 103, 105, 108, 110, 112, 114, 117, 119, 122, 124, 127, 129, 132, 134
Davidson, John, 22
Dawe, John, carpenter, 113
Delafawnte, Gyllam, 128
Derby, John, 45, 49
Dorking (Derkyn), Robert, 28, 128, 129
Draper, Martin, 5, 24
Droyse, John, 49, 52, 53
Dyer, Thomas, 119

Eagle, 20, 23
Edmund, clerk of St Stephen's, 74
Erle, Richard, 5, 131, 133
Erle, Thomas, 46, 61, 139, 141
Eyr, John, bailiff, 61

Fender, Richard, 133
Feoffment, deed of, 98
Fish, Thomas, 139
Forster, Joan, 18, 29
Forges, John, 13, 27, 49, 88, 139
Forster, Hugh, 18, 29, 136
Foster, Hugo, 116
Foster, Janet, 87
Foster, John, 85
Fredryck, John, 65, 66
Frith, William, 133, 137
Furbor, Sir Thomas, 119, 126
Fyler, Agnes, 7, 10, 25, 28, 48, 57, 72, 97, 138; her testament, 108
Fyler, Janet, 84
Fyler, Thomas, 7, 25, 28, 46, 47, 48, 58, 64, 72, 82, 83, 85, 87, 88, 89, 90, 93, 96, 139, 141
Fyler, Thomas the younger, 10, 48, 108–9
Fysche, Thomas, 48, 51, 58, 65, 67, 69, 73, 75

Galicia, 14
Garlond, 82
Gate, John, 5
Gaunts (Hospital of St Mark), 138
General Mind, 22, 30, 51, 52, 53, 54, 55, 56, 58, 59, 60, 62, 64, 66, 69, 70, 76, 78, 81, 83, 84, 86, 87, 89, 91, 92, 93, 95, 96, 97, 100, 101, 102, 103, 105, 107, 110, 120, 122, 124, 127, 135; itemized, 112, 115, 130, 132; rules on expenditure, 3; statement of purpose, 4
Gildeney, Henry, sheriff, 62,
Gillows Inn, 128
Glowe, Master, 137
Gnowsale, Stephen, 6
Gold, Thomas, 48, 101
Goldsmith, ?Gyeas, 67
Goldsmith, Joan, 61
Goldsmith, John, 89, 90
Goldsmiths, 12, 27
Goold, Thomas, 131
Gosselyng, John, 46, 61, 72
Gowe, John, 24
Green Lattice, 5, 9, 10, 25, 43, 89, 90, 93, 94, 95, 96, 98, 99, 100, 103, 105, 130; repairs to, 120, 127, 132, 133, 134 &c
Grenfeld, Pers, 91, 92, 94, 95, 96, 98, 123, 125
Grocesale, Stephen, 25
Gurdeler, Roger, 12, 13, 27, 44, 49
Gylmyn, (man of law?), 82

Haddon, Christine, 9, 13, 26, 42, 81
Haddon, John, 9, 13, 26, 42, 139
Haddon, Richard, 9, 15, 26, 34–43, 49, 81, 86, 87, 89, 90, 94, 95, 96, 97, 99, 100, 101, 102, 103, 105; costs of dispute with, 115
Haddons' deeds written, 81
Halleway, Joan, 14, 28
Halleway, Thomas, 5, 14, 17, 28, 45, 46, 53, 54, 61, 64, 67, 68, 72; and see also under chantries
Hardware, Katherine, 106, 108, 109, 110, 116, 118, 121, 125
Hardwareman, see James, Paul
Harper, Master Doctor, 30
Harrys, William, 75
Harsfeld, Harry, 5
Hatter, Richard, 97
Haunt, Thomas, 139
Hawkys, John, 9, 15
Hawley, John, rector of St Mary le Port, Bristol, 31, 138
Hayle, Alice, 5, 25
Haytfeld, William, 46, 58, 139, 141
Hervy, Ann, 30
Hervy, Humphrey, 25, 136
High Street, 5, 7, 10, 25, 49, 51, 54, 85, 88
Holme, Thomas, 5
Hoper, Nicholas, 58, 139
Hoper, Pers, 61, 65, 67, 69, 73, 75, 84, 85, 87, 88, 89, 90
Hoper, Robert, 82

Hosteler, William, 128
Hosyer, John, 65
Hosyer, Richard, 67
Houper, Peter, 141
Howell, Amy, 18, 121, 130, 131, 133, 134
Howse, John, 31
Huckford, William, 58
Hucksowe, mason, 63
Hussey, John, 70
Hychekocke, the summoner, 74
Hycks, Alson, 131
Hyend, Robert, 121
Hyll, John, carpenter and carver, 113, 132

Indulgence, 13, 27
Isgar, John, 88
Isgar, Richard, 88
Isgar, William, 48, 93

James, Paul (Hardwareman), 23, 30, 111, 125, 131, 133
Jay, John, 121
Jenkins, John, 16, 42, 119, 131, 137
Jenkins, William, 48, 95, 106, 117
Jenkyns alias Steyner, Agnes, 22
Jenkyns alias Steyner, John, 6, 22, 30, 111, 131
Jesus Guild, 3, 24, 136–7
Jesus Mass, 15, 21, 28
John, Thomas, 48, 101
Johnson, William, 61
Jose, John, 78, 82, 80, 84

Kalendars, 74; house of, 6, 7, 9, 25, 26, 44, 122; prior of, 64; Sir John Gyllarde, prior, 9, 13, 26, 81, 90; Sir John Herlow, prior, 12, 27; Sir Harry Colas, 9, 26, 27; Sir Thomas Haxby, 11, 27; Sir Thomas Furber, 12, 27; bill against, 97
Kemys, Roger, 110, 116, 117
Key, Isabell, 131
King, bell ringing for, 87, 88
Knight, Alison, 91
Knight, Richard, 91, 96
Knoking, William, 51
Knyght, Richard, 47, 48
Knyght, Stephen, 31, 32, 45

Lafyll (Layfyll), Martin, 47, 77, 78, 80
Lard, John, 24
Le Barres, 6
Ledbury, Pers, 77
Lenche, William, 31, 32, 45
Lente, John, 31
Lewins Mead, 5, 43, 46, 51, 52, 53, 58, 60, 62, 67, 69, 75, 77, 85, 87, 88, 89, 92, 98, 99, 100, 101, 109, 126, 131, 139

Lewis, Morgan 110, 116, 118
Lewys, Sir John, vicar of St Leonard's, 136
Leynell, John, 7, 17–8, 29, 41, 42, 46, 47, 48, 66, 77, 80, 82, 83, 84, 85, 86, 87, 88, 89, 91, 92, 93, 94, 95, 96, 98, 99, 100, 101, 103, 107, 116
Leynell, Katherine, 17–8, 29, 37, 41, 42, 123,
Library, 26
Like, William, 24
London, 74, 76, 96, 115, 128
Longe, Nicholas, 94
Longford, 66
Lonkodon, John, 104
Lybbe, Roger, 51, 60, 61, 62
Lynell, David, 99, 100
Lyvedon, Roger, mayor, 62
Lywe, Roger, 46, 65

Mangottesfeld, Richard, 6, 25
Manymoney, Margery, 6–7, 48, 106, 108, 109, 110, 116, 118, 119, 120
Marsh Street, 5, 8, 25, 43, 48, 49, 51, 52, 53, 58, 61, 67, 69, 73, 75, 77, 80, 84, 85, 87, 88, 89, 91, 92, 94, 95, 96, 98, 99, 100, 111, 114, 121, 128, 131, 132, 133, 134, 139
Martylment, John, 111
Mason, Hugh, 72
Mattson, Robert, 19, 29
Mawnell, John, 31
Mawnsell, (man of law?), 108
Mayowe, John, waxmaker, 112, 115, 118
Mede, Richard, 117
Meggys, Robert, 130
Mercer, Lawrance, 6
Mercer, Thomas, 25
Molle, Thomas, 86
Monke, Alison, 114
Monke, John, 45, 54
Morrow mass, 28
Morton, bishop of Worcester, 138
Myell, Richard, 24
Myllans, Chirstine, 123, 126

Nante, William, 116
Nele, John, 70
Newbery, William, 4, 14, 24
Newgate, prisoners of, 135
Newton, John, mayor, 61
Norton, Thomas, 32, 139
Norton, William, 68, 69

Olde, John, 67
Ornaments: 1395 inventory, 32–4; 1469 inventory, 34–5, 36–7, 41–3; bowls, 12, 13; candlesticks, 8,

14, 18, 19, 20, 21, 23, 24, 25, 27, 29, 30, 46 &c.; candlestick repair, 54; collection for, and expenditure on great candlesticks, 63; lending candlesticks, 75; censers, 13, 21, 23, 27, 30, 45; chalices, 13, 18, 20, 23, 27, 29, 53; cruets, 9, 18, 20, 23, 26, 29, 51, 92; cups, 12, 27; mazers, 14, 18, 27; monstrances, 14, 28; nuts, 22, 30; oilfat, 48; paxbreads, 9, 19, 22, 26, 51, 92; peces, 14, 18, 28; pyx, 27; ships of silver, 15, 28; spice dish, 30; spoons, 12, 19, 27

Osteler, Roger, 67

Pacy, Thomas, 137
Painter, Edward, 63
Painter, Richard the, 57
Painter, Richard, 63
Palm Sunday, 95, 97, 100, 103, 107, 108, 109, 119, 121, 124, 126, 128, 134
Palmer, Agnes, 111
Palmer, William, 28, 128, 129
Papnam, Julian, 13, 27
Parish clerk, duties, 2; assessment for, 2
Parishes: St Ewen's, 19, 29; St John's, 139; St Leonard's, 136; St Mary le Port, 139; St Nicholas's, 29, proctors of, 57; St Peter's, 25, 111, 114, 117, 118, 121, 131, 132, 133, 139; St. Stephen's, 12, 74, 139
Parken, Walter, 28
Parkhouse, man of law, 78
Parle, Andrew, bailiff, 61
Parnell, Thomas, 119, 128
Pavy, man of law, 68, 70–1, 74, 76, 82
Paynter, John, 111
Paynter, William, 119, 121
Perkyn, Walter, 14
Pernaunt, Thomas, 2, 19, 24, 42, 131, 133, 137, 138
Pers, John, 13, 27, 46, 47, 62, 66, 68, 76
Peynter, William, 47, 94, 97
Phylypps, Joan, 107
Philypps (Phelyppes, Phylypps &c), Thomas, 48, 91, 103, 104, 106, 107, 108, 109, 111, 116, 118, 121, 131, 136
Picard, Robert, 25
Plommer, Watkyn, 114
Plommer, John, 115
Pointmaker, Thomas, 101, 103
Poll's wife, 126
Portbery, vicar of, 65
Pyall, William, 5

Pykard, Robert, 6
Pynke, John, 18, 29
Pynke, Alison, 18, 21, 29
Pynner, John, 7

Raynes, Janet, 104
Raynes, William, 28, 45, 47, 54, 57, 46, 61, 75, 84, 98, 99
Red, Richard, smith, 113
Rede, John, 139
Redland, 6, 44
Regny, James, 25
Regny, Joce, 5
Relic Sunday, 16, 29
Rogation-tide, 112, 114, 117, 126, 128, 140
Roger, John, 7
Roper, John, 25
Rowe, William, 15
Rowley, Margaret, 131
Rowley, William, 10, 19, 29, 48, 107

Sadler, Hugh, 47, 48, 92, 99, 100
Saints: St Anne, 16, 33, 36; St Antony, 16; St Christopher, 14, 16, 20; St Dunstan, 14; St Erasmus, 16; St George's day, 65, 73, 77, 84, 85, 90; St Giles, 16; St James, 14; St James, pilgrims to, 65; St John the Evangelist, 16; St Katherine, 16; St Margaret, 16; St Mary Magdalene, 16, 33, 37; St Mary the Virgin, 16, 24, 32, 33, 35, 36, 37, 42 &c.; St Michael, 17; St Nicholas, 85; St Saviour, 9, 26, 68, 70; St Thomas Becket, 8, 25; St Ursula, 10, 26, 36
Schoppe, John, 34–43, 48, 49, 92, 97, 99, 100, 104
Schyre, John, tiler, 130
Selwod, man of law, 71
Selwood, Joan, 14, 27
Serle, Sir Thomas, 97
Sharp, John, sheriff, 61
Sherston, Nicholas, 25
Shipward, John, 6, 48, 100, 110, 116, 121, 128, 131, 133, 134; with-holding rent assize, 111, 114, 117
Shipward, John, younger, 6
Skey, Isabelle, 116
Skinner, Thomas, 131
Snygge, Alice (Alison), 21, 30, 41
Snygge, John, 7, 21, 29, 128, 136, 137, 138
Snygge, Thomas, 21, 133, 137, 138
Sokett, David, 46, 47, 61, 83
Somersett, Nicholas, 51, 52, 53
Somersett, Philip, 49
Spicer, Thomas, 123

Spicer, William, 45, 52, 53, 54
Spicer alias Baker, Thomas, 19, 22, 116, 136, 137, 138, 139
Spicer alias Baker, Maud, 19–21, 22–3
Spicer, Thomas the younger, 23
St Mark's Hospital (Gaunts), 138
St. Peter's Street, 6
Stayner, Robert, 75
Stephens, Joan, 30
Stephens, Richard, 2, 30, 138
Steyner, John, see Jenkyns alias Steyner
Stocke, Nicholas, 5, 48, 58, 61, 65, 69, 73, 75, 77, 80, 82, 84, 85, 87, 88, 89, 91, 92, 94, 95, 96, 98, 99, 100, 101, 111, 114, 128, 139
Sueg, John, 126
Suellard, Harry, 7
Summoner, 74
Suthfolk, John, 13, 46, 47, 70, 76, 85, 91
Sutton, Richard, 42
Sutton, Thomas, abbot of St. Augustine's, 9, 116
Syble, John, 5, 103, 105, 108, 109, 111, 116, 118, 121, 123
Symondson, Martin, 49, 109
Syson, Martin, 28

Tailor, Agnes, 139
Tailors, master of, 89, 91, 92, 95, 111, 116, 121, 133
Tailour, John, 75
Talbot, John, 45, 47, 52
Talbott, bailiff, 62
Tavener, Reynold, 31
Taverner, John, 115
Tempyll, William, 5, 45, 58, 63, 64, 66, 77
Testimonial, letter of, 98
Thorn, William, 31
Thornton, attorney, 74, 76
Tiler, Maurice, 31
Transfiguration, the, 20, 23
Trinity, the, 15, 16, 24, 32, 122
Troyte, John, bailiff, 62
Turner, John, 30, 44, 45
Turner, Thomas, 96
Twerty, William, 85
Twyte, William, priest, 74
Tyler, Harry, 49, 51, 52, 53

Vaghn, David, 123, 125, 131
Venney Lane, see All Saints' lane
Vestment: repairs, 119
Vestment-maker, false, 89, 90, 91
Vestments: 1395 inventory, 32–3; 1469 inventory, 40–41; pairs, 8, 10, 11, 13, 18, 19, 21, 25–6, 26, 27, 30; suits, 8, 13, 14, 18, 20–1, 23, 26, 28, 29, 48; unspecified, 20, 23, 45, 47, 50; chasuble, 27;

copes, 27, 28; collecting for, 53; payments for, 98, 99; purchase of orfreys, 76; hallowing, 110; press for copes and vestments, 30; repairs to, 49, 106, 112, 119
Vicars: Sir John Flook, 31; Sir Maurice Hardwick, 9–11, 26, 34, 37, 41, 94, 95, 96, 97, 99, 100, 101, 102, 104, 106, 107, 109, 138; Sir William Howe, 11, 26, 114, 116, 118, 121, 123, 125; Sir Walter Isgar, 7, 25; Sir William Lynch, 31; Sir Thomas Marshall, 5, 8, 49, 51, 52, 53, 54, 55, 57, 58, 59, 61, 62; Sir Thomas Parkhouse, 8, 26, 64, 67; Sir William Rodberd, 6, 8, 9, 26, 66, 69, 72, 75, 77, 84, 86, 88, 89, 91, 92; Sir William Scoche, 7; Sir William Selke, 5, 7, 25, 44; Sir John Thomas, 2, 10, 12, 22, 27, 42, 131, 133, 136, 138; Sir William Wer, 92
Vyell, 70–1, 74, 76

Wale, Richard, 24
Wall paintings, 20
Walshe, Joan, 101, 103
Walsche, Robert, 46, 47, 64, 69, 73, 75, 77, 79, 84, 85, 87, 89, 93, 94, 95, 99, 100
Walschote's wife, 77
Wanstre, William, 83
Ward, Joan, 89
Warde, Richard, 47
Warde, William, 46, 47, 58, 60, 61, 62, 65, 67, 69, 73, 75, 78, 80, 81, 82, 83, 84, 86; William Warde, sent to London, 76
Watson, John, 24, 30
Wele, Sir William, 128
Wells, John, 14, 27
Welschott, Sir William, 97
Welsh, Richard, 119
Went, Thomas, 121
Wente, Richard, 126, 130, 131, 133
Weston, Harry, 108
White, Thomas, 30
Whithypoll, John, 113
Whytsyde, John, 14, 27, 46, 58, 61, 65, 66, 67, 68, 69, 71, 73, 75, 77, 79, 139
William, John, 45, 51
Wilteshire, Clement, 19, 21, 29, 48, 102, 110, 114, 128, 133, 137, 138
Wilteshire alias Baten, Joan, 19, 21, 29, 41
Wine Street, 7, 44, 46, 47, 70, 76
Woad, 18, 19, 21, 29
Woddington, Maud, 23

Wodyngton, William, 116
Worcester Cathedral, 49, 51, 52, 53, 54, 55, 56, 57, 59, 60, 61, 64, 65, 68, 70, 73, 76, 77, 82, 84, 85, 88, 92, 93, 94, 96, 97, 98, 99, 101, 103, 105, 106, 108, 109, 112, 114, 117, 119, 122, 124, 126, 128, 140
Worcester; Morton, bishop of, 138; Robert, bishop of, 31; bishop of, 97

Wotton, Thomas, organmaker, 113
Wyell, T., 128
Wyn, Isabell, 112
Wytheford, John, 67
Wytteney, William, 14, 27, 88

Yonge, Janet, 73, 75
Yonge, Joan, 58, 61, 65, 139
Yonge, Thomas, 49, 51, 52, 54
Yonge, William, 49, 52, 53
Yowley, Thomas, 69